Published by:

The Emirates Center for Strategic Studies and Research

Enquiries may be addressed to:

The Emirates Center for Strategic Studies & Research
P.O. Box: 4567 – Abu Dhabi, United Arab Emirates
Tel: +9712 4044444 Fax: +9712 4044404
E-mail: info@ecssr.ae Website: http://www.ecssr.ae

ISBN: 9948-00-866-9
ISBN 13: 978-9948-00-866-8

The Emirates Center for Strategic Studies and Research

Annual Book 2006

The Emirates Center for Strategic Studies and Research

Contents

FOREWORD

The rapid developments witnessed by mankind in diverse fields at the beginning of the third millennium pose great challenges for all countries of the world. These challenges need to be met by adopting the necessary techniques to keep abreast of developments and by trying to comprehend and deal consciously with them.

The United Arab Emirates (UAE) is not isolated from such developments and has striven to adopt essential measures for keeping pace with the requirements of the age, including the establishment of a prominent scientific research institution, The Emirates Center for Strategic Studies and Research (ECSSR), which has shown itself to be one of the most dynamic and effective bodies in the UAE in monitoring and following up global events.

The Center is concerned with systematically tracking, analyzing and investigating local, regional and international developments on a structured, scientific and methodological basis that guides appropriate decision-making, inspired by the sound directives and the exclusive, unstinting support given to ECSSR by H.H. Sheikh Zayed bin Sultan Al Nahyan, the late founding father of the UAE. H.H. Sheikh Zayed always stressed the need to enhance the intellectual skills of UAE nationals and to help develop their potential as progressive citizens of the modern world.

Through its many concrete achievements, ECSSR has proved its ability to surmount all challenges and obstacles, and has consequently become a well-established intellectual institution, not only in the UAE but also in the Gulf and the Arab world. Furthermore, ECSSR has acquired a distinguished academic and research status at an international level.

The Center deserves our continued support in its efforts to strengthen the scientific and intellectual traditions which lay the foundation for the building of modern societies that aspire to follow a path of accelerated development and progress.

H.H. Gen. Sheikh Mohammed bin Zayed Al Nahyan
Crown Prince of Abu Dhabi
Deputy Supreme Commander of the UAE Armed Forces
President of the ECSSR

PREFACE

The Emirates Center for Strategic Studies and Research (ECSSR) is an academic research institution which was established with the objective of promoting scientific research methodology and encouraging academic traditions in society — an approach adopted by advanced nations in formulating strategies and taking decisions.

In this context, ECSSR has worked tirelessly, since its inception in March 1994, to support and develop scientific research in order to meet the needs and aspirations of the community.

ECSSR has many research achievements to its credit in its coverage of political, economic, social, information, military and strategic issues pertinent to the UAE, the Arab Gulf states and the Arab region, as well as the rest of the world in general. With the objective of serving the local community efficiently, the Center has also achieved tangible success in recruiting and developing the skills of promising national cadres in the field of research studies.

ECSSR conducts studies that serve current and future policies of the state. These studies are based on reliable information and accurate statistics, continuously developed and updated, aided by specialized and diverse sources provided by the databases unit of the Center.

With the help of Allah, and thanks to the sound directives under which the Center has been and is still privileged to function, ECSSR has fulfilled many of its goals. Amongst its most significant achievements is the publication of more than 515 books and monographs. These highly-regarded publications include both original and translated works covering various political, economic, social and information fields.

Concurrently, ECSSR has organized over 350 scientific conferences, symposiums, lectures and specialized seminars, covering vital issues particularly pertinent to the UAE and the Arab Gulf region. In addition, ECSSR, with its publication of daily newsletters which objectively monitor and analyze developments in the local, regional and international arenas, provides decision makers with speedy and reliable information.

The Center's varied achievements, some of which have been included in this Annual Book, could not have been accomplished without the honorable patronage, support and laudable interest of His Highness Sheikh Zayed bin Sultan Al Nahyan, the late founding father of the UAE (may Allah have mercy on him), His Highness Sheikh Khalifa bin Zayed Al Nahyan, President of the UAE and Supreme Commander of the UAE Armed Forces, and His Highness General Sheikh Mohammed bin Zayed Al Nahyan, Crown Prince of Abu Dhabi, Deputy Supreme Commander of the UAE Armed Forces and President of ECSSR.

They have spared no effort in supporting ECSSR, sponsoring its activities, monitoring them with great interest, and enriching the Center's course with their sound directives. God willing, this support will help the Center in its ambition to achieve excellence.

Jamal Sanad Al-Suwaidi, Ph.D.
ECSSR Director General

INTRODUCTION

The Emirates Center for Strategic Studies and Research (ECSSR), established on March 14, 1994, is an independent research center dedicated to enhancing the role of objective scientific research. The Center's fields of interest (political, economic, social and strategic) cover those current issues, topics and developments of greatest importance and pertinence to the UAE and the Arab Gulf region in particular, and the Arab world in general. The Center aims to keep pace with daily developments and anticipate the future in the light of tangible facts and data, using the latest advances in information technology (IT).

Since its establishment, ECSSR has sought to achieve a number of objectives through the organization of activities and studies. ECSSR's areas of activity include research and specialized studies undertaken either by the center's own researchers or in collaboration with other independent researchers within the UAE and abroad. ECSSR organizes conferences, symposiums, lectures and specialized workshops which strengthen cooperation with experts and specialists, and publishes all the research papers resulting from these occasions.

Recognizing the importance of exchanging information and ideas with similar institutions, both for stimulation and to ensure the expansion of the Center's work, ECSSR has sought to consolidate scientific cooperation with academic institutions, research centers and universities at local, regional and international levels, on issues falling within the scope of the Center's interest. Many local, Gulf, Arab and international dignitaries have visited ECSSR to acquaint themselves with its structure and objectives. Most of these visits were marked by the signing of scientific cooperation agreements, the delivering of lectures or the exchange of expertise with ECSSR officials on aspects of mutual interest.

One of ECSSR's prime objectives is the creation of a highly-skilled body of research staff. The Center has therefore undertaken an ambitious plan for training national research cadres who hold higher degrees in subjects relevant to its spheres of interest. Under this program, intensive training sessions are provided for its researchers to enhance their research and scientific skills. ECSSR also organizes specialized training sessions for individuals, institutions and local organizations to develop their skills in accordance with modern scientific elements and criteria.

Based on its constant monitoring of political, economic and military developments at both local and international levels, the Center conducts strategic research and studies and prepares specialized reports for decision makers and official bodies. Similarly, the Center creates and updates databases specifically for research purposes.

ECSSR exercises its functions and activities through three divisions: the Scientific Research Division, the Administrative Affairs Division and the Community Services Division. These are divided into departments, which, in turn, are sub-divided into units.

SCIENTIFIC RESEARCH DIVISION

Department of Strategic Studies
- UAE Studies
- GCC Studies
- Arab Studies
- Asian Studies
- European and North American Studies
- Military Studies

Department of Economic and Social Studies
- Economic Analysis
- Energy Studies
- Population and Labor Market Studies
- Social Studies

Department of Information
- Library
- Information Technology
- Statistics
- Information Sources
- Databases
- Information Research

ADMINISTRATIVE AFFAIRS DIVISION

Department of Personnel Affairs
- Personnel
- Recruitment
- Training

Department of Financial Affairs

Department of Services

COMMUNITY SERVICES DIVISION

Department of Conferences
 • Conferences

Department of Publications
 • Publications and Proofreading   • Journals
 • Translation   • Distribution and Exhibitions

Media Department
 • Media Monitoring   • Newsletters

Department of Public Relations and Scientific Cooperation
 • Public Relations   • Scientific Cooperation

Fields of Activity

Research and Studies
Preparing and Training Researchers
Community Services

Research and Studies

OBJECTIVES

- Collection of information and data and creation of databases for researchers and decision makers.
- Strategic research and systematic study of current issues to determine their impact on the UAE, the Gulf region and the Middle East.
- Study of international economic issues affecting the UAE and the Gulf region, especially those issues related to oil, international trade and economic blocs, in addition to local issues related to economic policies, organization of the labor market, population structure, development of national human resources and their contribution to the labor market.
- Monitoring of political, economic and social issues and any developments at local, regional and international levels which might influence the interests and policies of the UAE and the increasingly strategic Gulf region, assessing their significance and making scientific projections for the future.
- Identifying local and global issues of concern to the UAE in order of priority, assigning teams of researchers to analyze them and make relevant recommendations.
- Conducting studies based on factual data to anticipate and deal with developments prior to their occurrence, and avoid decision-making under pressure of real events. Such strategic studies must be based on realistic data and projections.
- Preparation of research digests for governmental institutions, research centers and universities.

PROGRAMS AND ACTIVITIES

ECSSR Research Activities

The main task of ECSSR researchers is to carry out research and prepare specialized strategic studies in the political, economic and social spheres. All ECSSR capabilities and resources are consequently dedicated to this purpose. Analytical and scholarly studies distinguish ECSSR's scientific research activity from those of other centers.

Research Scholarships

For the enrichment of research activity, ECSSR supprts special research projects and provides an opportunity for national researchers to become familiar with, and benefit from, the specialized research expertise available outside the Center. It runs an ambitious research scholarship program to recruit specialized researchers from within and beyond the UAE. Thus, the Center hosts the researcher or specialist who undertakes to prepare a study pertaining to ECSSR's fields of interest within a specified period. This enables the researcher to complete these studies, participate in a joint research project along with ECSSR researhers or devote attention to a subject that falls within the Center's scope. The visiting researcher may then submit the findings of the study at a seminar attended by specialists from within the Center and outside it. The Center may subsequently publish this study through one of its specialized periodicals.

Preparing and Training Researchers

OBJECTIVES

- Encouraging nationals to research issues relating to the UAE, through fellowships, awards and research support.
- Offering training sessions in specific fields for government employees to boost their performance.
- Organizing training sessions for ECSSR staff to improve their research skills.

PROGRAMS AND ACTIVITIES

Scholarship Program

ECSSR offers scholarships for UAE nationals to attend training courses or to obtain postgraduate degrees under the following terms:

1. Scholarships are offered for areas of study which are of interest to the Center. ECSSR has the right to choose the institute or university and the field of study.
2. Scholarships are of two types: postgraduate and training courses.
3. UAE nationals, whether ECSSR employees or otherwise, are eligible to apply for an ECSSR scholarship on condition that the applicant meets admission requirements and makes a commitment to study the specialization in the university chosen by the Center. Applicants must also undertake in writing to work at the Center immediately upon completion of their courses.
4. The right to attend a training session outside the UAE is confined solely to researchers working in the Center.
5. The period of the scholarship for the training session does not normally exceed one year, but may be extended by the Director General of the Center.
6. The Center bears the costs of travel and living expenses of the participating student in addition to all the study fees.
7. The Center's administration shall form a committee to assess applications and choose the candidates. The committee shall submit its recommendations to the Director General of the Center for a final decision.
8. Applicants shall be notified of the results of the assessment, which may be one of the following options: approval, deferred consideration of the application or rejection.
9. Immediately upon returning from the training session, the participant shall submit a detailed report to the Center on the activities undertaken during the session.

Training Programs for ECSSR Researchers

ECSSR aims to train and develop a qualified team of specialized researchers and spares no effort in strengthening research capabilities and practical skills. The Center's specialized 'Scientific Research Diploma' program initiates and trains participants to conduct scientific research in the political, economic, social and military fields and develops the skills of trainees in Arabic and English, as well as in computing and IT, within the framework of furthering scientific research. The duration of this program is nine academic months divided into three terms.

In addition to coordinating with foreign institutions to formulate programs for its researchers, ECSSR periodically organizes training programs within the Center, with a view to developing the skills and performance of researchers in computer usage, enabling them to deal with databases and information banks and use the Internet to exchange information on ways to obtain data relevant to the research subjects and projects undertaken by ECSSR.

Community Services

OBJECTIVES

- To enhance social and cultural awareness through the publication of studies and academic journals, and the organization of symposiums, conferences, seminars and lectures on issues that affect the UAE community.
- To encourage and develop research, authorship and translation, especially of studies dealing with topics of concern to the UAE, the Arab Gulf and Arab world in general.
- To organize seminars and research workshops at which strategic issues and their implications are discussed and investigated as academic matters in order to strengthen cooperative links with other academic institutions, to promote exchanges between lecturers and specialists through the convening of conferences, symposiums and seminars, and to participate in conferences organized within the UAE and abroad.

PROGRAMS AND ACTIVITIES

Research Projects Support Program
To promote scientific research, ECSSR has adopted a special scheme for supporting projects by specialized researchers who apply for scholarships funded from the Center's budget.

Assessment of Research Proposals: Criteria and Procedures
Criteria
1. The research should be relevant to ECSSR's interests.
2. The research should be conducted on issues related to the UAE and the Gulf region.
3. The research should be original and creative, and its findings should have an academic and practical value for the UAE and the Gulf.
4. The applicant should have the necessary expertise to conduct such research.
5. The proposed research budget should be commensurate with its academic value.
6. The research should be original and unpublished and should not be submitted to any other institutions for publication or otherwise.
7. The researcher should provide a detailed summary of the research project, including the expected time frame for completing the project, the methodology to be followed, the anticipated findings and the required budget.

Procedures
1. Researchers should submit a scholarship application with the required documents.
2. ECSSR will examine the application to ensure that all requisite information has been provided.
3. To maintain the distinguished scientific standards set by the Center, all scholarship applications shall be subject to professional assessment by a committee formed by ECSSR.
4. The assessment committee shall submit a detailed report on whether the project is suitable for financing and offer its recommendations to the administration of the Center.
5. The committee's recommendation shall be one of three options: approval, conditional approval or rejection.
6. In the event of approval, a contract shall be signed between the Center and the applicant stipulating all the conditions to be observed by the researcher.
7. In the event of conditional approval, the proposal shall be returned to the applicant to make the required revisions and returned thereafter to the Center for consideration.
8. In the event of rejection, the proposal shall be returned to the applicant.
9. The researcher may not submit more than one proposal at a time.
10. The researcher should submit a progress report mid-way through the research project along with a summary of the most important findings. The final report shall be submitted upon completion of the project.
11. The scholarship shall be granted in installments in proportion to the completed stages of the research. The applicant shall provide all the vouchers to the Center after completing each stage of the research.
12. All equipment bought for research purposes shall be the property of ECSSR.
13. ECSSR shall be the copyright holder of all research funded from its budget.

Books and Periodicals

This program aims to attract outstanding manuscripts and research studies conducted by researchers from the UAE and abroad. Such research shall be published by ECSSR in accordance with the following conditions:
1. The subject should fall within the scope of ECSSR's interests.
2. Both authored or co-authored studies submitted to the Center can be accepted.
3. Research studies proposed by the Center and conducted outside shall be on a contractual basis.
4. Research studies written both in Arabic and English may be accepted only if they are accurate and original.
5. The researcher should observe the rules and principles of scientific research methodology, including bibliography and endnotes.
6. Publications may include previously unpublished academic papers that were submitted to symposiums and local or international conferences. These papers should fall within the scope of the Center's interest and deal with issues related to the UAE and the Arab Gulf region.

7. All studies shall be refereed by a specialized scientific committee formed from among the competent editorial staff. The recommendations of the committee shall be one of three options: approval, conditional approval or rejection.
8. Authors shall be notified of the committee's decision. The unpublished papers shall not be returned to their authors.
9. The editorial staff shall assess the papers in terms of language and content.

Authorship, Translation and Publishing

ECSSR promotes research, authorship, translation and publishing with the aim of enriching Arab libraries with outstanding scholarly research studies on political, economic and social issues concerning the UAE and the GCC, as such studies remain limited. ECSSR therefore encourages and provides support for specialized researchers seeking to conduct such studies.

Application forms with detailed procedures are available from the Center for the following purposes: book writing, book translation, book publishing, publishing of research papers and research scholarships.

The applicant shall be notified of ECSSR's decision. In the case of approval, the two parties shall sign a contract stipulating the material and intellectual rights of the author and the publishing rights of the Center.

Conferences, Symposiums, Lectures and Workshops

To promote the image of the country in intellectual circles and among specialized research centers, ECSSR prepares an annual program of cultural activities. This includes lectures, symposiums, workshops and specialized conferences to foster an atmosphere for the exchange of research expertise inside the UAE and abroad, with a view to furthering research and publishing endeavors in the Center.

The Center has a multi-purpose meeting room equipped with state-of-the-art technological equipment that displays information in a sophisticated manner and facilitates ease of communication at many levels. Among the meeting room's most important facilities is the Worldnet, a global television network that specializes in broadcasting political, economic and cultural programs relevant to the Center's interests. The Worldnet provides an opportunity to record the required programs and replay them. It also permits live electronic dialogue via satellite between guests in the meeting room and guests at television studios in the USA and many other countries. Thus, interaction and dialogue can be conducted live via satellite, saving time, effort and money. Over one hundred satellite channels can be received by means of dish antennas available in the Center. The meeting room is also equipped with a computer, visualizer, slide projector and audio-visual equipment. All these devices are designed to display information on a super-screen with the help of a back projection system. Both presenter and audience benefit from the employment of such multi-media techniques, that present ideas with speed and clarity.

Organizational Structure

Scientific Research Division
Community Services Division
Administrative Affairs Division

Scientific Research Division

STRATEGIC STUDIES DEPARTMENT

The main objective of this department is to investigate and analyze the political and military aspects of current or anticipated events that may affect UAE national security in the local, regional and international arenas, propose appropriate recommendations and conduct prospective studies and research on ways to handle these issues.

The department includes the following units:

UAE Studies

Follows up, studies and analyzes domestic, political and security issues directly or indirectly affecting national security and decision making in the UAE and is also involved in the process of developing a comprehensive research plan to identify and study crucial issues in the UAE.

GCC Studies

Studies, follows up and analyzes Gulf issues related to UAE national security and prepares strategic reports related to these issues.

Arab World

Follows up, studies and analyzes political and security issues which directly affect UAE national security, or that of the Arab world in general, and the Middle East in particular. This unit also prepares analytical reports that support the decision making process in the UAE.

Asian Studies

Follows up and analyzes Asian political and security issues which have a direct or indirect impact on UAE national security.

European and North American Studies

This unit monitors European and North American political and security issues that have a direct impact on UAE national security. It also prepares studies and reports on issues related to European and North American countries.

Military Studies

Investigates and analyzes military and security crises that have a direct or indirect impact on UAE national security, with the aim of aiding UAE strategic military planning. It also prepares studies and research on more general military issues.

ECONOMIC AND SOCIAL STUDIES DEPARTMENT

The mission of this department is to conduct economic and social research leading to recommendations to formulate future UAE economic policies and to study and analyze economic transformations that influence UAE security and stability at the local, regional and international levels. The department also develops plans and programs intended to preserve the high standard of living for UAE citizens, as well as national stability and economic growth.

To realize its mission, the department defines long-term developmental trends that influence elements of the national economy, analyzes energy variables and their impact on the UAE economy and identifies and examines pioneer sectors and industries to develop and diversify the economy base and increase its competitive capability. The department also monitors local, regional and international developments and the changes which reflect their impact on the national economy in order to present the findings to policy makers. Moreover, the department conducts studies and research on the UAE labor market and population structure and develops standard economic models that assist in planning and economic forecasting. All information is regularly updated. This department comprises the following units:

Economic Analysis

Promotes studies relevant to the UAE's strategic position within the framework of the global economy. This units studies UAE macroeconomic policies, makes proposals for developing these policies, conducts studies seeking to minimize dependence on oil as a main source of UAE gross domestic product (GDP), and outlines the private sector's role in this strategy. It also:

- Identifies the potential strengths and weaknesses of the UAE economy.
- Evaluates current policies and their medium and long-term impact on UAE economic growth.
- Suggests alternative policies – if necessary – to realize desired economic objectives.
- Develops research plans to strengthen the UAE's economic base through diversifying sources of income instead of totally depending on oil, while taking into consideration the private sector's contribution.

Energy Studies

Given the importance of the oil sector within the UAE economy, this unit aims to assess the impact of world energy markets on the domestic economy, and the means that enable optimum use of oil and natural gas revenues. To realize this objective, the unit:

- Follows up on developments that affect oil and natural gas markets as well as other energy sources.
- Studies the effect of fluctuations in oil and natural gas production on the UAE economy.
- Proposes means and ways to alleviate the negative effects endured by the UAE economy.
- Makes proposals on the best means of using the surplus funds resulting from oil and natural gas sales.

Population and Labor Market Studies

Studies various domestic issues relating to the labor market and population, which may directly or indirectly affect the UAE's national security. The aim of the unit is to draw up the best policies that aim to organize the labor market and develop appropriate polices to expand job opportunities for UAE nationals and ensure their effective contribution to the workforce. The main functions of this unit are to:

- Analyze trends and policies of foreign labor and population.
- Develop and improve databases purposely designed for the labor market and population.
- Prepare questionnaires and surveys on the situation of the various labor communities.
- Provide analytical policy studies and practical recommendations.

Social Studies

The discovery of oil, the massive development achieved by the UAE and the GCC states within a short period of time, and the subsequent influx of foreign labor to the Gulf region have drastically affected the structure of the society and generated a host of social problems. Therefore, this unit is concerned with studying these effects and phenomena and proposing applicable solutions and policies.

INFORMATION DEPARTMENT

The mission of this department is to create comprehensive databases to support strategic planning, effectively and efficiently, in all circumstances, for serving the researchers and decision makers in the UAE, through application of the latest information and communication technologies.

To achieve its objectives, this department: provides and updates information sources in all fields of research; statistically analyzes data; designs research questionnaires; publishes specialized pamphlets and summaries; monitors the latest developments in the field of information; prepares relevant reports and studies; and develops administrative and library information systems in the Center. It also collects, classifies and summarizes information from various sources which include online services, data collected from information centers, CDs, and the information available in the Center's specialized data bases.

The department is also involved in monitoring daily news, events and articles for the benefit of researchers.

The Information Department comprises the following units:

Website Section

The Website Section is responsible for maintaining the ECSSR's comprehensive portal, through which politicians, strategists, researchers, students, and others can access diverse, accurate, and updated information, data, and analysis. The Section also allows visitors to communicate ideas through forums and opinion polls as well as to read about the latest local, regional, and international developments. Center activities and publications are closely followed and updated on the site and e-commerce options are available.

Public Opinion Polls Section

The objective of this section is to evaluate public opinion trends, in addition to undertaking field surveys and studies on various domestic, regional and international issues of interest to the ECSSR. The Center provides researchers and decision makers with data and the findings of its surveys to enhance their ability to make decisions on a systematic basis. So far the Section has undertaken several studies and surveys on local, regional and international issues.

Statistics Section

This unit develops the ECSSR's statistical base through:

- Establishing and updating specialized databases in all fields that concern the state, policy makers and researchers.
- Developing tools for statistical analysis.
- Conducting polls to measure public opinion trends regarding specific issues that concern the Center.
- Preparing statistical reports.

Information Sources Section

This section is responsible for collecting, storing and documenting information, acting as quickly as possible to provide the required information, and developing the Center's information capabilities. Information sources include subscriptions to international information centers, CDs, electronic archives, the internet and the library.

Databases Section

This section prepares general, specialized and statistical databases.

Information Research Section

This unit prepares specialized information reports and research.

Community Services Division

CONFERENCES DEPARTMENT

This department makes the necessary plans for organizing the activities of the Center, including conferences, symposia, lectures and workshops, and follows up their implementation stage by selecting vital issues, expert speakers, thinkers and specialists. The department focuses on political, economic, social, strategic and military issues that concern the UAE in particular and the Arab World in general. This unit has organized 31 conferences, 37 workshops, 20 symposia and 262 lectures covering political, economic, social and security issues that attracted the attention of decision makers, elites and intellectuals as well as Arab and international media.

PUBLICATIONS DEPARTMENT

This department has been established to enhance social and cultural awareness through the publication of specialized research and studies, encouraging and promoting research, writing and translation, and enriching Arab libraries with refereed academic books and periodicals. To attain these goals, the department seeks to publish distinguished works (original or translated) and serious scientific studies (in both Arabic and English) which deal with political, economic, social, informational, military and strategic issues of interest to the UAE and the Gulf region in particular, as well as the most important current events in the Arab and international arenas.

The ECSSR has published through this department more than 515 publications in Arabic and English.

Within this context, the department explores avenues of cooperation and communication with the largest possible group of researchers, academics and research institutions, at Arab and international levels, with the aim of translating and producing their work in the form of books and academic studies that observe scientific methodology and have a formal style of presentation. All units contribute to these efforts through translation, proofreading and editing. The department seeks to publish books and studies that meet the highest standards of design and printing.

Main duties:

- Publishes original books (in Arabic and English) which comprise the research papers presented at conferences, symposia and workshops organized by the Center throughout the year, with the aim of studying and analyzing the most important issues at local, regional and international levels. It also publishes original books written by authors cooperating with the Center on relevant issues.
- Publishes translated books that convey to the reader the latest intellectual thought through outstanding publications that were in great demand when first published in the original language.
- Publishes refereed studies and research papers in the Strategic Studies and Emirates Occasional Papers series that cover political, economic, social and strategic fields related to the UAE and the Arab Gulf region and deal with current issues and developments in the regional and international arenas.
- Publishes studies and research originally published in distinguished international periodicals and outstanding scientific journals, which investigate issues of concern to the Center. These research studies are published in the International Studies series after obtaining Arabic translation and publication rights.
- Publishes the Emirates Lecture Series, both in Arabic and English, which comprise lectures organized by the ECSSR within the framework of its various academic activities conducted during the course of the year. This series aims to make information accessible to readers, promote constructive dialogue and serious research and broaden horizons for interested readers.
- Contributes effectively to translating, editing, proofreading, revising, and preparing various texts published by the Center.
- Assists in the Center's efforts to recruit highly qualified candidates in the fields of editing, translation and proofreading.
- Follows up and maintains constant communication with interested parties (researchers, academics, readers, subscribers and research institutions) with the aim of acquainting them with the means and ways of strengthening research collaboration with the Center, and contributing to the Center's publications.

This department consists of the following sections:

Publications

This section is responsible for the editing and proofreading of texts and academic publications (original books, translated books, periodicals in Arabic and English).

Its responsibility starts with the selection of the research projects to be translated and published in the Center's translated books series or regular periodicals.

It maintains links with researchers and specialists in the Center's fields of interest, adopts and publishes distinguished studies in the form of original monographs in the strategic studies series or in the Emirates Occasional Papers.

This section is also responsible for promoting publication activity, through adopting new ideas to publish scientific book series and specialized books for the purpose of serving the reader and keeping pace with the Center's aspiration of publishing books that serve the interest of the largest possible section of readers and researchers, regardless of their age or level of education.

Translation

This unit undertakes various projects (books, studies and articles), translating them into the Arabic language, taking into consideration extreme accuracy and skill upon translation, primarily to serve the Arab reader and Arab libraries, through providing them with the latest and most distinct studies, without loosing the essence of the original text.

Distribution and Exhibitions

This unit undertakes distribution of the Center's publications to the largest possible number of concerned bodies, specialists, readers and libraries in the UAE and abroad. It also sets plans for participating in local and international book fairs.

Publications are distributed directly through the Center; through libraries inside and outside the UAE; certified agents and the Internet; and through participation in local, regional and international book fairs. These participations are greatly welcomed by exhibition organizers. Many publications have won prizes at local, regional and international levels. The title "Iran and the Gulf: A Search for Stability," edited by Dr. Jamal S. Al-Suwaidi, Director General of the ECSSR, won the 1st Prize for Humanities and Social Sciences, and the Best Authored prize at the International Book Fair, Sharjah, November 1997. Also, "Gulf Security in the 21st Century" received the Ben Torki award for Futurist Research and Planning in Medina, KSA 1998, which was awarded by the Ben Torki Institution for Poetic Innovation, Intellectual and Heritage Research sponsored by the Arab League.

The ECSSR's publications are greatly welcomed by researchers, concerned bodies and readers. More than one book has won a "best seller" title in more than one exhibition. By the end of January 2006, the Center had participated in more than 200 local, regional and international book fairs.

MEDIA DEPARTMENT

Monitors political, economic and military events and developments of particular relevance to UAE national security, by covering five main research areas; the UAE, the GCC countries, the Arab world, EU, US and Asian countries and the rest of the world.
This department comprises two units:

News Monitoring
This unit is responsible for monitoring various information resources. It follows up on television news programs and interviews related to political, military, and social subjects at the local, regional, and international levels. It records and saves such material by using the latest technologies in this field.

Newsletters
This unit undertakes the publishing of the *Akhbar Al-Sa'ah* and *Al-Alam Al-Youm* newsletters and the *Afaq Al-Mustaqbal* magazine.

LIBRARY DEPARTMENT

Caters to the needs of beneficiaries, including researchers and policy makers, from inside or outside the Center, through providing them with information covering all fields of knowledge (Political Science, Economics, History, Strategic Studies, Statistics, Labor and Population, and Military Sciences). The department also provides circulation services and reference services as well as selective dissemination of information.

Administrative Affairs Division

HUMAN RESOURCES DEPARTMENT

The main task of this department is to ensure application of the Center's rules, regulations, by-laws, and administrative decrees. It makes proposals for developing these regulations, in relation to the procedural and personnel dimensions.

This department undertakes and follows up on all procedures pertaining to the selection and recruitment of new staff for the filling of vacant positions, provides quality services for the Center's employees, and responds to their comments, suggestions, and complaints. It is also involved in developing staff skills and improving their professional performance by providing appropriate training programs.

This department is composed of three units:

Personnel Affairs
Supervises the implementation of all personnel procedures, starting with recruitment and finishing with end-of-service procedures in accordance with the effective rules and regulations. To achieve this end, the unit undertakes the following tasks:

- Organizes and documents employment and promotion procedures, change of status procedures and the assessment of staff performance.
- Oversees and facilitates personnel affairs regarding transportation, leave, official assignments, termination of service, renewal of contracts, and resignations.
- Maintains and updates staff files according to their departments, ranks, categories and academic qualifications.

- Facilitates service procedures for new and old employees regarding housing, expertise certificates, special permissions, residence permits, travel tickets and educational services for ECSSR staff children.
- Prepares reports and statistics reflecting the size of the Center's manpower resources.

Recruitment

This unit recruits highly competent personnel who are qualified to join the ECSSR, in accordance with the Center's regulations and procedures. It also undertakes the following:

- Contributes to determining the Center's needs in terms of human resources, and takes initiatives to meet such needs on the basis of merit, and to attract qualified persons to join the Center.
- Develops and proposes mechanisms for advertising vacant positions, receives and classifies applications, verifies candidates' credentials and prepares their files.
- Contributes and coordinates with other departments regarding the development of relevant tests with the aim of selecting the best candidates.

Quality Control

Undertakes assessment of the Center's policies with the aim of increasing departmental productivity.

Training

Since its inception in 1994, the ECSSR has been primarily concerned with promoting the skills of UAE national cadres in the fields of studies and research. To attain this objective, the Center has established a special training unit to train these research cadres.

Objectives
- Providing unique opportunities for UAE national researchers and employees to acquire new skills, knowledge and experience.
- Developing job descriptions for UAE national researchers and employees.
- Improving and refining the capabilities and skills of UAE national researchers and employees.
- Promoting cultural and knowledge levels of UAE national researchers and employees.

Assets

The Center aims to provide the technical and scientific assistance necessary for the training unit to function. Therefore, the Center focuses on:

- Recruiting distinguished teaching staff to participate in the implementation of the specialized training programs offered by the Center.
- Providing space for the training unit that includes three computer and language labs with a seating capacity of 14 trainees, in addition to a major seminar room that accommodates 40 trainees, a lecture room and 6 class rooms.
- Equipping the labs and classrooms with state-of-the-art audio-visual teaching aids, including DVDs and screens. All computer sets are linked to a local area network (LAN) which is connected to the Internet, in addition to a closed circuit TV system.

Programs

The ESCCR offers programs that aim to promote academic skills and train UAE national workers and employees to undertake their duties in a more effective and efficient manner. These programs include:

- Scientific Research Diploma: This aims to provide training on how to conduct academic research on political, economic, social and military issues, while taking care to improve the trainees' skills in Arabic and English languages, computing, and IT. The program's duration is nine months, distributed over three sessions.
- Specialized Training Courses: This aims to meet the training needs of national employees, technicians and administrators. They include: typing, word processing, SPSS (statistics), Arabic Language for Administrative Purposes, Specialized English Language, Personnel Management, Communications Skills, Reporting etc. The session duration varies from one week to three months.

ADMINISTRATIVE AND FINANCIAL AFFAIRS DEPARTMENT

This department undertakes the organization and administration of the ECSSR's administrative and financial affairs. It comprises three sections:

Financial Affairs

Organizes and administers ECSSR's financial affairs, and works towards developing and promoting these aspects in accordance with the effective financial regulations. Its duties include:

- Preparing the ECSSR's annual budget in coordination with the other departments and units.
- Monitoring expenditures and preparing periodic financial reports.
- Monitoring funding of research projects, scientific delegations and training sessions.

Purchasing

Provides all units with their needs, including equipment and services.

Public Relations

Formulates and imparts a clear image of the ECSSR through providing information about the Center, developing mutual ties and effective channels of communication between the Center and its internal environment on the one hand, and the Center and its external environment on the other, through strengthening bonds with local, regional and international research institutions. This unit aims to achieve the following:

- Enhance the mission, role, activities, and achievements of ECSSR.
- Establish and strengthen mutual ties between the Center and the local community.
- Establish reciprocal relations between the Center and various local and international news media.
- Foster mutual interaction between the staff and the Center's administration, with the aim of creating the ideal environment for collective work to ensure better performance.

Information Technology

This unit conducts research on IT and provides the relevant technologies to facilitate effective access to information sources. It also undertakes automation of procedures in the Center's departments to ensure easy flow of work and promptness, besides development of the electronic systems in the library.

Services Department

This department is responsible for providing administrative services for the various departments and units of the Center, including maintenance and cleaning services, security and safety, transportation, communication, and housing services.

Scientific Cooperation

ECSSR attaches great importance to establishing and developing cooperation with similar regional and international institutions, think tanks and research centers in order to conduct scientific research and exchange expertise, printed material and publications. Accordingly, the Center has concluded a number of agreements and scientific cooperation protocols with counterpart institutions at local, regional and international levels.

SCIENTIFIC COOPERATION AT THE LOCAL LEVEL

ECSSR supports active cooperation with the UAE University faculties such as the Faculty of Management and Economics and the Faculty of Humanities and Social Science.

The Center cooperates with ministries such as the Ministry of Foreign Affairs and the Ministry of Culture, Youth and Community Development, and with other public and private institutions in the country.

ECSSR seeks to develop mutual ties with these institutions and bodies in the following spheres:

- Joint research projects.
- Consultation and exchange of expertise and cadres.
- Exchange of printed material and specialized periodicals.
- Coordinating with the above-mentioned bodies to host their delegates at conferences, lectures and seminars.

SCIENTIFIC COOPERATION AT ARAB AND REGIONAL LEVELS

ECSSR is interested in developing ties with universities, institutes, scientific colleges, regional research centers and organizations that share the Center's fields of interest. Regional and Arab cooperation includes:

- Joint research projects.
- Exchanging expertise, visits, printed material and information.
- Reciprocal benefit from conferences, lectures, symposiums, seminars and training programs, organized either by the Center or the above-mentioned bodies.

SCIENTIFIC COOPERATION AT THE INTERNATIONAL LEVEL

ECSSR maintains close ties with prominent international scientific institutions and organizations through:

- Exchange of expertise, printed material, consultation and academic visits.
- Mutual coordination with a view to organizing conferences, lectures, symposiums, specialized seminars and training programs held by the Center throughout the year.

SCIENTIFIC COOPERATION AGREEMENTS AND PROTOCOLS

ECSSR has signed Scientific Cooperation Agreements with the following research institutions and centers:

Name of Institution	Date of Agreement
Middle East Institute (Washington, DC, USA)	October 1996
Netherlands Institute for International Relations, Clingendael (Gravenhage, Holland)	September 1996
Deutsches-Orient-Institut (Hamburg, Germany)	February 1997
Russian Center for Strategic and International Studies (Moscow, Russia)	February 1997
Center for Iranian Research and Analysis (Mobile, Alabama, USA)	February 1997
The Institute of Strategic Studies (Islamabad, Pakistan)	December 1997
Al-Urdun Al-Jadid Center for Studies (Amman, Jordan)	January 1997
Qatar Center for Futuristic Studies (Doha, Qatar)	February 1997
Egyptian Armed Forces Center for Strategic Studies (Giza, Egypt)	September 1997
Arab Thought Forum (Amman, Jordan)	December 1997
Jordanian Studies Center (Yarmouk University, Irbid, Jordan)	September 1998
Arab Research Center (Kuwait)	May 1999
Middle East Studies Center, Arizona University (Arizona, USA)	January 2000
The Center for Studies and Research in Damascus University, (Damascus, Syria)	February 2000
Lebanese American University (Beirut, Lebanon)	June 2000
Cornell University (New York, USA)	July 2000
The Turkish Foreign Policy Institute (Ankara, Turkey)	November 2000
Ukrainian National Institute of International Security Problems (Kiev, Ukraine)	January 2001
Zayed University (UAE)	May 2002
International Studies Association (Tunis, Tunisia)	October 2003
Tarik Ibn Zyad Center (Rabat, Kingdom of Morocco)	January 2004
Hashemite Jordanian Center for Documentation (Jordan)	June 2004

ECSSR looks forward to implementing these agreements & concluding other agreements in the future.

ECSSR has organized numerous conferences, lectures, symposiums and workshops in fields that fall within the scope of its interests and which concern the UAE, the Arab Gulf region and the Arab World. Elite UAE decision makers, outstanding academics at Arab and foreign universities and specialized scholars from research centers and academic institutions, as well as political personalities both from the UAE and abroad, have been invited to participate in these activities. This is in accordance with a comprehensive strategy that aims to make an effective contribution to the study of contemporary issues in order to promote scientific research and submit objective studies pertaining to these issues.

Activities

Recent Events
(January 2005–June 2006)

Conferences

11th Annual Energy Conference
Gulf Oil and Gas: Ensuring Economic Security
(September 25–27, 2005)

This conference investigated the economic and geopolitical impact of the recent record-high oil prices, and the projected long-term benefits for Gulf countries. In addition, the conference traced emerging trends in the energy sector, such as the globalization of the gas trade and the global supply and demand for different grades of oil. The conference also examined avenues for closer cooperation between consumers and producers and between national and foreign oil companies. It also focused on future trends in oil production, reserves, and the projected demand for Gulf energy.

Conference Papers:
1. Keynote Address: H.E. Sheikh Ahmad Fahad Al-Ahmad Al-Sabah, Kuwaiti Minister of Energy, Chairman of Kuwait Petroleum Corporation & President of OPEC (delivered by a delegate).
2. Dr. Herman T. Franssen, "Oil Prices: Challenges for the Producers."
3. Dr. Tarik M. Yousef, "Towards Economic Competitiveness: Strategies for Future Economic Security of the Gulf."
4. Dr. Edward L. Morse, "Highlighting Price Concerns: Hurricane Katrina and its Aftermath."
5. George S. Littell, "The Regional Instability Factor: Consequences for Long-Term Market Stability."
6. Peter I. Hughes, "The Emerging Gas Commodity Market: Globalization of Gas Trade."
7. Pedro Antonio Merino García, "Future Crude Quality Availability: Implications for Oil Markets."
8. Dr. Alberto Cisneros-Lavaller, "Oil Producer-Consumer Relations: Cooperation Opportunities within the Framework of Interdependence."
9. Prof. Jean-Pierre Favennec, "Investment Prospects for Foreign Oil Companies: Risks and Potential."
10. Aloulou Fawzi, "The Future Importance of the Gulf in US Energy Requirements."
11. Dr. Kang Wu, "Supplying Asia-Pacific Oil Demand: Role of the Gulf."
12. Nawaf E. Obaid, "Saudi Arabia's Sustainable Capacity and Security Issues."
13. Prof. Peter R. Odell, "The Market for Gulf Oil: Present Situation and Future Challenges."
14. Roger Diwan, "Diversity of Oil Supply: Implications for the Demand Security of Gulf Oil."

A session of the conference

H.H. Sheikh Mansour bin Zayed Al Nahyan, Sheikh Talal Khaled Al-Ahmad Al-Sabah and H.E. Mohammed bin Dhaen Al Hamli

H.E. Mandisi Mpahlwa, Minister of Trade and Industry, South Africa, and other conference attendees

Dr. Mohammad Ibrahim Al-Rumaithi chairing the first session of the conference

H.H. Sheikh Mansour bin Zayed Al Nahyan, Sheikh Talal Khaled Al-Ahmad Al-Sabah,
H.H. Sheikh Fahim bin Sultan Al Qassimi, H.E. Mohammed bin Dhaen Al Hamli and other attendees

11th Annual Conference:
Current Transformations and their Potential Role in Realizing Change in the Arab World
(March 12–14, 2006)

The ECSSR organized this conference under the patronage of H.H. Gen. Sheikh Mohammed bin Zayed Al Nahyan, Crown Prince of Abu Dhabi, Deputy Supreme Commander of the UAE Armed Forces and President of the ECSSR.

The conference examined the nature of reform in Arab countries in the light of significant changes that have occurred over the past few years. The conference explored the link between economic growth and political change as well as challenges arising from international terrorism. It also addressed crucial issues raised by the series of three Arab Human Development Reports issued by the United Nations Development Program (UNDP), with the focus on education and the changing nature of Arab society.

Conference Papers:
1. Keynote Address: H.E. Abdulrahman Al-Attiyah, Secretary General of the Gulf Cooperation Council (GCC).
2. The Honorable William S. Cohen, "New and Future Leadership: Implications for Change."
3. Dr. Bourhan Ghalioun, "The Problem of Reform in the Arab World."
4. Dr. Clovis Maksoud, "Arab Political Reform and the Middle East Peace Process."
5. Prof. Metin Heper, "Modernity and political Transformation: The Turkish Experience."
6. Dr. Amitav Acharya, "Protecting Sovereignty in an Age of Regionalism."
7. Dr. Marina Ottaway, "The Role of Non-State Actors in Promoting Change."
8. Dr. Gary Hart, "Encouraging the Independence of State Institutions."
9. H.E. Yasser Abed Rabbo, "The Role of External Pressure in Encouraging Home-Grown Reform."
10. Dr. Adnan Pachachi, "Iraq as an Example of the "Spread of Democracy" through the Arab World."
11. Dr. Amr Hamzawy, "Political Transformation in the Arab World: The Role of Islamist Actors."
12. H.E. Dr. Mohammed Bin Ali Kouman, "Causes of Terrorism and Ways to Combat it in the Arab World."
13. H.E. Sheikh Nahyan Mubarak Al Nahyan, UAE Minister of Higher Education and Scientific Research, "The Importance of Education in Regional Development."
14. H.E. Dr. Faisal Al-Rufouh, "The Position of Education as a Catalyst for Social Change: The Arab World as a Case Study."

15. H.E. Dr. Ibrahim Guider, "Losing Talent to Other Countries: Halting the Arab 'Brain-Drain'."
16. Dr. Rafia Obaid Ghubash, "One Goal and Different Agendas: Expanding the Scope of Education in the Arab World and Addressing the Needs of the Labor Market."
17. H.E. Dr. Massouma Al-Mubarak, Kuwaiti Minister of Planning & State Minister for Administrative Development, "Activating the Role of Women in Development: Current Realities and Future Prospects - A Case Study of Kuwaiti Women."
18. Dr. Matar Ahmed Abdullah, "International Emigration and Population Composition in the GCC Countries."

H.E. Sheikh Nahyan Mabarak Al Nahyan delivering his lecture

H.E. Abdulrahman Al-Attiyah, Secretary General of the Gulf Cooperation Council (GCC)

Dr. Rafia Ghubash, Dr. Faisal Al-Rufouh, Dr. Ibrahim Guider and Panel Chair Dr. Fatima Al-Sayegh

H.E. Yousef bin Alawi, H.E. Abdulrahman Al-Attiyah, H.E. William Cohen,
Dr. Jamal Al-Suwaidi and other attendees of the conference

H.E. Yousef bin Alawi, H.E. Abdulrahman Al-Attiyah,
H.E. William Cohen and Sheikh Mohammed bin Hamad Al-Sharqi

H.E. Yousef bin Alawi talking with Dr. Jamal Al-Suwaidi

H.E. William Cohen during his lecture

Symposiums

Turkey and the Arabian Gulf
(December 18–19, 2005)

This symposium examined common interests between GCC countries and Turkey. It focused on issues of regional stability, the problems of Iraq, Iran and the Middle East and the strengthening commercial and economic relations between the GCC and Turkey in light of the current negotiations towards a Turkey–GCC free-trade agreement.

Papers Presented:

1. Welcoming Remarks: The Emirates Center for Strategic Studies & Research (ECSSR), H.E. Khalid Ghanim Al-Ghaith, Ambassador of the UAE to Turkey, and H.E. Selim Karasomanoğlu, Ambassador of Turkey to the UAE.
2. Prof. Dr. Ali Lutfi Karaosmanoğlu and Dr. Mustafa Kibaroglu, "Turkey's Security Policy in the Middle East and the Arabian Gulf."
3. Dr. Ahmad A. Shikara, "Threat Perceptions of the Gulf States and Their Security Policies."
4. Dr. Ali Tekin and Seyfullah Nejat Tashan, "Turkey's Relationship with the EU and Its Implications for the Middle East and the Arabian Gulf."
5. Ahmet Necdet Pamir, "Turkish Energy Security: Role of the Arabian Gulf and the Caspian and Black Sea Basins."
6. Dr. Mohammad Al-Asoomi, "Development of Bilateral Trade and Investment."

Iraq's Constitution: Implications for Iraq and beyond
(December 27, 2005)

This symposium studied the strengths and weaknesses of the new Iraqi constitution, assessed how it would contribute to the modernization and development of the country, assessed the position of religious and ethnic groups, the position of Islam and civic society in the constitution, and the impact this may have on the security and the stability of Iraq. It also aimed to give an understanding of the outlook of various powers toward the constitutional amendment in the wake of the elections of the Iraqi National Assembly.

Papers Presented:
1. Humam Hammoudi, "The New Constitution: Strengths, Weaknesses, and Consequences."
2. Dr. Faleh Abdul Jabar and Dr. Muwafaq al Rubaii, "Iraq's Factions, Regional Interests and the Constitution."
3. Shukri Saleh Zaki and Dr. Muwafaq al Rubaii, "Islam, Society, the State and the Constitution (in Iraq)."

Iran's Nuclear Program: Realities and Repercussions
(February 26, 2006)

This symposium and the related discussion assessed the current and future trends pertaining to Iran's nuclear program, its overall impact on international stability and its particular effects on regional security. It also examined the potential role that regional diplomacy can play in addressing the problems posed by the Iranian nuclear program.

Papers Presented:
1. Welcoming Remarks: Aida Abdullah Al-Azdi, ECSSR Deputy Director General for Community Services.
2. Prof. John Simpson, "Iran's Nuclear Capability: The Potential to Develop Atomic Weapons."
3. Dr. George Perkovich, "Iran's Nuclear Program after the 2005 Elections."
4. James H. Noyes, "Iranian Nuclear Program: Impact on the Security of the GCC."
5. Geoffrey Aronson, "Iran's Nuclear Program and its Impact on Israeli Foreign Policy."
6. Sverre Lodgaard, "Prevention of Iranian Nuclear Proliferation: The Role of Regional Diplomacy."

France and the Arabian Gulf
(June 3–4, 2006)

This symposium examined common interests between France and the countries of the Arabian Gulf. The first day of the symposium focused on France's role in contributing to regional stability and security. The military relationships between France and the GCC countries were also discussed, with a special focus on those GCC states with which France has concluded defense agreements. The symposium also explored ways to strengthen commercial and economic relations between France and the GCC in the light of the current negotiations towards an EU-GCC free trade agreement, as well as the broader relationship between the GCC and the European Union.

Papers Presented:
1. Welcoming Remarks: Ms. Aida Abdullah Al-Azdi, ECSSR Deputy Director General for Community Services and H.E. Patrice Paoli, Ambassador of France to the UAE.
2. H.E. Abdullah Ahmed Al-Saleh, "Overview of Economic and Trade Ties between France and the UAE."
3. Mr. Denis Bauchard, "French Foreign Policy towards the GCC States: Strategic Issues and Considerations."
4. Mr. Jacques Boyon, "The Role of France in Conflict Management in the Middle East."
5. Dr. Fatiha Dazi-Heni, "Military and Security Cooperation between France and the GCC."
6. Mr. Charles Saint-Prot, "EU-GCC Relations: The French Perspective."
7. Amb. Bernard Savage, "EU-GCC Relations: The EU Perspective."
8. Dr. Ali Mohammed Fakhro and Mrs. Nathalie Meriem Goulet, "The Role of France in Cross-Cultural Communication with the GCC States."

Workshops

Earthquake Disaster Mitigation: Why is it Necessary?
(February 12, 2006)

This workshop was organized under the patronage of His Highness General Sheikh Mohammed bin Zayed Al Nahyan, Crown Prince of Abu Dhabi, Deputy Supreme Commander of the UAE Armed Forces, and President of the ECSSR. A number of seismographers participated in the workshop, which provided a valuable opportunity for discussion on the risks of seismic activity in the UAE, and how to reduce its effects. The predictability of earthquakes is very limited. Therefore, structural improvements must be introduced to buildings and urban structures.

Opinion Polls in the Arab World: Opportunities and Challenges
(April 17–18, 2006)

A number of experts from research centers and universities participated in this workshop, which deliberated upon available opportunities for conducting opinion polls, the challenges that face them, methodological and other issues associated with the design and implementation of public opinion research, and conducting surveys and social research. It also addressed the problems, topics, strengths, and weaknesses of social research, the dependability of Arab social research on the priorities of regimes in the fields of economic and social development.

Ways of Motivating Employees
Dr. Abdulla Alawadi
Advisor, Center for Labor Market Research and Information
The National Human Resources Development and Employment Authority
(May 16, 2006)

This workshop dealt with one of the basics for administration, namely effective employee motivation. In its first session, the workshop focused on the definition of motivation, motivation theories such as the one propounded by Maslow, and the importance of social motivation. In the second session, a survey questionnaire based on the theory by psychologist David McClelland was distributed to the participants. The aim was to understand the role of suitable incentives for each respondent separately, when the matter relates to his/her career or why he/she aspired to certain jobs to the exclusion of others.

Lectures

(250–262)

The Palestinian Question and the Gaza Withdrawal Plan: Real or Illusory Detente?

Dr. Ahmed Al-Tibi & Mr. Mohammed Baraka
Arab Members of the Knesset
(February 22, 2005)

Details of the Israeli plan for withdrawal from Gaza reveal that it includes the evacuation of settlements, redeployment of forces and imposition of a land, sea and air blockade on the territory. The plan is to give up a small piece of land in order to retain the greater part of the Occupied Territories; evacuate 8000 settlers from the West Bank in order to ward off international pressure that calls for a permanent solution, which is unacceptable to Israel. It is also aimed at creating a scenario that hinders negotiations.

Russian Relations with Europe and the US: Implications for Global Security

Prof. Vitaly V. Naumkin
President of the International Center for Strategic and Political Studies, Moscow, Russian Federation
(March 29, 2005)

In recent years, Russian relations with the West have suffered setbacks. In the West, Vladimir Putin is often criticized for resurrecting authoritarianism, using excessive force in Chechnya, and for attempting to turn the post-Soviet space into a zone of Moscow's influence. The USA has expressed concern over Russian cooperation with Iran in the field of nuclear energy and is alarmed by Moscow's intention to sell anti-aircraft missile complexes to Syria. In Russian political circles, the West is criticized for seeking to oust Russia from a region where it has security interests, and to impede the process of Moscow's integration into Western structures. Despite sharp rhetoric, the process of Russia's rapprochement with the West continues: Russia is preparing to join the WTO, the energy dialogue is developing, the Russia-NATO Council continues to function, and the two sides are cooperating in combating terrorism and countering WMD proliferation.

Azerbaijan's Place in the Modern World
H.E. Elmar Mammadyarov
Minister of Foreign Affairs, Republic of Azerbaijan
(April 6, 2005)

The Republic of Azerbaijan is facing the first steps towards economic and political integration into the international community (membership of the United Nations, the Organization for Security and Co-operation in Europe, the Council of Europe, and the Organization of the Islamic Conference). It is furthering its ties with its neighbors, Russia and Iran, and is seeking to strengthen its relationship with the Arab League and the Gulf Cooperation Council (GCC). The goal of achieving a lasting peaceful settlement with Armenia remains, as does the need for international mediators to assist in the process. The role of Azerbaijan's energy policy will play a crucial role in promoting its ideals of sovereignty and independence and in diversifying its economy (especially in light of the 'Contract of the Century' agreement between Azerbaijan and a consortium of foreign oil companies, which opened up the Caspian Basin).

Challenges & Opportunities in the Middle East: An American Perspective
Dr. Richard N. Haass
President, Council on Foreign Relations, USA
(May 4, 2005)

The Middle East today presents several opportunities: for an Israeli withdrawal from Gaza and parts of the West Bank and a move from there towards a comprehensive settlement of the Israeli-Palestinian issue; for the consolidation of democracy and order in post-Saddam Iraq and post-Syria Lebanon; and the promotion of political, social, educational and economic reform throughout the entire region. None of these opportunities, however, will be easy to realize and in no case is success inevitable. For that reason, all of these opportunities can also be described as challenges. There are also challenges posed by Iran's nuclear program, the existence of terrorist groups, and basic demographic realities. Although progress toward realizing one set of opportunities (or meeting one set of challenges) can help with others, it is equally true that setbacks in one area can complicate attempts to make progress in others.

Global Oil Markets, US Demand & the Impact of Hurricane Katrina

Guy F. Caruso
Administrator at the Energy Information Administration (EIA)
United States Department of Energy
(November 13, 2005)

Continued high crude oil prices had been expected prior to Hurricanes Katrina and Rita. International factors, such as low oil spare capacity, low supply growth and other uncertainties had led to tight global markets. The complete recovery of the energy infrastructure affected by the hurricane will take many months. However, considerable recovery should be achieved by the end of 2005. The restart of two major refineries in western Louisiana and another in Pascagoula, Mississippi during the first week of October is particularly encouraging, as is the resumed – although limited – operation of the Henry Hub. However, energy market projections are subject to considerable uncertainty. Price projections are particularly uncertain, because small shifts in either supply or demand, which are both relatively insensitive to price changes in the current market environment, can necessitate large price movements to restore the balance between supply and demand.

NATO's Role in Southwest Asia and the Arabian Gulf

Dr. Philip H. Gordon
Director, Center on the United States and Europe
The Brookings Institution, USA
(December 20, 2005)

Only about a decade ago, NATO member states were still engaged in serious debate about whether the organization should take on missions and responsibilities beyond the Alliance's traditional borders. However, NATO invoked its Article 5 defense clause for the first time ever after the September 11 attacks in the United States. It has deployed a peacekeeping force of nearly 10,000 troops to Afghanistan; launched a training operation for Iraqi forces; created the NATO Response Force; launched the Istanbul Cooperation Initiative to develop its political and military relations with members of the Gulf Cooperation Council; and expanded its Mediterranean Dialogue to facilitate political dialogue with Middle Eastern countries including Israel and Egypt. Therefore, the trend toward greater NATO involvement in and around Southwest Asia is clear and NATO's role there is likely to continue to grow.

Syrian–Lebanese Relations: Origins and Prospects
Mr. Hazem Saghia
Journalist with Al-Hayat Newspaper, U.K.
(January 3, 2006)

Syria and Lebanon have had a complex and difficult relationship since their independence in the mid-1940s. The relationship was further complicated by growing conflicts in the Middle East. Having political disputes with Egypt and a contentious relationship with Iraq, Syria felt that Lebanon was the only arena for settling its problems and strengthening its influence for reclaiming the Golan Heights that were occupied by Israel in 1967.

Healing the Transatlantic Rift:
Moves towards US–European Cooperation in the Middle East
Dr. Charles A. Kupchan
Senior Fellow and Director of European Studies, Council on Foreign Relations
Professor of International Affairs, Georgetown University, USA
(January 29, 2006)

Dealing with the Middle East has for decades proved to be a very divisive issue for the United States and Europe. During the long decades of the Cold War, heated transatlantic disputes emerged over a host of issues, including the Suez Canal, the Palestine–Israel conflict, and the containment of Iran. However, these differences did not significantly impair transatlantic relations, due to the solidarity engendered by the Soviet threat in Europe. With the demise of the Soviet Union, common tasks in Europe no longer overshadow differences over other regions and the Middle East is now at the top of the transatlantic agenda. Differences over Middle East policy have therefore become more consequential and have contributed to the erosion of transatlantic amity in the post-Cold War era. However, recent trends indicate a gradual convergence of approach, suggesting that the transatlantic divide of the past few years may be on the mend.

Asia: The Strategic Picture in 2010
Nasim Zehra
Senior Fellow, Harvard University Asia Center
Visiting Professor at the School of Advanced International
Studies, Johns Hopkins University
(March 25, 2006)

In the opening years of the first decade of the twenty-first century, Asia has established itself as the locale for all the major themes of contemporary international affairs. These include economic growth; energy security; trade relations; nuclear proliferation; political conflicts; the war on terrorism; and inter-civilizational issues, all of which are powerful determinants effecting change in the modern world. This lecture explored the likely strategic scenario in 2010, covering Asia's key relationships and key conflict areas. Significant relationships including those between China and America; North Korea and South Korea; India and China; and Pakistan and India were covered. The likely outcome of the conflicts extending through the Arc of Crisis was also reviewed.

South Africa's Foreign Policy Perspective and its Impact on the Arabian Gulf
Dr. Chris Landesberg
Director, Centre for Policy Studies (CPS)
South Africa
(April 24, 2006)

In order to advance African and Middle East agendas, South Africa has engaged in deft and carefully calibrated geo-strategic diplomacy both within the continent and in the Middle East. It has developed strategic partnerships in these regions and has built support bases and alliances with key states in the Middle East. South Africa is committed to an "African Agenda" and a "South–South" agenda, in which the Middle East features prominently. South African, African and Middle Eastern politics are inextricably intertwined. There cannot be a peaceful Middle East without a peaceful Africa and vice versa. Therefore, the government has keenly pursued a "quiet leadership" approach, towards the broader continent of Africa, as well as the Middle East.

Renewed Conflict in Sri Lanka: A Return to War?

Dr. Chris Smith
Associate Fellow, Chatham House
London, UK
(May 9, 2006)

In 2002, Sri Lanka looked set to bring an end to the civil war that had plagued the island for nearly twenty years and claimed the lives of 64,000 soldiers and civilians. As the peace process got underway, the main questions that remained concerned the extent of devolution and federalism that the Sri Lankan government would be prepared to grant the Liberation Tigers of Tamil Eelam (LTTE). One year later, however, serious differences emerged between the two sides and eventually the LTTE refused to negotiate any further. By February 2006, it was clear that the LTTE had encouraged the beginnings of an uprising in Jaffna and then Trincomalee. To all intents and purposes, the peace process is in ruins.

Iraq and American Empire:
Can Arab-Americans Influence Middle East US Policy?

Prof. Rashid Khalidi
Director, the Middle East Institute
Columbia University, USA
(June 5, 2006)

The lecture addressed the broader implications of the invasion of Iraq. It then considered briefly the degree to which Arab-Americans affect the formulation of American Middle East policy, and how this may change in the future. The invasion, occupation and subsequent restructuring of Iraq by American hands have taken place without justification in international law. Earlier forms of US global domination were generally exercised indirectly and through multilateral alliances or indigenous governments. These indigenous governments were generally not created as a result of the invasion and occupation of these countries, and their restructuring by American hands from the ground up. However, this is what has happened in Iraq since March 2003. To understand the limits of the political influence of Arab-Americans, although there are perhaps 4 million of them, it is essential to understand how poorly assimilated most of them are into American society. Many were not educated in the United States and do not understand how the American political system works. Furthermore, many of them live isolated from the larger society around them. It is not hard to understand that the impact on American politics of people in such circumstances is limited.

Activities

Record of Past Events
(March 1994–January 2005)

The following is a complete list of conferences, symposiums, workshops and lectures that have taken place since the inauguration of the Center, classified according to subject. Those entries appearing again under the same or a revised title in the chapter entitled "ECSSR Publications" are marked either by date of publication (books) or by the series in which they are published, *Emirates Occasional Papers* (EOP) and *Emirates Lecture Series* (ELS). These cross-references relate only to the English publications.

In November 1996, the 25th anniversary of the UAE's formation, ECSSR hosted a ten-part lecture series, "25 Years of a United Federation of Arab Emirates: Challenges and Horizons," on the achievements of the UAE and the late President H.H. Sheikh Zayed bin Sultan Al Nahyan (may Allah have mercy on him). These lectures appear under their subject headings.

ARAB/ISRAELI PEACE PROCESS

Arab-Israeli Peace: Prospects and Regional Implications (6/19–20/94) S
This event was held within weeks of the historic peace agreement signed between the PLO and Israel. Scholars and policy practitioners from the region and beyond participated in this symposium.

Papers presented:
Dr. Ann Lesch (EOP1), "The Relations among Arab States" – The paper discussed possible changes in the event of a resolution of the Arab–Israeli conflict. It also highlighted the likely impact on domestic politics in key Arab countries.
Dr. Khalil I. Shikaki (ELS6), "Palestinian Relations with the Arab States" – The focus was on possible future Palestinian foreign policy. Factors pushing the Palestinian leadership toward "radical" foreign policy alternatives and those encouraging a more "moderate" tone were examined.
The Hon. Michael P.W. Stone, "Security in the Middle East: Is Israel the Only Issue?" – The Gulf War emphasized the need for powerful military coalitions and well-trained and equipped soldiers when faced with a regional threat. Opportunities for the region's political actors following the Gulf War and ongoing Arab-Israeli peace talks were pinpointed.
Dr. Shibley Telhami (ELS7), "The US and the Middle East" – The absence of an active role by the US in the Oslo Accords was highlighted. Domestic and international variables driving US policy in the post-Gulf War period were analyzed.
Dr. Mark Tessler (EOP2), "Israel at Peace with the Arab World" – Issues tackled included the position Israel is likely to seek in the Middle East if conflict with the Arab world is resolved, the likely impact on Israel's ties with key actors outside the region and the ways in which peace will affect the political dynamics inside Israel.

Other participants: Ambassador Richard Murphy (US Council on Foreign Relations); Dr. Anwar Gargash (Department of Political Science at UAE University); Dr. Shafiq Al-Ghabra (Department of Political Science at Kuwait University).

The Peace Process: the Gulf and Israeli Calculations (4/21/96) L
Dr. Mohammad Muslih
Asst. Professor of Political Science and International Relations
Long Island University, USA

This lecture examined the peace process, focusing on aspects of the permanent solution of the Palestinian track; causes of the Syrian track deadlock; possible solutions; sources of tension in the peace process from Israeli and Arab perspectives; the dynamics of interaction between regional developments and the peace process; and the nature of the American role. Also discussed were Israeli interests in the Gulf from the Israeli perspective, indicating the importance of the Gulf in Israeli strategic calculations, and emphasizing the Israeli assessment of the Iraqi and Iranian roles, and of US strategies in the region.

The Arab–Israeli Peace Process in the Wake of the American Elections (10/21/96) L
Dr. Kamil Abu Jaber
Former Foreign Minister and Member of the Senate
Hashemite Kingdom of Jordan

This lecture provided an analysis of the reasons for the current obstacles in the Arab–Israeli peace process, and the future dimensions of that process. The rise to power of Benjamin Netanyahu as Israeli premier has not only hampered the peace process but has also threatened Middle East security. Dr. Abu Jaber discussed the effect of Netanyahu's childhood on his political outlook and also noted the pivotal role that the US must play to get the peace process back on track.

The Israeli Political System (10/19/99) (ELS27) L
Dr. Peter Gubser
President of American Near East Refugee Aid

The Israeli political system has absorbed laws and institutions from Ottoman rule and the British Mandate. Equally important were Zionist institutions based in Europe and their relocation in Palestine. These institutions and political forces continue to influence the Israeli political system. Aspects discussed included the historical antecedents of the Israeli system, the principal institutions and how they interact with major political forces in the country, the result of the Israeli elections of 1999 and the reasons for the change in leadership.

Jerusalem and the Peace Process in the Middle East (12/27/99) L
Mr. Naser El-Deen El-Nashasheebi
Writer and Journalist, Palestine

This lecture demonstrated the continuing judaization of Jerusalem effected by the Israeli government. In addition to the policy of settlement, which is intended to change the features of the holy city, Israel continues to destroy Arab homes, exercising a search policy, and withdrawing identity cards from the Palestinians. It claims that Jerusalem is the "eternal capital" of Israel. Although Israel joined the UN in 1949 under the condition of recognizing the international status of the holy city, it still rejects this status. Jerusalem remains the cornerstone of a comprehensive peace.

Constants and Variables in the Arab-Israeli Struggle and the Form of the Next War (2/25/01) L

Major General (Ret.) Tal'at Ahmed Mussallam
Former Chief-of-Staff, Infantry Brigade, Egyptian Army
Reporter, Labor Party Political Office
Managing Director of Al Shaab

Arab imperatives were abandoned due to variables in the Arab–Israeli conflict, as shown by the recognition of Israel and the abandonment of the three "Nos" of the Khartoum conference. Unchanging realities are the inevitability of struggle, the rise of Israel as the result of occupation, racist colonization and dependence on a foreign power. Israeli "invincibility" collapsed after the 1973 war and the triumph of Lebanese resistance. Confrontation may include a popular liberation war, electronic and information warfare, air and missile strikes and limited operations.

Jerusalem: Realities and Prospects in the Light of Regional and International Developments (4/23/01) L

H.E. Dr. Jawad Al Anani
Former Jordanian Deputy Prime Minister and Foreign Minister and Member of the House of Notables

The speaker reviewed the changes witnessed by Jerusalem since the Israeli occupation in 1967. Muslims ought to play an important role in order to secure their legitimate rights in the holy city in any comprehensive settlement of the Palestinian issue.

ASIAN/ARAB RELATIONS

Conceptual Sources of Iranian Foreign Policy (1/24/95) L

Prof. Mahmood Sariolghalam
Research Director, Center for Middle East Studies
Tehran, Islamic Republic of Iran

Following the 1979 Islamic revolution, Iranian foreign policy underwent several key changes. Dr. Sariolghalam explored two distinct periods: the period prior to the 1988 ceasefire in the Iran–Iraq War, and the period that followed. He also introduced four concepts fundamental to the understanding of Iranian foreign policy, namely authenticity, historical negativism, ideological egalitarianism and revolutionary idealism, and focused on the strong links between domestic and foreign politics.

UAE–Pakistan Roundtable (3/30-31/96) W

This forum assessed aspects of the UAE–Pakistan relationship – political dimensions, security, joint economic development, and the role of expatriate labor in bilateral relations. Prominent scholars from both countries participated in the workshop. Representing Pakistan were: Senator Aitzaz Ahsan, former Minister of the Interior; The Honorable M. Akram Zaki, former Ambassador of Pakistan to China and the US; Brigadier (Ret.) Mohammad Yusuf and Fazel ur-Rehman of the Institute for Strategic Studies in Islamabad.

Asian Perspectives Towards the Arab Gulf (11/15–16/97) C

This conference analyzed the dynamics of expanding bilateral and unilateral relationships between the countries of the Arabian Gulf and the Asian continent. The diverse and growing interdependence between the two groups calls for investigation of how they view each other and what each can learn from the other's experiences. The conference projected the views of several Asian countries in relation to the states of the Arab Gulf. The panel included speakers from China, Japan, South Korea, India, Pakistan, Malaysia, Indonesia, the Philippines and Singapore.

Conference papers:

Dr. Jamal S. Al-Suwaidi, ECSSR Director General, "Opening Speech."

Mr. K. S. Balakrishnan (EOP25), "Pacific Asian Security and the ASEAN Regional Forum: Lessons for the GCC States."

Dr. Chong-Ki Choi, "Asian Perspectives Towards the Arab Gulf: A Korean Point of View."

Mr. Omar Halim, "Strengthening Links Between Indonesia and the GCC Countries: An Indonesian View."

Dr. Tsuyoshi Kurokawa, "Japan's Foreign Policy on Major Middle East Issues."

Dr. Wu Miaofa, "Chinese Foreign Policy Towards the Arab Gulf Region and the Middle East."

Dr. Mohammed Aslam Qureshi, "Pakistan's Security Options After the Second Gulf War."

Dr. Julius Caesar Parreñas (EOP26), "Economic and Security Considerations: The Role of the GCC States in the Stability and Development of ASEAN."

H.E. Veluthevar Kanaga Rajan (EOP28), "Asia Towards the Gulf: Prospects for Cooperation."

Air Commodore (Ret.) Jasjit Singh (EOP27), "Indian Perspectives on West Asia and the Potential for Enhancing Peace and Cooperation."

The Balance of Power in South Asia (10/11–12/98) (Publ. 2000) S

This symposium analyzed the political and military ramifications of South Asia's regional security in the light of nuclear detonations by both India and Pakistan and their impact on the Gulf. As many migrants from the sub-continent reside in the UAE, South Asian developments are of strategic concern. Potential instability arising from the South Asian arms race and the alignments of other members of the nuclear club in response are an additional cause for concern.

Air Commodore (Ret.) Jasjit Singh, Director of the Institute for Defense Studies and Analyses in New Delhi, delivered a paper on "India and Regional Security in South Asia." He assessed the difficulties of the continuing conflict in Afghanistan, the East Asian financial crisis, ballistic missile deployment, drug trafficking and strategic uncertainties associated with China. The differences in the nuclear rationale of India and Pakistan and the resulting political consequences were reiterated. Mr. Najam Rafique, speaking from Pakistan's perspective, emphasized the significance of the rapid emergence of a new world order, based on equitable political growth, sustainable economic development and the integrity of stable frontiers. The rationale behind Pakistan's subsequent detonations was explained.

Dr. Christian Koch explored the intricate implications of the Chinese influence on the region, while Professor Marvin Weinbaum offered a US perspective on the limits of regional *realpolitik*. Dr. Mohammed Al-Rumaihi examined the impact of nuclear proliferation on the Gulf region and Dr. Eric Arnett compared the potential outcomes of an air battle between India and Pakistan, and assessed the force posture between the two countries.

The Security Environment in Central Asia (3/16/99) (ELS22) L
Prof. S. Frederick Starr
Chairman, Central Asia-Caucasus Institute
Johns Hopkins University, USA

The newly established states in Central Asia and the Caucasus are surrounded by major regional and international powers, three of which have nuclear weapons. Several security threats now challenge the stability of the region. Domestically, the real implications of the conflict over new wealth, i.e. oil and gas, have to be considered, as well as issues like the scarcity of water, inequality in income, population growth, ethnic tension, rapid urban development, the conflict over religion versus secularism, corruption and drug trafficking. Any effective security system needs to enhance the security environment of the whole region.

Emirati-Indian Relations in the Next Decade (I) (4/13–14/99) S
This symposium was organized in collaboration with the Institute for Defence Studies and Analyses (IDSA) in the Indian capital, New Delhi. The consolidation of existing research ties was stressed as the world enters a new century in which new international relations with different concepts and constants are expected to prevail. Three main topics were tackled from both Emirati and Indian perspectives: Emirati-Indian relations, economic and commercial relations, and security cooperation. A joint research paper presented the framework for future research cooperation between ECSSR and the IDSA.

The Future of Afghanistan and its Relations with Iran (6/29/99) L
Ms. Nasim Zehra
Analyst on National Security Affairs
Pakistan

The birth of the Taliban in Afghanistan is among the most significant political events of the last decade in Southwest Asia, and poses a challenge to international and regional politics. The Taliban emerged in a particular domestic and regional context. The Taliban dominates 80–90 per cent of Afghanistan's territory. Iran remains a player in the battle for gaining influence in Afghanistan through the Afghan Unity Party, and by offering military aid to the Northern Alliance. The Taliban and Iran, although on the brink of war in August 1998, are eschewing escalation and confrontation.

The Gulf and Central Asia (2/20/00) L
Dr. Peter Huenseler
Chief Researcher, German Association for Research and Scientific Application (ASRI)
Federal Republic of Germany

The balance of power in the Gulf region is constantly undergoing crucial changes. Recent developments include: the emergence of six new Muslim states in Central Asia; international jockeying for power in this area; the dispute over Caspian energy and pipeline issues; the diversification of demand for Gulf oil, and unresolved domestic and regional conflicts. Lastly, Iraq and Iran may acquire nuclear capabilities, while producing weapons of mass destruction.

The Political System in Pakistan (6/18/00) L
Ms. Nasim Zehra
Analyst on National Security Affairs
Pakistan

The death of the main political leaders in less than four years after the founding of Pakistan, marked the beginning of a tussle between weak politicians and powerful members of the defense and civil establishments. Pakistan has been under semi-martial law for at least 25 years of its 50-year history. Inter-institutional relations are often marked by competitiveness and conflict. Consequently, the state has become vulnerable to the influence of powerful institutions. The army has now assigned itself the role of final arbitrator and the task of reforming the state structure.

Emirati-Indian Relations in the Next Decade (II) (11/18–19/00) S
This forum constituted the second part of 1999 ECSSR/IDSA New Delhi symposium. Issues included: the Middle East peace process, the latest events in the Palestinian occupied territories and India's position on those events, and the Indian stand on the Iranian occupation of the three Emirati islands. Five areas dominated, namely Gulf regional security from Emirati and Indian perspectives, the dangers of WMD, the impact of the information revolution, the UAE's economic diversification, as well as international terrorism and transnational organized crime.

South Asia in the Twenty-First Century: Challenges and Opportunities (11/24/00) L
Lt. Gen. Jahangir Karamat
Former Chief-of-Staff of Pakistan Armed Forces

Violence has been increasingly used in South Asia to settle disputes. The Indo-Pakistani conflict is the most dangerous, since more than 70 per cent of territory and more than 75 per cent of the population and GDP belong to India, while Pakistan takes the second place. The level of danger has heightened since May 1998 after both countries acquired nuclear capability. South Asia faces challenges that stem from economic circumstances. Lt. Gen. Karamat hoped that agreements such as SAARC and SAPTA would be activated to promote economic development.

Sri Lanka and the Arab World (2/27/01) L

H.E. Lakshman Kadirgamar
Minister of Foreign Affairs
Democratic Republic of Sri Lanka

Sri Lankan-Arab ties date back to the pre-Islamic era, when trade flourished. Arab immigrants came to Sri Lanka in the fourteenth and fifteenth centuries, leading to the introduction of Islam. While preserving their Islamic identity, Muslims integrated socially and played an important role, constituting 7.5 per cent of the population and currently occupying important positions, including four ministerial posts. Sri Lankan-Arab links include their Asian identity, Non-Aligned Movement membership and Colombo's support for Palestinian rights in the Arab–Israeli conflict.

The Future of Pakistan in the Aftermath of September 11, 2001 (6/9/02) (ELS 41) L

Dr. Maqsudul Hasan Nuri
Senior Research Scholar, Institute of Regional Studies
Islamabad, Pakistan

The Musharraf government's decision to join the US-led coalition against the Taliban regime in Afghanistan brought some immediate gains. However, some long-term problems are also casting their shadows, including the deteriorating economy and a recrudescence of terrorism.

The Current Crisis between India and Pakistan (6/18/02) L

Ms. Nasim Zehra
Analyst on National Security Affairs
Pakistan

The roots of the current crisis between India and Pakistan lie in the aftermath of the attacks of September 11, 2001 on the USA. The bombing of the Indian parliament and related developments have all contributed to the tension and military standoff between the countries.

Afghanistan and Continuing Challenges (9/24/02) L

Ms. Nasim Zehra
Analyst on National Security Affairs
Pakistan

The present situation in Afghanistan has an ethnic dimension that is evident in the internal balance between political and military powers. The security situation in Afghanistan still contains a number of challenges, partly due to a lack of funds and state soldiers.

The Japanese Strategy Towards the Middle East After 9/11 (9/5/04) L

Dr Massoud Daher
Professor of Modern and Contemporary History, The Lebanese University

This lecture examined five major points of the above subject. These features cover the role of Japanese foreign policy in reflecting the higher interests of the country;

Japan's firm support for the US in the wake of the 9/11 attacks; its support for the US against global terrorism and terrorism-supporting states; Japan's participation in the war on Iraq and its sending of peacekeepers to back the coalition forces; Japan's stand regarding the Arab–Israeli conflict and its adoption of the principle of "cultural dialogue" with Middle East states.

DEMOCRACY AND POLITICAL DIALOGUE

The Concept of Liberal Democracy (2/28/95) L
Mr. Khalil Ali Haidar
Kuwaiti writer

After defining the term liberal democracy and its political implications, Mr. Haidar analyzed the different political experiences that the Arab world has faced and the split among the intelligentsia over the very concept and understanding of democracy. He went on to discuss the different liberal currents that have passed through European communities. He argued that the Western view of liberal democracy has never been equal to that of the East, and he predicted that Middle East governments will confront many problems if they attempt to adopt the Western democratic system of governance.

Civil Society in the Middle East: A Long-Term Political Challenge (3/15/95) L
Dr. Emile Nakhle
Researcher and Analyst, United States Information Service

This lecture concentrated on the emergence of civil society throughout the Middle East, which has surfaced as a major focus of study within the last two decades. Dr. Nakhle discussed the relationship between the emergence of civil society and the political changes facing the states of the region. These societies, currently in political transition, are characterized by continuous fluctuation between cooperation and conflict. There are already 70,000 civil society groups spread throughout the Middle East, and the number is likely to increase.

The Future of Bosnia: Peace or War? (11/20/95) (ELS19) L
The Rt. Hon. Lord David Owen
Co-Chairman, International Conference on the Former Yugoslavia
H.E. Dr. Hassan Muratovic
Minister of the State Committee for UN Cooperation
Bosnia–Herzegovina

Discussing the Bosnia–Herzegovina war, Lord Owen stressed that nationalist leaders filled the vacuum left by departing authoritarian unifying forces after the end of the Cold War. He said that the intransigence of the Serbs and Bosnians complicated the solution to the conflict. Dr. Muratovic argued that the war was in defense of Bosnian lives and land, and requested international assistance to help rebuild the Bosnian economy and bring Serbian war criminals to justice, a prerequisite for a just and permanent peace.

Britain and the Middle East: Into the Twenty-First Century (11/4/96) (ELS1) L
The Rt. Hon. Malcolm Rifkind
Secretary of State for Foreign and Commonwealth Affairs
United Kingdom
　　The interaction of Britain with the Middle East goes back a long way, especially with the UAE, which has maintained political, commercial and cultural relations with Britain for over a century and a half. The speaker talked about peace, prosperity and progress, and stressed that states enjoying domestic stability and peace with their neighbors are able to create a better life for their citizens and establish a strong economic and social base. The UAE, under the leadership of H.H. Sheikh Zayed bin Sultan Al Nahyan, testifies to this.

Democratization in Jordan: Aspects and Prospects (5/25/97) L
Dr. Hani Hourani
Director, Al Urdun Al-Jadid Center for Studies
　　The speaker reviewed democratic dimensions in Jordanian political life since the founding of Transjordan in 1921 to the elections of 1989, which marked the beginning of a new democratic era. He focused on the indicators and the significance of political participation. One result was that martial law and emergency law were annulled. Democratic legislation, such as the laws on political parties and publications, was also introduced. The legislative elections of 1993 and all developments that influenced parliament in the period 1993–1997 were assessed.

The Political, Economic and Security Situation in the Russian Federation (1/7/98) L
Dr. Victor Lebedev
Director, Russian Regional Media Center
Abu Dhabi, UAE
　　The Russian economy witnessed a major change in 1997 when Moscow demonstrated its determination to build its national economy and curb its GDP decline. However, growing conflicts between the state and its civic institutions have led to the growth of pressure groups, mainly financial and industrial unions, which control almost half of the economic sector. A confrontation may result from such a rapid buildup, endangering the emerging political and economic institutions in Russia.

The Arab-European Partnership: A Case Study of Jordan (2/17/98) L
Dr. Ahmed Qassim Al-Ahmed
Researcher and Member of the Royal Scientific Society
The Hashemite Kingdom of Jordan
　　This review of Arab-European cooperation since the early 1970s revealed that although economic and technical cooperation agreements were implemented, political dialogue was mostly absent. Since the 1995 Barcelona Conference, strategic ties with the European Union have grown significantly and may lead to the creation of a Free Trade Zone. In the case of Jordan, a cooperation agreement has existed with the EU since 1977 through which much financial assistance was received. A comparison between similar agreements signed with Israel and Tunisia was also made.

Fifth Annual Conference
2000: The Making of the Future (10/9–11/99) C
This conference attempted to predict the characteristics of the new millennium and seek appropriate techniques for addressing emerging patterns of change. Participants included prominent leaders, thinkers, scholars and Nobel Prize winners who have played a pioneering role in enriching human life and furthering its development through their contributions in various fields.

Conference papers:
Dr. Fred Bergsten, "International Monetary Policies and their Effects on Developing Economies."
Dr. Zbigniew Brzezinski, "Determinants of the New World Order in the 21st Century."
Lord Marmaduke Hussey, "Future of the Media."
Prof. Paul Kennedy, "Challenges Confronting Humanity in the 21st Century."
Dr. Paul Krugman, "Global Competition in the New World Economic Order."
Dr. James McGroddy, "Information and Telecommunications Technology of the Future."
Dr. Christopher Murray, "Global Trends and Challenges to Health and Health Systems in the 21st Century."
Prof. Nicholas Negroponte, "Future Schools."
Dr. Kenichi Ohmae, "The Nature of the State in the 21st Century."
Mr. Jeremy Rifkin, "Genetic Engineering and its Effects on Humanity."
Mr. Alvin Toffler, "Transformation of Cultures: Implications for the Individual, Family and Society."
Ms. Jody Williams, "Human Rights in the 21st Century."
Dr. Earl Tilford, "Warfare in the 21st Century."

Dialogue among Civilizations (11/10/00) L
Dr. Udo Steinbach
Director, Orient Institute, Hamburg
Federal Republic of Germany
Professor Steinbach focused on modern cultural transformations in Western Europe entailing a reassessment of the stereotyped cultural model. In the Muslim world, such reassessment focused on adopting the Western model while adhering to roots. Culture is a key element as it defines the relations associated with globalization and the danger of cultural assimilation. Adherence to culture is a decisive factor in opposing uniculturalism. In order to have integration without fusion or merger, Western Europe would need to move from the instruction culture to the learning culture & achieve pluralism peacefully.

The Jewish Component in Contemporary Culture (10/23/01) L
Prof. Sa'd bin Abdel-Rahman Al-Bazi'ee
Professor of Literary Criticism
King Saud University, Saudi Arabia
Both the Jews who assimilated and those who maintained their character played an important role in the globally dominant Western culture. The Jews have contributed to different aspects of this culture, including ideologies like communism and scientific disciplines like psychoanalysis.

Patterns of Change in International Relations: Actors, Polities and Globalization
(9/4/01) (ELS 36) L
Prof. Kiichi Fujiwara
Professor of International Relations
Tokyo University, Japan
    The neo-realist school maintains that as long as the world is comprised of sovereign states, the main structure of international relations will be the same. Another school of thought states that the process of globalization and the interdependence of nations have challenged the isolated autonomy of sovereign states. The lecture adds another factor to the equation, namely, the entry of non-Western actors and powers.

The Aftermath of September 11: Clash of Civilizations or Opportunity for a Dialogue Renewal Between the East and the West? (11/12/01) L
Prof. Gilles Kepel
Institute of Political Studies
Paris, France
    The September 11 attacks fundamentally changed the ways in which people look at the world. So far, dialogue has taken place mainly at the inter-governmental level. In a number of Islamic states, this has generated tensions between governments and anti-American segments of the population.

Ukraine and the United Arab Emirates: Partnership in the Era of Globalization
(1/15/02) L
H.E. Anatoliy Zlenko
Foreign Minister of Ukraine
    Ukraine is among the "newly emerging economies." Its growth figures and Ukraine's regulatory reforms have highlighted the country's potential for investment and partner-ship. Ukraine is seeking a closer partnership with the Arabian Gulf countries, and partic-ularly the United Arab Emirates.

International Zionism and its Impact on Islam's Relations with the West (3/17/02) L
Dr. Abdel Wahab El-Misseery
Author, Encyclopedia of Jews, Judaism and Zionism
    Zionism owes its success to its close links with Western civilization. Zionism is not an international phenomenon, but rather a Western ideology, with interests that are closely related to those of the West. Furthermore, its imperial and racist perspective is a byprod-uct of Western imperialism.

The German Role in Developing European Socio-Political Dialogue with the Arab World (1/19/04) L
Ambassador Dr. Gunter Mulack
Commissioner for the Dialogue with Islam/Dialogue Among Civilizations
Ministry of Foreign Affairs, Germany
    Traditionally, Germany enjoys good relations with the Arab countries. At present, the

relations between Europe and the Arab world are facing new challenges. The aim behind encouraging dialogue and discourse is to eradicate aggression and terrorism. Through the necessary expertise and knowledge, we shall be able to realize better common understanding and to analyze, for instance, the role of political Islam & its impact on security.

The Role of Public Opinion in Decision-Making and Forecasting (4/16/03) L
Dr. Basyouni Ibrahim Hamadeh
Professor, Mass Communication, UAE University
   Public opinion is important in political decision-making, as it represents a form of democratic participation. Public opinion polls are also important in the field of communication. The information and technological revolution has partly helped to develop the role of public opinion in decision-making.

ECONOMY/TRADE

The Role and Function of GATT (2/25/95) L
Mr. Mohammed Saleem
Former Director, GATT
   Mr. Saleem concentrated on the General Agreement on Tariffs and Trade (GATT) as an institution. He provided an overview of the emergence of GATT and elaborated on the objectives underpinning current trends toward the expansion and liberalization of the contemporary international trading system. He also discussed the elimination of discrimination in international trade, the basic principles and rules of GATT, and the latest developments in multilateral trade negotiations, including the development of the World Trade Organization.

Implications of GATT for the GCC and UAE (2/26/95) (ELS2) L
Mr. Mohammed Saleem
Former Director, GATT
   Mr. Saleem's second lecture was more specialized, looking at the implications of GATT for member states of the Gulf Cooperation Council (GCC) in general, and for the UAE in particular. After giving an account of the current status of the GCC countries in GATT with respect to the WTO, Saleem underlined the implications of WTO membership for the GCC countries and the UAE. He also discussed the effect of GATT on petrochemicals, the textile and clothing industry, the agricultural sector, and subsidies for domestic industries, and he examined the significance of GATT for the smaller countries.

After Amman: The Economic Prospects for the Middle East (11/1/95) L
Mr. David Lay
Managing Editor, Oxford Analytica Daily Brief
   Mr. Lay analyzed the proceedings of the Amman Economic Summit in the light of the global economy, specific aspects of the Arab regional economies and the considerations of political risk. In the global economy, the Middle East is now competing with other regions for increasingly limited resources. Regionally, it is important to tap into the flow

of available investment capital, and ensure sufficient investment in the areas of tourism and infrastructure. Ultimately, if the social conditions do not improve, there is the potential consequence of serious disaffection and increased political risk.

Arab Economic Cooperation: An Outside Perspective (4/23/96) L
Dr. Volker Perthes
Research Fellow, Stiftung Wissenschaft und Politik
Ebenhausen, Germany

The Arab world and the Middle East are debating the options, prospects and risks of the new division of labor expected to emerge from the Arab–Israeli peace process. A major issue is whether and to what extent the Arab states should accept Israel as an integral part of the region, or whether these states should unite to safeguard their own economies, culture and identity against Israeli penetration. Dr. Perthes stressed the importance of analyzing the gains of inter-Arab cooperation.

Rentier Wealth and Unruly Law: The Political Economy of Oil States (5/12/96) L
Dr. Gwenn Okruhlik
Professor of Political Science
University of Arkansas, USA

Throughout the Middle East, there have been increasing demands for social justice, meaningful economic development and political reform. The presence of such demands is especially interesting in the oil-producing states. In these countries, the majority of state revenue accrues from abroad, and the state generally does not depend on the populace for taxation revenues. Distribution, rather than extraction, becomes the primary function of government.

The Implications of GATT and the Future of the Arab Economy (5/7/96) L
Dr. Abdel Rahman Sabri
First Secretary, General Administration for Economic Affairs
Arab League

Dr. Sabri explained the GATT agreement in relation to developments in the Arab economies. Three components are of specific interest to the GCC: the financial sector (effects on insurance, exchange and the money market), the investment sector (especially trade investment procedures), and the effect on the garment industry through the multi-fiber textiles agreement (MFA), especially in the UAE. He suggested that all affected governments should make use of the adjustment periods, and called for a strengthening of Arab cooperation.

Australia's Experience in Immigration and Linkages to the Labor Market (10/1/96) L
The Hon. Philip Ruddock
Australian Minister for Immigration and Multicultural Affairs

Previously, immigration to Australia comprised mainly permanent settlers. Now, immigration has become more diversified and Australia has, in turn, expedited its process to allow companies to attract foreign labor. Streamlined entry for long-term arrangements gives business more flexibility to build international competitive links. The current Australian program for permanent migrants balances its social, economic and humanitarian objectives, has widespread community support, and will allow it to meet international obligations.

Economic Perspectives of the UAE (11/25/96) L

Dr. Mohammad Al-Assoumi
Manager, Economic Research Section
Emirates Industrial Bank

Dr. Al-Assoumi focused on the economic aspects of the UAE's achievements over the past 25 years. Following a discussion about the current economic situation and subsequent future challenges, the lecture led to an open discussion on the topic. Dr. Al-Assoumi stated that the country had made significant progress in the economic field, and that these advancements are the result of its efficient leadership and an efficient economic decision-making process. He praised the existence of healthy competition among the emirates, the aim of which is to improve and advance the UAE's overall economic development.

Implications of WTO Membership and the Role of the UAE in the Global Economy (5/5/97) (ELS9) L

Prof. Lawrence Klein
Nobel Laureate for Research in Econometric Forecasting
Professor of Economics
University of Pennsylvania, USA

Dr. Klein dealt with the relationship between international trade and domestic economic performance. He presented a brief overview of the generally accepted principles of free trade, and some historical facts regarding trade, economic development and economic growth. On the important role of international trade, he noted that the world is experiencing greater economic openness, which facilitates the initiatives of the World Trade Organization (WTO). He reviewed WTO activities since its inception and shed light on the main difficulties obstructing it.

Labor Markets and Policy in the GCC: Micro Diagnostics and Macro Profiles (5/31/97) (ELS12) L

Dr. Sulayman Al-Qudsi
Economics Department
University of California, USA

This lecture analyzed the structure of labor markets in the GCC states, based on an investigation of economic data from the Sultanate of Oman, a GCC member. The speaker applied a group of Poisson models to a sample derived from the 1993 census in Oman, in order to assess the micro-forces that support macro-profiles and policy drivers. The lecture critically analyzed the consistency of demographic and labor market policies in achieving the main long-term development objective, namely the nationalizing of domestic labor markets.

Aluminum: Metal of the Twenty-First Century (1/24/98) L

Mr. Mohammed Al-Naqi
Chairman, Board of Directors
Kuwaiti Industries Company

Since the early 1950s, the growth in aluminum consumption has been higher than consumption of any other metal. Developments in alloy manufacturing methods suggest that this growth rate is likely to be sustained well into the next millennium. As the third most common metal on earth, aluminum accounts for about 8 per cent of the earth's crust and has been the subject of the most intensive research and development this century. Estimated reserves are likely to meet demands for the next ten centuries and to outstrip the use of iron, steel and copper.

Economic Crisis in Southeast Asia: Origins and Outcomes (11/17/98) (ELS21) L

Prof. Richard Robison
Director, Asia Research Center
Murdoch University, Australia

Asia's economic and financial meltdown appears to confirm the end of "Asian capitalism" and a new era of free global markets. Among neo-classical economists and within the IMF, it is generally proposed that recovery does require structural changes to end market-distorting systems. Critics argue that the solution lies in proper regulation of capital markets. The origins and outcomes of the crisis are best understood in terms of the impact of structural changes upon the rivalry between coalitions of power and interest to define the rules that govern economic activity.

Arab Gulf Economies: Challenges for the 21st Century with Reference to the UAE Economy (5/11/99) (ELS26) L

Prof. Ibrahim Oweiss
Department of Economics
Georgetown University, USA

The speaker presented an interpretation of future challenges, followed by examination of the region's indigenous and exogenous factors. The Gulf economies have witnessed growth, mainly as a result of exogenous factors. While any review of the Gulf economies needs to bear in mind the region's dependence on oil and its price, a statistical estimate of the price elasticity of demand for oil can be made, given the fluctuations in oil prices from peaks in 1979 to low levels in the mid-1980s and in early 1999.

Future of the National Economy: Economic Diversification Strategies for the Next Century (11/21–22/99) W

The focus of this workshop was the presentation and discussion of the results of the 1997 ECSSR project, "Diversification of the Economic Base in the UAE." Among the issues discussed were the macroeconomic performance of the UAE economy and its competitive environment, improving the information infrastructure's capacity to acquire reliable and comprehensive statistics, the promotion of the economic diversification process, and the maintenance of an advanced system of social and economic welfare.

Money Laundering (5/10/00) (ELS30) L
Mr. Michael McDonald
President, Michael McDonald & Associates,
Miami, USA
   The lecture focused on anti-money laundering initiatives as international tools to fight organized crime, and also explored legislative programs in different countries. Mr. McDonald urged setting up Financial Investigation Units at the national level to review financial reports and intelligence, and to manage financial information. The lecture presented a ten-point regulatory program recommended by experts in the Money Laundering Alert that would allow financial institutions to protect themselves from criminal exploitation. A summary was also given of the Financial Action Task Force recommendations.

A New Vision of Turkish-Arab Economic Relations and Economic Cooperation in the 21st Century (11/14/00) L
Ambassador Yüksel Söylemez
Co-Chairman, Turkish Foreign Policy Institute
Ankara, Turkey
   Arab and Turkish societies are undergoing a difficult transition, torn between modern and traditional forces and confronting economic challenges. Problems obstructing trade, banking and investment activity between Turkey and the Arab East were discussed. Regional stability and prosperity depends on Arab-Turkish relations, based on a common history, culture and intellectual tradition. Four principles govern Arab-Turkish ties: non-discrimination; reciprocal trade privileges; accessibility to markets and fair competition.

Investment in the UAE: Present Status and Future Prospects (1/13–14/01) C
   This conference was organized in collaboration with the Abu Dhabi Chamber of Commerce and Industry. The aspects discussed included the nature of current investments in the UAE and their role in comprehensive economic development; the infrastructure of investment in the country; factors and mechanisms to attract investors; ways of creating the appropriate investment climate; the obstacles impeding investment; the legal framework of investment; investment sectors and the future scope of investment, taking account of international variables, economic openness, the rapidly growing role of multinational companies, free trade and free movement of goods and services.

Conference papers:
H.E. Mohammed Omar Abdullah, H.E. Abdul Malik Al-Hamar, Mr. Eyyad Khalil Matar, Dr. Mohammed I.R. Al-Rumaithi, "General Discussion."
Mr. Faruk Al-Arabi, "The Legal and Legislative Framework for Investment in the UAE."
H.E. Ahmed Saif Belhassa, "Current Status and Investment Prospects in the Construction Sector in the UAE."
Mr. Mubarak Saeed Al-Dhahiri, "The Privatization of Public Undertakings and its Impact on Investment Promotion in the UAE."
Dr. Ibrahim Ismael, "Current Status and Investment Prospects in Oil, Gas and Petrochemicals in the UAE."

Mr. Aoun Al-Junaibi, "Current Status and Investment Prospects in Small and Medium Industrial Projects."

H.E. Sheikh Khalid bin Zayed bin Saqr Al Nahyan, "Current Status and Investment Prospects in the Information Technology Sector in the UAE."

Dr. Ahmed Al-Qasim, "Prospects and Strategies for Promoting Investment in the UAE."

Dr. Mohammed I.R. Al-Rumaithi, "The Role of Free Zones in Developing and Promoting Investment in the UAE."

Dr. Fatima Al-Shamsi, "Foreign Investments in the UAE: Current Status and Available Opportunities."

H.E. Mohammed Ali bin Zayed, "Investing in the UAE: A General Assessment."

Determinants of Capital Flows in Emerging Markets: A Case Study (2/11/01) L
Dr. Gilbert Wesso
Research Department
South African Reserve Bank

Dr. Wesso outlined policies essential for developing countries to attract foreign investment, in order to achieve economic growth, to support tax reform, financial systems, liberalization of exchange control and deficit reduction, and to increase returns. All this may be achieved by examining capital movement with the assistance of widely used determinants in the field of capital flow and developing economies. Dr. Wesso's technique aimed to determine the dynamics between capital flows and other economic variables, using quarterly data relating to South Africa through 1991–2000.

Determinants and Possibilities for Economic Integration among the GCC Countries (2/13/01) L
Dr. Mohammad Al-Assoumi
Manager, Economic Research Section
Emirates Industrial Bank

Implementation of the GCC economic agreements has been modest in comparison with blocs such as WTO and the European Common Market. Dr. Al-Assoumi advocated more GCC economic integration to withstand international competition. The key points stressed were: exploiting human resources and infrastructure surplus for diversification; unifying customs tariffs; issuing a unified currency; preference for Gulf federal laws and abolishing investment restrictions for Gulf nationals.

The Gulf–EU Trade Relationship: Challenges and Opportunities
(11/13/01) (ELS 37) L
Prof. Rodney J. A. Wilson
Centre for Middle Eastern and Islamic Studies
University of Durham, United Kingdom

This lecture reviewed how far EU exports to the GCC region have depended on oil pricing and production developments. Privatization and provisions for the restructuring of utilities present opportunities for European multinational companies, as do reforms of investment laws in the GCC states.

Findings of the Project on Economic Diversification in the United Arab Emirates
(3/23/02) W

This workshop examined a comprehensive strategy for economic diversification in the United Arab Emirates. A series of in-depth reports offered a comprehensive and comparative assessment of the UAE economy since the early 1970s, the competitive edge of UAE exports and the information infrastructure.

Monetary Policies and Economic Development in the Arab World
(3/24/02) L
Dr. Jassim Al-Mannai
Director General, Chairman of the Board
Arab Monetary Fund

The lecture discussed direct monetary policy as well as indirect monetary policy and their relative effects on economic development. The lecture analyzed the link between monetary policy and financial policy in the Arab world.

The UAE Economy: An Analysis of Factors Affecting Stability and Future Development (3/5/02) L
Dr. Mohammed Ibrahim Al-Rumaithi
Professor of Economics, UAE University

Economic growth refers to the average growth of per capita income and economic development, comprising quantitative material growth, while qualitative knowledge growth cannot be measured in figures. Economic development requires human resource development, stability and capital.

E-Commerce (1/6/03) L
Mr. Rami Jaghoub
Director, Business Development and Customer Service, Tejari.com Dubai, UAE

The lecturer reviewed the historic development of e-commerce. He examined the difference between e-commerce and traditional commerce, besides discussing its types, requirements, benefits, obstacles, risks and future.

Population, Development and the Global Economy (5/12/03) L
Dr. Hasan Yousuf
Emirates Center for Strategic Studies and Research (ECSSR)
United Arab Emirates

The lecture explained the concepts and terminology which form an important part of awareness of population and development issues. He reviewed the relevant theories and developments that have arisen during the past two centuries and stressed the importance of becoming acquainted with the policies and programs prepared by other countries for addressing their population problems.

An Analysis of the Impact of International Changes on the UAE Economy
(10/14/02) L
Dr. Mohammed Ibrahim Al-Rumaithi
Professor of Economics, UAE University

Factors like political stability and trust constitute the basis of economic development in any state, and ways must be sought to promote stable and balanced economic development in all sectors. These considerations are especially important in a turbulent international and regional environment.

The Iraqi Economy: Present State and Future Challenges (4/25/04) L
Dr. Muhammed Ali Zainy
Senior Energy Economist and Analyst, Center For Global Energy Studies (CGES)
London, UK

To rebuild the Iraqi economy and set it in a direction of self-sustained growth, several challenges have to be addressed. To achieve a measure of stability for the economy, inflation rates have to be reduced and the exchange rate has to be stabilized for the Iraqi dinar. It would be essential to get the oil industry up and running and to resume oil exports. However, even if oil exports are achieved, the revenues generated will have to cover several financial commitments, such as the general imports bill, financing reconstruction projects and economic development, servicing of foreign debts and paying off war reparations.

EDUCATION, MEDIA AND THE INFORMATION AGE

Media in the UAE (11/26/96) L
Dr. Ali Qasim Al-Shuaibi
Mass Communication Department
UAE University

Dr. Ali Al-Shuaibi emphasized the need to refine and improve the quality of mass media in the Arab Gulf. The steps taken by the media, particularly TV stations, have achieved limited success in projecting all the country's achievements. In the process, entertainment has overshadowed other media functions, such as preparing the public for future challenges of the information revolution. His proposals included proper coordination among media authorities and implementation of a strategic media development plan.

Positive and Negative Phenomena in the Arab Media (11/26/96) L
Mr. Hisham Dabbagh
Broadcaster, Abu Dhabi Television

The speaker shed light on the importance of reconciling local Arab media and the official Arab media regarding objective and balanced coverage, and in terms of building a sense of citizenship based on a true Arab identity. The various media should also identify the trends and developments among Arab youth and direct it to serve the objectives of the nation. He stressed the necessity to emphasize heritage and also to examine the contemporary issues of the Arab people.

Third ECSSR Annual Conference
**The Impact of the Information and Communications Revolution on Society
and State in the Arab World** (1/4–7/97) (Publ. 1998)

The effects of communications technology on society and state in the Arab world were highlighted at this conference. The growing importance of the Middle East in the international arena and regional interest in utilizing the information revolution and communication technology to boost development programs were emphasized. Topics included mass communication, the role of mass media and information in shaping the political process, the role of international news agencies, the current status of institutions in the information age and the dimensions of the "global village" concept. An exhibition covering state-of-the-art information and communication technologies attracted the participation of major international companies specializing in manufacturing and marketing communication technologies.

Conference papers:
Dr. Abdellatif Aloofy, "What Makes Arabian Gulf TV? A Comparative Analysis of the Volume, Origin and Types of Programs."
Mr. Peter Arnett (ELS3), "The Media and the Gulf War: An Eyewitness Account."
Dr. Mohammed Ayesh, "Telecommunication Policies and Trends in the United Arab Emirates and their Implications for National Development."
Mr. Henri Conze, "The Art of Information and Disinformation Technology."
Mr. Francis Fukuyama (via satellite), "Social and Digital Networks."
Mr. George Hawatmeh, Mr. Salah El-Din Hafiz, Mr. Abdel Rahman Al-Rashid, Mr. Abdel-Qader Tarish, "Will Newspapers be Something of the Past?"
Dr. Mustapha Masmoudi, "Challenges of the Communication Revolution on the Arab World."
Mr. Dusan Mihajlovic, "Waiting for the Next Revolution? It's Already Happened on the Internet."
Dr. David Morgan, "Mass Media and the Policy Process."
Dr. Hamid Mowlana, "Triumph of the Image: The Gulf War as Media Ecology."
Mr. Jamil Rabah, "Public Opinion Polling: The Palestinian Experience."
Dr. Saqer Abdel-Rahim, "The Impact of the Information Revolution on Society and State in Jordan."
Ambassador Eric Rouleau, "The Use of Information Technology by Dissidents."
Mr. Michel Saloff-Coste, "The Impact of the Information Revolution on Society and State in the Next Century."
Dr. Jamal S. Al-Suwaidi, Dr. Mohammed Al-Rumaihi, Dr. Sami Al-Damegh, "The Impact of the Information Revolution on Secondary School and University Students in GCC Countries: Result of Field Studies in UAE, Bahrain, Kuwait and Saudi Arabia."
Mr. Amir Taheri, "The Iranian Media Since 1979."
Dr. Mark Tessler, "Studying Citizen Orientations: The Contribution of Public Opinion Research to an Understanding of Information Revolution & its Impact on North Africa."
Dr. Lester Thurow, "The Economy, Financial Markets, and the Information Revolution."
Dr. Julian West, "The Quiet Revolution: Information Technology and the Reshaping of the Oil and Gas Business."

Education for and in the 21st Century (3/15/97) (ELS5) L
The Hon. Jerzy Wiatr
Education Minister
Republic of Poland
   The twentieth century saw education spreading to every corner of the world and all sectors of society. Professor Wiatr discussed the expansion and change in the role of higher education from a broad to a more specialized system, as well as developments in knowledge and educational systems, the diversity of equipment and the widespread use of new information technologies. On educational reform, Professor Wiatr recommended that character-building be highlighted. Education should return to a more general system and become more international, emphasizing teacher and student exchange programs and the rapid transfer of knowledge.

Setting up a Research Support Center (3/18–23/97) W
Interactive Workshop with the Congressional Research Service
   ECSSR staff gained valuable insight into the requirements for running a modern research organization both in terms of providing comprehensive decision-making support as well as acquiring latest technology to facilitate the research process. The workshop featured presentations by three senior analysts of the Congressional Research Service (CRS) in Washington DC. An overview of CRS divisions and topics of managing and chartering an institution was followed by discussions on how to conduct research in a largely open-source environment; how to communicate research results and how to deal with staff recruitment, evaluation and promotion. The importance of IT in searching for data and tracking the latest international events were explained, as were guidelines for research and writing. Staff presentations were made on previously selected topics. These briefings were analyzed and critiqued by presenters, providing a valuable tool for ECSSR staff to further their skills as researchers, analysts and information providers.

The Impact of Space and Computer Technology on Arab Media (6/10/97) L
Mr. Muhammed Arif
Head, Science & Technology Section
Al-Hayat, London, United Kingdom
   There are several ongoing international initiatives that will lead to a revolution in the field of information technology. The speaker dealt with the extent of such a technological impact on the production and services of the three main forms of media, namely newspapers, television and radio. The Arab world is facing formidable challenges because of the technological revolution. Several steps need to be taken, particularly since the Arab world possesses human resources and communities living abroad that can participate strongly in the information revolution. Education in the Arab world needs to be given more emphasis.

Media, Internet and National Security (1/25/98) L
Prof. Barry Lowe
English Language Faculty
City University, Hong Kong
   The salient characteristics of the new information age (particularly the Internet revolution) and their impact on modern nation-states were examined. Both the benefits and potential risks of these developments were explored, such as aspects relating to national security, fraud and censorship. The experiences of other countries were commented upon, together with the appropriateness of current policy strategies relating to online communication.

The Arab World and Space Research: Where Do We Stand? (1/27/98) (ELS14) L
Prof. Farouk El-Baz
Director, Center for Remote Sensing
Boston University, USA
   Advances in space exploration have raised the levels of science and technology in countries with viable space programs, with tangible benefits. Dr. El-Baz reviewed the available satellite imaging systems and their data, and outlined a proposal for the planning, launch and operation of "Desertsat," an imaging satellite to be dedicated to photographing arid lands, particularly in the Arab world. He gave examples of the practical uses of space images in solving problems, particularly those relating to a better understanding of the origin and evolution of the Arab deserts.

Fourth ECSSR Annual Conference
Challenges of the Next Millennium: Education and the Development of Human Resources (5/24–26/98) (Publ. 1999) C
   Heightened global competitiveness has made economic success dependent on the scope of achievements in education. With ongoing technological developments and the information revolution, educational systems and labor markets are undergoing major changes, which not only affect patterns of education, but also the nature of skills and abilities required of graduates and new employees. In examining the role of education and its importance in the development of nations, the conference sought to highlight the most crucial educational and training issues in GCC countries and to examine appropriate implementation strategies in order to develop the form and content of the field of human resources for the future. Such strategies should be in harmony with social dimensions characteristic of Arab Gulf countries. Additionally, the conference offered insight on the academic experiences of states such as Japan and Singapore through the participation of experts from these countries.

Conference papers:
H.E. Sheikh Nahyan bin Mubarak Al Nahyan, Minister of Higher Education and Scientific
   Research and Chancellor of UAE University, "Opening Address."
Dr. Adnan Badran, "Human Capital and Quality Management: Strategies for an Era of
   Globalization."

Dr. William Becker, "The Role of Education and Training in Economic Development."

Dr. Roger Benjamin, "Developing the United Arab Emirates Workforce for 2015."

Dr. Robert Cornesky, "Applications of Total Quality Management in Education and Training."

Dr. Don Davies, "Education and Society: Looking Toward the 21st Century."

Dr. William F. Halloran, "Zayed University: A New Model for Higher Education in UAE."

Dr. Masanori Hashimoto, "Education in Modern Japan: Formal Schooling and Learning on the Job."

Dr. Norman Henchey, "The Future of Education and Work: A Perspective from Canada."

Dr. Abdullah Mograby, "Human Development in the United Arab Emirates: Challenges and Prospects."

Dr. Daphne Pan, "The Singapore Education System: A Quality Model?"

Dr. Margaret Riel, "Just-In-Time Learning and the Course of Intellectual Development in the 21st Century."

Mr. Jeremy Rifkin, "Educational Challenges for the 21st Century: Learning in a Changing World."

Dr. Monther Al-Share, "Investment in Human Capital: A Cost-Benefit Approach."

Mr. Robert Spielvogel, "Technology and the Reform of Education."

Mr. Geoff Spring, "Future Schools: Getting the Balance Right."

H.E. Dr. Hamad Ali Al-Sulayti, "Education and Training in the GCC Countries: Some Issues of Concern."

Mass Education, the New Media and Implications for Political and Religious Authority (6/20/98) (ELS18) L

Prof. Dale F. Eickelman
Chair, Department of Anthropology
Dartmouth College, USA

Recent shifts in religious consciousness in the Muslim world have blurred the existing line between religion and politics. The fragmentation of political and religious authority, associated with mass education, multiple channels of communication, and intensified migration and travel, has added multiple voices to the political arena. This lecture assessed the prospect for Islamic liberalism in the Middle East. It commented on accommodation between Muslim identity and the transformative power of economic and political forces.

Arabic Media in Britain (11/29/98) L

Dr. Sa'ad Mohammed Al-Ajmi
Director, Kuwaiti Media Center
London, United Kingdom

This study highlighted the reasons behind the establishment and unprecedented success of "Migrant Media," the new Arabic network service based in London. Although past attempts have failed, this system of press and television coverage has been enormously influential within the Arab community resident in the UK, more than justifying its choice to concentrate in the capital city rather than the provinces.

Freedom of the Press in Arab Gulf States and Kuwait: Nine Years after Liberation (2/5/00) L

Dr. Sa'ad Mohammed Al-Ajmi
Information Minister
State of Kuwait

The lecture demonstrated ways in which the media in the Arab Gulf states is increasingly witnessing freedom of the press and freedom of speech. The media is seeking to keep pace with new technology. The study urged more independence for the Gulf press, to enable it to contribute through constructive criticism. The lecture also focused on the role of the Kuwaiti media after nine years of liberation. It showed how media reports could project major national issues, such as missing POWs, and how the media could coordinate its efforts.

The Jordanian Experience in Building an Information Infrastructure (4/9/00) L

Dr. Yousef Nusseir
President, National Information Center
Hashemite Kingdom of Jordan

Dr. Nusseir dealt with the Jordanian experience in organizing, coordinating and managing information to utilize it as a major resource in the development process. The National Information Center (NIC) aims to build and administer an integrated information system at the national level, while the Jordanian National Information System (JNIS) coordinates data provision for policy makers, decision makers and researchers.

News Monitoring: Concept and Objectives (11/9/00) L

Dr. Saleh Abu Osha
Head of Media Department
Sultan Qaboos University
Muscat, Oman

News monitoring provides abundant information and trends from various sources for decision makers. It is indispensable for politicians, economists and those concerned with public opinion, security and national security affairs. It is a communication process concerned with checking and documenting daily and periodical reports from different news media to identify trends and views regarding current affairs. The lecturer focused on the concept and objectives of news monitoring. He suggested that the process should involve practice, by presenting news monitoring models covering Arab media.

Public Opinion and its Importance in Decision-Making (4/23/01) L

Dr. Basyouni Ibrahim Hamadeh
Department of Mass Communication
UAE University

Public opinion has gained more significance because of the information revolution and communication technologies, which have given people greater opportunities to express their opinion on political issues. This development has an impact on political decision-making.

The Development of Public Universities in the UAE: A Case Study of Zayed University (2/3/02) L

Dr. Hanif Hasan Al-Qasemi
Director, Zayed University

The lecture highlighted the mission of the Zayed University, its curricula, programs and colleges, giving a brief description of its contribution to scientific research, its academic staff, its buildings and equipment, and how it relates to the local community and the world at large.

Assessment of the Arab Media after the War on Iraq (5/20/03) L

Mr. Jamil Mroue
Editor-in-Chief and Publisher, Daily Star, Lebanon

This lecture poses important questions: What kind of media do we want? What type of media coverage do we need to understand our circumstances and environment? The media is the mechanism which society employs for understanding the environment and its interactions.

Trends in Strategic-Administrative Leadership in the Information Age: Modern Applications in the Face of Crises (2/22–26/03) W

Dr. Mustafa Alawi

This workshop examined the definitions of basic concepts, the importance of information in promoting awareness of the leadership responsible for handling a crisis, the elements that form a crisis, the factors of maturity or immaturity in handling and managing a crisis as well as the strategy levels for crises management.

The Information and Telecommunications Revolution and its Impact on State and Society (2/17/03) L

Mr. Mohammed Aref
Advisor, Arab Institute for Science and Technology
UAE

The lecturer pointed out that most aspects of life have been subject to the impact of modern telecommunication technologies and information systems. The rhythm of technological and informational accumulation has become amazingly fast. It has developed from mere PCs that process, save and digitally exchange information to the present level, that affects all forms of human activity.

Freedom of the Media in the Internet Age (5/27/02) L

Dr. Mohammed Ayesh
Head, Faculty of Communications
University of Sharjah, UAE

The lecture discussed the issue of media freedom in the Internet age, and the concept of the content of media reflecting the nature of ideological and cultural contradictions between the various communities in the world.

Tenth Annual Conference
Arab Media in the Information Age (1/9–11/06) (Publ. 2006) C
   The Conference discussed the impact of cultural and regional factors on the media, and the role these factors play in promoting or hindering cross-cultural understanding. The Conference examined the relationship between education and the media, and evaluated the impact of round-the-clock international news channels on modern life.

Conference Papers:
Keynote address: H.H. Sheikh Mohammed bin Rashid Al Maktoum, Vice-President and Prime Minister of the UAE and Ruler of Dubai, "The Gulf Media and Global Developments."
H.H. Sheikh Abdullah bin Zayed Al Nahyan, UAE Foreign Minister and Former Minister of Information and Culture, "Address by the UAE Ministry of Information and Culture."
Dr. Ali Mohammed Fakhro & Dr. Mai Al-Khaja, "The Influence of Media on Education: Reality & Ambitions."
Dr. Ali Qasim Al-Shuaibi & Abdul Rahman Al-Rashid, "The Role of Arab Media: Between Education and Entertainment."
Greg Dyke, "Impact of Global News Channels on International Relations."
Waddah Khanfar, "Credibility of News Channels: Competing for Viewers."
Jihad Al-Khazen and Jean AbiNader, "The Role of Arab Media in Shaping the Western Perspective of Arabs."
Dr. Jack Shaheen, "The Content and Presentation of Arab Media: The Impact of Western Media."
Mohammed Ibrahine, "Communicating with the Muslim World: US and German Public Diplomacy Since 9/11."
Mohammed Al-Jassem, "The Influence of Online Media on Arab Socio-Political Development."
Ahmad Julfar and Fahd Al-Othman, "Enriching the Arabic Content on the Internet: Current Problems and Future Prospects."
Khaled Al-Hroub and Dr. Musa Shteiwi, "The Contribution of Arab Media to Creating Social Change and Developing Civil Society in the Arab World."
Dr. Mohammed Al-Sayed Sayeed, "The Role of Media in the Formation of Arab Public Opinion."
Dr. Hussein Ibish, "The Role of Media in Cross-Cultural Communication."
Dr Michael Hudson and Dr James Zogby, "The Role of Political Influence in Global Media."
Dr Naomi Sakr, "The Impact of Commercial Interests on Media Content."
Dr Richard Caplan and Robert Hodierne, "Media Credibility in War: The Phenomenon of Embedded Reporters."
Abdel Wahab Badrakhan and Hussein Sinjari, "Impact of Occupation on Freedom of the Press: Iraq and Afghanistan."
Edmond Saab, "The Margin of Freedom of the Arab Press."
Ahmad Abdul Aziz Al-Jarallah, Abdullah Rasheed, Daoud Al-Shiryan and Abdullah Al-Olayan, "The Influence of Arab Governments in Shaping Arab Media."

German-Arab Media Dialogue: Media Culture and Challenges of Globalization
(5/16–17/04) S
The ECSSR organized this symposium in collaboration with the Institut fur Auslandsbeziehungen (IFA) (i.e. Foreign Relations Institute), which drew the participation of an elite group of politicians, media specialists and academics from the UAE, Arab countries and the Federal Republic of Germany.

ENERGY

Comments on OPEC's Low-Price Strategy (2/7/95) L
Dr. Thomas Stauffer
International Oil and Finance Consultant
Washington, DC, USA
This lecture gave an overview of the current international oil market, presenting Dr. Stauffer's views on the most pressing issues and current OPEC strategy in determining and evaluating oil prices. Dr. Stauffer highlighted the main elements that will affect future oil prices and outlined the most likely strategy to be pursued by OPEC members in assuring optimum revenue streams.

The Oil Industry Value Chain: Concepts and Issues (11/11–13/95) W
Prof. Paul Stevens
This workshop focused attention on five vital stages of the oil industry value chain: exploration; development and production; crude transportation; refining; and marketing and distribution. For a solid understanding of the industry, a working knowledge of each stage as a separate entity and how each interacts in the value chain is imperative.

First ECSSR Annual Energy Conference
Gulf Energy: Challenges and Threats (11/14–15/95) (Publ. 1997) C
The importance of the Gulf region as a provider of oil and natural gas for industrialized countries was acknowledged. The energy sector has encountered problems, sometimes caused by regional disturbances and oil fluctuations, prompting predictions regarding stability and prospects for future growth. This conference dealt with various energy dimensions, economic and political alternatives available to energy producers and consumers, and forecasts relating to the future of energy. ECSSR's Energy Report was considered a comprehensive assessment of energy trends and analysis of the future role of oil and natural gas in the economy.

Conference papers:
Dr. Abdul-Razak Faris Al-Faris, "Forecasting the Demand for Gasoline in the GCC Countries."
Dr. Walid Khadduri, "Gulf Optimization Strategies."
Dr. Ken Koyama, "Growing Energy Demand in Asian Countries: Opportunities and Constraints for Gulf Energy Exporters."
Mr. Michael Lynch, "Petroleum from the Former Soviet Union: The Shortest Road from Socialism to Capitalism?"

Dr. Clinton W. Maffett, "World Oil Market Scenarios."

Dr. Thomas Stauffer, "Economic Impact of Natural Gas on the Gulf Oil Exporters."

Prof. Paul Stevens, "The Role of the Gulf in World Energy: Lessons from the Past."

Mr. Vahan Zanoyan, "A Relevant Framework for Understanding the Global Crude Oil Market."

Sustainable Development for Oil-Producing Countries (3/12/96) L

Dr. James Gustave Speth
Executive Director, UNDP

Dr. Speth noted the Gulf region's rapid economic development over a period of three decades. According to the 1995 UNDP Human Development Index, the UAE was among the states that achieved the highest comprehensive human development in terms of per capita GDP, standard of education and average life expectancy. The contribution of the UNDP to salient developmental areas was also discussed, including the formulation of regional programs to analyze the expertise of Arab countries in the field of public administration, and UNDP support for initiatives aimed at reinforcing the UAE's capacity to formulate development strategies.

The Oil Industry: Value Added (5/20–22/96) W

Prof. Paul Stevens

OPEC and OECD policies, as well as events in the Gulf, have played a significant role in the international oil industry. Trends and forecasts of the oil market and oil prices were discussed at this workshop. Forecasting oil trends, prices and market forces is a complicated task. Not only do economic, geological and technical factors interplay, but also political factors. Energy policy in producing and consuming countries should be investigated, in addition to other ecological and demographic factors.

Second ECSSR Annual Energy Conference
Strategic Positioning in the Oil Industry: Trends and Options
(10/26–27/96) (Publ. 1998) C

The crucial role of oil and energy in the comprehensive development of the UAE and other Gulf countries was reiterated. The region's role as a global exporter of energy was reviewed. Strategic positioning can determine whether a country, or company, should invest in the latest technologies, contract to sell oil in the international market, or profit from oil price fluctuations in the commodity market.

Conference papers:

Mr. Andrew Barton, "The Challenge of Resource Constraints for International Major Oil Companies."

Dr. Alfred Boulos, "The Past and Present Contractual Make-Up: Options for Negotiating Future Concessions."

Dr. Tilak Doshi, "The Future of the Oil Industry and the Strategic Importance of Consumer Needs."

Mr. Charles El-Hage, "Emerging Structural Changes in the Petroleum Industry: Current Trends and the Significance of Strategic Planning."

Dr. Giacomo Luciani, "A Strategy for Managing Risks: Vertical Integration in Mature Markets vs. Developing Markets."

Dr. Wael Al-Mazeedi, "Back-door Privatization of National Oil Companies in the Gulf: A Blueprint for Private Sector Participation."

Dr. Majid Al-Moneef, "The Strategies of National Oil Companies in Terms of Downstream Operations."

Mr. Keiichi Yokobori, "Strategic Options and Opportunities for Gulf Oil Companies in the Asian Markets."

The Oil Industry: Value Added (4/26–29/97) W
Prof. Paul Stevens

Five vital stages of the oil industry's value chain – exploration, development and production, crude transportation, refining, and marketing and distribution – collectively create the industry's ability to add value. To understand how the industry "adds value," the workshop expounded on each stage, transmitting the necessary working knowledge of each as a separate entity and as part of the complete value chain. Also discussed were oil markets and oil prices, the future of the oil market, and prospects for oil revenues in the GCC.

Third ECSSR Annual Energy Conference
Privatization and Deregulation in the Gulf Energy Sector
(10/25–26/97) (Publ. 1999) C

The Arabian Gulf region is a pivotal player in the energy market with huge oil and gas reserves, and is likely to maintain a major share in future growth in demand for world oil. However, the structure of energy demand and supply, aided by rapid technological advances, is undergoing significant changes, which will impact on the competitive position of oil as a strategic commodity in the global economy. These and other changes necessitate an ongoing evaluation of the energy market, its indicators, underlying currents, future challenges and the considerations necessary to meet the needs of environmentally-conscious consumers. The privatization experiences of India and Britain were also considered at this conference.

Conference Papers:

H.H. Sheikh Diyab bin Zayed Al Nahyan, "Opening Speech."

Dr. Achilles Adamantiades, "The Reform and Privatization of the Power Sector in Developing Countries: Implications, Pros and Cons for the GCC States."

Mr. Abdulla Al-Ahbabi, "Privatization of the Water and Electricity Sectors in Abu Dhabi."

Dr. Sharif Ghalib, "The Financial and Capital Market Implications of Privatizing the Energy Sector in the Arab Gulf."

Dr. Paul Horsnell, "Issues in Deregulation, Privatization and Re-regulation of the Energy Industries."

Dr. Gordon MacKerron, "Electricity Privatization in England and Wales: A Case Study."

Dr. Colin Robinson, "Privatization: An Overview of Current Directions."

Dr. Abdul Hafeez Sheikh, "Privatization of Energy in the Arab Gulf: Selected Issues and Options."

Dr. Leena Srivastava, "The Indian Oil Experience: A Case Study."
Mr. Andrew Ward, "The Legal Framework for Privatization in the UAE."

Fourth ECSSR Annual Energy Conference
Caspian Energy Resources: Implications for the Arab Gulf
(10/25–10/26/98) (Publ. 2000) C
The conference focused on the significance of energy production in an area with particular political and commercial risks. Topics covered were the politics of pipelines, oil transport and natural gas projects in the wake of regional instability following the demise of the Soviet Union, the legal status of the Caspian Sea, the economic repercussions for the Gulf and global economy. The geo-strategic and environmental consequences of exploiting the world's last major untapped hydrocarbon resources were analyzed.

Conference Papers:
H.E. Sheikh Ahmed Zaki Yamani, "Opening Remarks."
Dr. Shirin Akiner, "Risk Assessment for Azerbaijan, Kazakhstan and Turkmenistan."
Dr. Fadhil Chalabi, "The Caspian Sea and Its Impact on Gulf Oil."
Ms. Sarah Emerson, "The Relevance of Caspian Oil for the Global Energy Market."
Dr. Paul Gregory, "Developing Caspian Energy Reserves: The Legal Environment."
Ms. Amy Myers Jaffe, "Price vs. Market Share for the Arab Gulf Oil Producers: Do Caspian Oil Reserves Tilt the Balance?"
Dr. Geoffrey Kemp, "Caspian Regional Politics: Prospects for Cooperation and Conflict."
Dr. Wilfrid Kohl, "The Caspian Oil Development: Implications for OPEC."
Ms. Julia Nanay, "The Industry's Race for Caspian Oil Reserves."
Dr. Laurent Ruseckas, "Caspian Oil Development: An Overview of the Issues Concerned."

The Y2K Problem and its Impact on the Oil Industry in the Middle East and Africa
(5/4–5/99) C
This conference was held in cooperation with the International Energy Agency to address the possible implications of the Y2K problem for the strategically important oil sector in the Middle East and Africa. Particular areas of concern included oil production, transportation and refining.

Conference Papers:
Mr. Khalil Aburizk, "How the Y2K Problem can Affect the Telecommunications Sector: Implications for the Oil Industry."
Mr. Mohammed Ali Ahmed, "Y2K Contingency Planning at the Bahrain Petroleum Company."
Dr. Mohammed El Amin, "A Regional Report from the Telecommunications Sector."
Mr. Ken Bell, "Schlumberger and Y2K."
Mr. Gary Foote, "ABB's Y2K Initiative."
Ms. Lynn Fourroux, "Introduction to Supply Chain Management."
Mr. Robert J. Glynn, "Y2K and Insurance Issues in the Oil Industry."

Ms. Jane Gunn, "Mediation and Settlement of Y2K Issues."

Mr. Jeya Jeyathevan, "Overview of Y2K Issues in Information Systems."

Mr. O. Louis, "Business Continuity and Contingency Planning."

Mr. Brice Martin-Castex, "The Y2K Problem in the Shipping Industry and its Implications for the Oil Industry."

Mr. Theo van der Meulen, "How can the Y2K Problem Affect the Electricity Sector? Questions You Should Ask your Electricity Provider."

Mr. Keith Miller, "The National and Global Implications of the Y2K Problem for the Oil Industry."

Mr. Keith Narayansingh, "The Human Factor in Contingency Planning."

Mr. Bjorn-Tore Viste Solheim, "Y2K Contingency Planning in the Oil Industry: The North Sea Experience."

Mr. Simon Stoddart, "Information Resources Available to Oil Companies for Addressing the Y2K Problem."

Mr. Barrie Toner, "How are Oil Equipment Vendors Responding to the Y2K Problem?"

Mr. Jack Townsend, "The Y2K Problem in the Port Industry: Identification and Solutions."

Ms. Janet Valades, "Overview of the Embedded Systems Problem."

Mr. Saleh Al-Zaid, "Supply Chain Management: A Case Study."

Mr. Bellhassen Zouari, "Tunisia Faces the Y2K Problem."

Fifth ECSSR Annual Energy Conference
The Future of Natural Gas in the World Energy Market
(10/30–31/99) (Publ. 2001) C

The worldwide focus on natural gas is expected to increase. This conference assessed the position of natural gas in the world energy market; the future of the natural gas industry and market; areas of commercial exploitation of world gas reserves; experiences of other countries in fields of capital investments in the natural gas; sector and new technologies pertaining to the effective exploitation of natural gas. A futuristic vision of the position of natural gas and oil in the world energy market was presented.

Conference Papers:

Dr. Suresh Babu, "New and Prospective Technologies for Natural Gas Development."

Dr. Judith Dwarkin, "Government Regulation and Natural Gas Industries and Markets: The Canadian Experience."

Dr. Paul Horsnell, "Deregulation of European Natural Gas Industry and its Implications."

Prof. Robert McRae, "The Development of Natural Gas Markets in Asia: The Importance of Economic Growth."

Prof. Øystein Noreng, "The World Natural Gas Market and its Implications for the World Oil Market."

Dr. Dennis O'Brien, "Medium and Long Term Geopolitical Issues in Asia and their Implications for Natural Gas Industries and Markets."

Prof. Adam Rose, "An Overview of Natural Gas in the World Energy Market."

Energy Statistics (2/26–28/00) W

This workshop, conducted by International Energy Agency experts, was intended to contribute towards the integration of UAE and GCC energy statistics into the international energy statistical system.

Predicting Oil Prices in the Year 2000 and the Role of OPEC (4/11/00) L
Dr. Ibrahim Ismael
Chief Engineer, Petroleum Consultant
Ministry of Petroleum and Mineral Resources, Abu Dhabi, UAE

Oil markets have always experienced heavy fluctuations because of global events, such as conflicts, speculations, rumors and statements, and market forces of supply and demand. Market conditions led to the fall in oil prices during the last two years. The economic crisis in Southeast Asian countries directly influenced the fall in fuel consumption and led to an imbalance between global oil supply and demand. The speaker reviewed OPEC's role in restoring the stability of oil markets after the period of instability from late 1998 and early 1999.

Sixth ECSSR Annual Energy Conference
The Future of Oil as a Source of Energy (10/7–8/00) C

The unique position of the Arab Gulf region in global energy markets is due not only to the size of its oil reserves, but also to the growing demand for energy. Potential challenges to this position in the global energy markets were outlined. These include the rapid development of technology based on alternative sources of energy. Taking into account the latest developments in the global energy markets after the record rise in oil prices, and anticipating that the increase will persist, ECSSR convened this conference with the aim of identifying the future prospects of oil as a source of energy.

Conference Papers:
Dr. Cutler J. Cleveland, "Energy Quality, Net Energy and the Coming Energy Transition."
Mr. Seth Dunn, "The Impact of Environmental Concerns on the Future of Oil."
Dr. David Hart, "Alternative Energy Sources: An Assessment."
Dr. Mohan Kelkar, "New Technologies in the Oil Industry."
Mr. Jean Laherrère, "Oil as a Source of Energy: Present Realities and Future Prospects."
Dr. Timothy E. Lipman, "Renewable Energy: Now a Realistic Challenge to Oil."
Mr. Michael C. Lynch, "Seeking Stability in the Oil Market."
Dr. Marian Radetzki, "The Future of Natural Gas in the Energy Market."

Seventh ECSSR Annual Energy Conference
Energy Markets in Asia (1/13–14/02) C

This conference focused on the determinants governing energy supply and demand in Asian countries, including global energy prices, regional political stability, domestic economic policies, and changing consumption patterns of the local population.

Conference Papers:

Dr. Jamal Sanad Al-Suwaidi, Welcoming Remarks.

Mr. Ahmed Ali Al-Sayegh, Keynote Address, "The Energy Markets in Asia."

Mr. James P. Dorian, "Future Supply and Demand Trends in the Energy Markets in Asia."

Ms. Amy Myers Jaffe, "Energy Trade In Asia: Securing Asia's Energy Supply."

Mr. Philip Andrews-Speed, "Regulation and Deregulation of the Energy Markets in Asia: A Case Study."

Mr. David Von Hippel, "The Present Status and Future Prospects of Energy Supply and Demand in East Asia."

Mr. Romeo Pacudan, "World Energy Prices and Implications for the Electricity Supply Market in Southeast Asia."

Mr. Ronald Soligo, "The Present Status and Future Prospects of the Energy Market in China."

Ms. Leena Srivastava, "The Present Status and Future Prospects of Energy in India."

Eighth ECSSR Annual Energy Conference
Risk and Uncertainty in the Changing Global Energy Market: Implications for the Gulf (9/19–02) Publ. 2004 C

This conference first highlighted views on conventional energy sources, then focused on market-related and technological-related changes in addition to energy strategies in the main oil and gas importing regions. The conference aimed to offer options for Gulf oil producers on how to manage the implications of these changes in the long run.

Conference Papers:

Mr. Michael C. Lynch,"The Future of Oil and Gas in the Changing Global Energy Market: The Geopolitics of Oil and Gas in the 21st Century."

Mr. David Hart, "The Future of Energy: Are We Moving Towards a Hydrogen Economy?"

Mr. David J. Jhirad, "Energy Policy of the United States."

Mr. Ken Koyama, "Energy Policies in Asia."

Mr. Giacomo Luciani, "Energy Policies in the European Union."

Mr. Robert J. Weiner, "The Future of Oil Price Volatility: The Roles of Supply, Demand and Speculation."

Mr. Jean-Francois Seznec, "Managing Risk and Uncertainty in the Energy Sector: Towards Economic Diversification in the Gulf."

World Oil Market: Present and Future Prospects (4/19–23/03) W
Mr. Tayel Al-Hajji

This workshop examined the problems of the global oil market through discussing major issues of Energy, oil supply, oil demand and its determinants, challenges facing the oil industry, the future of oil and the importance of the Arab Gulf in this framework.

The Future of Oil and Natural Gas in the World Economy (1/15/03) L
Dr. Ibrahim Abdel-Hamid Ismael
Advisor to H.E. the Minister of Oil and Mineral Resources
United Arab Emirates
The lecturer envisages that the global economy will continue to expand and develop during the next two decades, first at a fast rhythm, then at a more stable pace. This, he believes, will be coupled with increasing energy demand, particularly of oil and gas. He contends that gas demand is likely to be stronger.

Ninth Annual Energy Conference
Gulf Oil in the Aftermath of the Iraq War: Strategies and Policies (10/19–20/03) C
This conference discussed the vital issues that will determine the future of Gulf oil and the global energy markets in the aftermath of the Iraq war. The participants also discussed the strategies and policies deemed necessary for managing the long-term implications of a changing energy market.

Conference Papers:
Dr. Jamal Sanad Al-Suwaidi, Welcoming Remarks.
Mr. Richard L. Paniguian, Keynote Address on "Gulf Oil in the Aftermath of the Iraq War."
Mr. Walter van de Vijver, "A New Era for International Oil Companies in the Gulf: Opportunities and Challenges."
Mr. Fatih Birol, "Gulf Oil Investment Outlook: Trends and Issues."
Mr. Thomas E. Wallin, "Stabilizing the World Oil Market During Unstable Times: Economic Dilemmas for the Gulf."
Mr. Herman T. Franssen, "The Future of Iraqi Oil in the Global Energy Market: Strategic Options in the Aftermath of the War."
Robert Emile Mabro, "Gulf Oil in a New Map of World Oil Supplies."
Mr. Paul Stevens, "The Changing Dynamics of OPEC and Non-OPEC Relations: Present Status and Future Prospects."
Dr. Fereidun Fesharaki, "New Energy Markets in Asia: Opportunities for the Gulf."
Mr. Christophe de Margerie, "Oil and Gas Prospects in the Atlantic Basin: Expanding Petroleum Production."
Prof. Vitaly V. Naumkin, "Russia's Expanding Role in the Oil and Gas Markets: Strategic Objectives and Future Policy Choices."
Ms. Dorothea H. El Mallakh, "Post-War Iraq and OPEC: Present Status and Future Prospects."
Mr. Vahan Zanoyan, "Strategic Options for Energy Decision-Makers in the Gulf: Energy Policy Planning for the Future."

Tenth Annual Energy Conference
The Gulf Oil and Gas Sector: Potentials and Constraints (9/26–27/04) C
In their attempts to draw and apply policies for developing hydrocarbon resources, the Arab Gulf States might need to strike a balance between their own strategic requirements and the requirements of energy needed for the global economy. The Conference was held to examine and analyze this vital issue.

Conference Papers:

Keynote address: H.E. Abdullah bin Hamad Al-Attiyah, Second Deputy Prime Minister, Minister of Energy and Industry, Qatar.

Dr. Adnan A. Shihab-Eldin, "The Future of OPEC in a Globalized World Energy Market: Opportunities and Constraints."

Luis Giusti, "Maintaining Cohesion Within OPEC: Implications for Cooperation Between Member Countries."

Dr. Muhammad-Ali Zainy, "Iraq's Oil Sector: Scenarios for the Future."

Ms. Vera De. Ladoucette, "Saudi Arabia's Oil and Gas Industry: Strategic Outlook and Policy Options."

Mehdi Varzi, "World Oil Prices: Impact on Global Economic Growth."

Prof. Kjell Aleklett, "The Influence of Markets and Technology on Regional Oil and Gas Reserves."

Dr. Fatih Birol, "Investment Requirements and Capabilities in the Gulf."

Dr Valerie Marcel, "National and International Oil Companies: Existing and Emerging Partnerships."

James T. Jensen, "The Future of Gas Transportation in the Region: LNG, GTL & Pipelines."

Ian Seymour, "The Impact of Gas Development on the Future of Gulf Oil."

Dr. Oystein Noreng, "The Norwegian Experience of Economic Diversification in Relation to the Petroleum Industry."

Youssef M. Ibrahim, "Towards Sustainable Economic Diversification: Long-Term Challenges for the Gulf."

The Future of Funding the Oil Industry in Iraq (4/11/04) L
Dr. Ali Hussein
Oil and Gas Industry Consultant, Abu Dhabi, UAE

The oil industry in Iraq has suffered destruction in recent decades due to wars, sanctions, negligence, plunder and sabotage operations. The restoration and expansion of Iraq's oil industry would need huge investments ranging from $30 billion to $40 billion over the next few years. At present, the Iraqi options for local investment in the oil sector are extremely limited. There is an evident need for foreign investment. However, there has been a split in Iraqi opinion over foreign investment in this all-important sector of the country's economy.

GLOBALIZATION

Globalization and Regionalization: New Trends in World Politics
(1/18/98) (ELS13) L
Dr. Richard Higgott
Director, Centre for the Study of Globalisation and Regionalisation
University of Warwick, United Kingdom

Globalization offers four common interpretations: a specific historical epoch, the confluence of specific economic phenomena, the so-called "American values," and a technological and social revolution. Globalization represents a more fundamental shift in the behavior of the modern world economy, with implications for politics. Higgott discussed economic integration and also institutional economic cooperation as major trends of regionalization, outlining how the management of global and regional orders cannot be undertaken separately.

Globalization: Scenarios and Questions (9/12/00) L
Dr. Nayef Ali Obeid
Political Expert, Ministry of Presidential Affairs
H.H. the Crown Prince's Court
Abu Dhabi, UAE

"Globalization" refers to transnational ties or the economic penetration of foreign markets. Some think that this will mean the end of the nation-state in favor of an international form of government while others stress that globalization helps the nation-state to adapt to the new world. The presentation traced this phenomenon and its effects on the economic, social and national policies of countries. It also focused on the anticipated effects of globalization in the economic, political, environmental and social spheres.

Globalization and its Impact on UAE Society and State (2/4–5/01) S
This symposium reflects ECSSR's interest in investigating the characteristics and complexities of the globalization phenomenon and the transformation it has caused in economic, social, cultural, political and security fields.

Papers presented:
Dr. Talal Atrissi, "National Security and the Sovereignty of the State in the Age of Globalization."
H.E. Ambassador Abdullah Bishara, "Concepts of State and Sovereignty in the Age of Globalization: The Case of the Gulf."
Dr. Ahmed Sidki Dajani, "Globalization: An Analytical View of the Present and Future of this Phenomenon."
Dr. Abdel Hadi Al-Jawhari, "Globalization and National Identity: The Case of Egypt."
Dr. Bahjat Korany, "The Future of Economic Blocs in the Age of Globalization."
Ms. Niveen Abdul Mounim Mussad, "International Relations and the Future of the International Order in the Age of Globalization."
Mr. Abdul Mounim Mussad, "International Relations and the Future of the International Order in the Age of Globalization."
Dr. Khaldoun Hassan Al-Naqeeb, "Globalization: The Cultural Traits of Society and the Future of Civilizational Interaction."
Dr. Munther Sharé, "Globalizing National Economies: Challenges and Available Opportunities."

Islam and Globalization (3/12/02) L
Mr. Fahmi Huwaidi
Islamic Scholar and Deputy Editor-in-Chief
Al-Ahram Daily, Egypt

The lecture focused on the impact of globalization on the cultural and economic interests of societies. One should differentiate between the concepts of globalization and universalism. For example, Islam is a universal religion. Globalization has positive and negative implications for Muslims.

INTERNATIONAL LAW

The Contemporary United Nations: The Next Fifty Years (11/11/95) L
Dr. Richard Langhorne
Director, Wilton Park Conference Center

As its fiftieth anniversary approached, Dr. Langhorne discussed the United Nations (UN) in the light of its structural characteristics, changes within the international system since its establishment, its response to those changes and the necessary requirements for the near future if the UN is to evoke a more positive response. Dr. Langhorne indicated the need for such reforms as the incorporation of other entities, the introduction of a variegated system of weighted voting, and an alteration in the arrangement and duties of the Security Council.

International Law, International Political and Economic Relations (1/20–22/96) W

This workshop was specifically organized by ECSSR to assist in the orientation of candidates for the position of UAE Military Attaché at UAE embassies. Topics included international law, international relations, Gulf security, information warfare, the Middle East peace process, weapons of mass destruction, international economic organizations, the economics of oil, foreign expatriates in the Gulf and the UAE economy. Speakers who participated in the workshop included a panel of experts, comprising both ECSSR staff and intellectuals from the local community. These included:

Dr. Ali Al-Arai and Mr. Tareq Za'al, "Overview of the Internet."
Dr. Anwar Gargash, "World Order: Its Development and Future."
Dr. Najeeb Ghadbian, "Future of Peace in the Middle East."
Dr. Abdulla Juma Al-Hajj, "Future of Gulf Security."
Dr. Joseph Moynihan (EOP7), "Information Revolution and Information Warfare."
Dr. Mustafa Rashash, "Oil Economics."
Mr. Abdullah Al-Sharafi, "Foreign Labor: Advantages and Disadvantages."
Dr. Abdullah N. Al-Suwaidi, "International Economic Organizations and the Economics of the United Arab Emirates."

The Issue of Borders and the UAE (11/27/96) L
Dr. Nasreen Murad
Assistant Professor, Political Science Department
UAE University

Dr. Murad discussed border disputes within the Gulf region. Three disputes were highlighted: the UAE–Iran dispute over the islands of Greater Tunb, Lesser Tunb and Abu Musa; the Saudi Arabia–Qatar dispute over the area of Al Khafoos; and the Qatar–Bahrain dispute over the Hawar Islands. Disputes were categorized as regional, functional, local, and resource disputes. Dr. Murad mentioned the absence of clear border agreements and illegal status quo by the stronger party as reasons behind regional border disputes.

Territorial Issues in the Gulf Region (3/2–4/97) W
Dr. Richard Schofield

Territorial issues in the Gulf region came under the spotlight. The workshop examined how the contemporary territorial framework of the region is derived; the region's more serious and enduring territorial problems; how the Gulf states have dealt collectively with the issue of territorial definition and boundary disputes through the offices of the GCC; the land and maritime boundaries agreed upon in the region (and in selective cases beyond the region) and the basis on which agreement was reached. Participants were introduced to the language and terminology of international boundary studies, and certain types of primary evidence which are deemed important in arbitration cases.

International Law: Sources and Application (2/8/00) (ELS28) L
Prof. Christoph Schreuer
Professor of International Law
University of Salzburg, Austria

The sources of international law are listed in the relevant clause of the Statute of the International Court of Justice: treaty law; customary international law; general principles of law and the decisions of courts and tribunals; and scholarly writings as subsidiary means of determining rules of law. The decisions of international organizations should be added to this list. These sources are interrelated, and depend on the cooperation and consent of states. The development of more efficient methods of lawmaking remains a major challenge for the future.

The Evolution of International Environmental Negotiations (5/16/00) (ELS29) L
Ambassador Marc Gedopt
Ambassador of the Kingdom of Belgium to the UAE

The lecture reviewed how international environmental negotiations evolved from a concern for local problems in the industrialized world, to cover transnational issues and global issues. The two UN Conferences on Environment, in Stockholm (1972) and Rio de Janeiro (1992), are taken as the two poles in this evolution. The policy instruments used evolved from remedial actions to preventive measures and the use of economic instruments. These shifts signify the movement of environmental negotiations from their former peripheral status to their current position as a core issue in international politics.

Border Issues in the Arab Gulf Region: Causes, Realities and Future Challenges
(11/17/00) L
Dr. Mohammed Hassan Al-Aidrouss
Member of the General Secretariat of the Arab Historians Union
Chief Editor, *Islamic Studies* magazine of Rotterdam University
Political borders in the Arab Peninsula were drawn during the British colonization. Britain's success in thwarting the Damascus Pact Project proclaimed by Arab leaders enabled the colonizer to draw political borders and create colonial entities to prevent Arab unity. Border disputes in the Arab Gulf region and the resulting political and social effects were examined. The speaker also highlighted the related challenges and their impact on regional stability, and collective Arab national security. He also proposed mechanisms for tackling such border disputes.

Implementing Treaties and International Law: between Unilateralism and Multilateralism (4/28/03) L
Dr. Ahmed Shikara
Emirates Center for Strategic Studies and Research (ECSSR)
United Arab Emirates
Two trends dominate international relations in the age of globalization, namely unilateralism and multilateralism. The lecturer discussed the driving force behind unilateralism and multilateralism, the development of international relations, the emergence of international challenges and whether international law can deal with them. He also discussed the United States and the future of international systems in the context of unilateralism and multilateralism.

The UN, the US, the EU and Iraq: Multiple Challenges for International Law?
(12/21/03) (ELS 51) L
Mr. David M. Malone
President, International Peace Academy
New York, USA
Since the attacks of September 11, 2001, the US has been more averse to any attempts to constrain US power, at the UN or elsewhere. The invasions of Afghanistan and Iraq were conducted without a UN resolution, although the Security Council would have been willing to authorize action in the former case. The aftermath of the war has again renewed the UN's importance, and many member states are trying to lessen US dominance in the Security Council.

Border Disputes and their Means of Resolution According to International Law
(10/10/04) (ELS 59) L
Dr. Giovanni Distefano
Professor of International Law, University of Geneva, Switzerland
The lecture examined the Qatar–Bahrain territorial dispute on which the International Court of Justice passed its verdict on May 16, 2001, thus putting an end to a protracted territorial, islands, and maritime dispute between the two states. The lecture focused on the court proceedings, and the contribution made by this lawsuit to the law related to territorial and maritime disputes.

INTERNATIONAL PEACEKEEPING

Assessing the Role of the UAE Armed Forces in Relief Operations for the Albanians in Kosovo (3/11–12/00) S

This symposium was convened to highlight the outstanding role played by the UAE Armed Forces, following the prudent national policies of H.H. Sheikh Zayed bin Sultan Al Nahyan, the former President of the United Arab Emirates, in bringing relief to the Albanians through its positive and active participation in relief efforts of international peace-keeping forces in Kosovo. Difficulties and dangers to which members of the UAE Armed Forces have been exposed while performing their duties were identified, while the symposium also revealed the benefits and experience gained by UAE military units participating in this humanitarian mission.

International Peacekeeping Operations: The Jordanian Armed Forces Experience (3/13/01) L
Staff Lt. General (Ret.) H.E. Eid Kamil Al-Rawdan
H.E. Ambassador of the Hashemite Kingdom of Jordan to the UAE

As former UN Secretary General Dag Hammarskjöld observed, "Peacekeeping operations are not military operations but can only be performed by the military." Peacekeeping operations involve humanitarian, diplomatic, political and military action. Operations are managed through the UN Secretariat General, and directed by the Assistant Secretary General for Peacekeeping Operations. He is assisted by a consultative military body presided over by an officer holding the rank of General. If the UN Security Council theoretically represents the executive council of the world, this body is equivalent to a central military administration for the world. Jordanian Armed Forces participated in peacekeeping forces from 1989, numbering 20,068 peacekeepers covering states such as Mozambique, Georgia, Tajikistan, Liberia, Somalia, Congo, ex-Yugoslavia, East Timor, Sierra Leone and Eritrea. For a peaceful country located in a troubled area, international peacekeeping is viewed as a means of promoting regional peace and national security. Peacekeeping reflects Jordan's policy of justice and peace and enhances the expertise, efficiency and readiness of its armed forces.

Preventing, Managing, and Resolving International Conflicts (10/6–8/02) W
Dr. David Carment, Mr. David Nyhcim, Ms. Hannelore Wallner

The main issues covered by this workshop were: Introduction to conflict analysis and conflict prevention; conflict analysis; structural risk assessment and events analysis; response strategies; and evaluating information and identifying responses.

The Peaceful Use of Nuclear Energy: The Contribution of the International Atomic Energy Agency (12/15/02) (ELS 43) L
Dr. Mohammed El Baradei
Director-General of the IAEA

The IAEA promotes the concept of "Atoms for Peace," which includes the non-proliferation of nuclear weapons and their eventual elimination, and the use of peaceful nuclear technologies. The IAEA works in three basic areas: nuclear technology, nuclear safety and security, and nuclear monitoring.

ISLAM/POLITICS

The Islamic Political Movement and the Future (2/20/95) L
Dr. Radwan El-Sayed
Editor-in-Chief, Al-Ijtihad
Director, Higher Institute for Islamic Studies
Beirut, Lebanon

Dr. El-Sayed addressed some of the more important aspects of contemporary Islamic movements and focused on the political thoughts of Ibn Taymieh and his book *Al-Fatawi Al-Kubra*. He argued that most contemporary Islamic groups are not well-informed about the historical and political context in which Ibn Taymieh's ideas were formed. He went on to discuss the reasons behind the politicization of the Islamic movements, attributing it to specific social, political and religious crises in the region. These dispositions appear in the books of famous Islamic leaders and scholars.

The Issues of Al-Shura, the Written Law and the Nation's Historical Experience
(2/21/95) L
Dr. Radwan El-Sayed
Editor-in-Chief, Al-Ijtihad
Director, Higher Institute for Islamic Studies
Beirut, Lebanon

Dr. El-Sayed presented an understanding of *Al-Shura* (consultation), as found in the books of famous Islamic scholars, and discussed its historical and religious significance. A link between *Al-Shura* and governance by representative, constitutional law was established, Dr. El-Sayed analyzed the relationship and contrasted its dynamics with issues of modern democracy. He also covered the differences between the various forms of leadership during the first century Hijri, and the military tendencies in Islamic countries in the Turk and Seljuk era.

Islamic Political Systems (2/27/95) L
Mr. Khalil Ali Haidar
Kuwaiti writer

This lecture took a historical view of the development of Islamic movements, focusing on their popular bases and their categorization. Khalil Haidar suggested alternative methods for Islamic countries and societies to deal better with problems of violence, economic and social stagnation, and the environment. He concluded that the future of an Islamic country depends on the ability of its citizens to find a balance between the basic principles of Islam and those of modernization.

Islamic Activism in the Gulf: Saudi Arabia in Comparative Perspective (6/8/96) L
Dr. Mamoun Fandy
Professor of Political Science
Center for Contemporary Arab Studies
Georgetown University, USA

The lecture focused on Islamic activism in the Gulf and its implications for regional stability. Four Islamic groups in Saudi Arabia were studied: the Shi'a Reform Movement (1975–1993), the Committee for the Defense of Legitimate Rights (1993 to present) and the groups following Sheikh Safar Al-Hawali and Sheikh Salman Al-Auda. Dr. Fandy examined the effectiveness of state strategies used to deal with the threat of Islamic activism, and how the various groups circumvent these tactics.

Islam, Western Democracy and the Third Industrial Revolution: Convergence or Clash? (11/3/97) (ELS17) L
Prof. Ali A. Mazrui
Director, Institute of Global Cultural Studies
Binghamton University, New York, USA
Islamic history reflects a long struggle for social unity and monotheism. Christian history reflects a long search for freedom and political pluralism. Do religious monotheism and political pluralism clash? Is Western political pluralism part of Christian Trinitarian pluralism? Islamic philosophy recognizes the existence of other monotheistic religions. The speaker also called for a bridging of the gap between Islam and modern technology, stressing that Islam encourages creative thinking and innovation.

Islamic Movements in the Arab World (1/18/98) L
Mr. Khalil Ali Haidar
Kuwaiti writer
The implications for GCC states of the growth of the modern Islamic movement were evaluated through an in-depth examination of Iranian Shi'a groups, the Muslim Brotherhood as well as the Al-Jihad and Takfeer organizations in Egypt, and subsequent clashes with Nasserism culminating in the assassination of President Sadat. In addition, the upsurge in the popularity of such organizations in Algeria, Tunisia, Sudan and the Levant was scrutinized, particularly their development at the expense of nationalism and liberalism, with legislative positions being conceded and social institutions radicalized.

Political Islam and Political Pluralism from an Islamic Perspective (3/19/02) L
Dr. Mohammed Imareh
Islamic scholar and Member of the Islamic Research Academy, Al-Azhar
The lecture examined the evolution of Islamism and the attitude of different Islamic schools of thought towards political pluralism, as opposed to the nationalist, liberal and leftist perspectives. It also compared the perspectives of Islamic philosophy and Western philosophies towards political pluralism.

Relations between Islam and the West: Repairing Cultural Bridges (10/6/03) L
Mr. Mobashar Akbar
Editor-in-Chief, The Asian Age
New Delhi, India
Differences of opinion might become dangerous when the competing cultures attribute civilization and civilizational accomplishments to themselves, and barbarism and backwardness to others. To settle such differences, our responses must emanate from a genuine desire to remove the causes of such differences in order to pave the way for smooth future relations.

The Attitude of Islamists toward Population Problems and Birth Control (10/28/02) L
Mr. Khalil Ali Haidar
Kuwaiti writer
Islamist writers and experts of *fiqh* and population policies have differed on the need for population and birth control policies in support of development. Birth control as such is not directed against Muslims and countries like India and China have applied stricter policies in this field.

The Future of Political Islam in the Aftermath of the Iraq War (1/6/04) L
Dr. Graham E. Fuller
Former Vice-Chairman of the National Intelligence Council
Central Intelligence Agency (CIA), USA
The diverse armed guerrilla forces participating in resistance against the US occupation in Iraq have enabled many international jihadi forces and Iraqi radical forces to cooperate against the US presence. If the US is seen as withdrawing from Iraq under pressure, it will be a major victory for the jihadist view of the world. There is no peaceful environment in the region today, but radical Islamists would be weakened when people have a chance to express their will.

MANAGEMENT ISSUES

Crisis Management (5/28–6/4/94) W
Dr. Frederick Holborn
Assistant Professor of US Foreign Policy
Paul Nitze School for Advanced International Studies
Johns Hopkins University, USA
This workshop outlined the principal concepts of crisis management, including elements of contingency planning and policy planning, design methods for crisis simulation and gaming examples which have heavily influenced crisis management. Case studies, starting with the Suez Crisis (1956), Cuban Missile Crisis (1962) and Falklands War (1982) were studied. More recent examples included increasing tensions between India and Pakistan in the last ten years and the Gulf War (1990–1991). The workshop included a lecture on the "pathologies" of crisis management, videos, video-taped role-playing and assessment. Concluding lectures focused on current trends in the management of international affairs, methods of crisis management in post-Cold War world, the influence of middle/small powers and alliance politics. US security and foreign policies of the Clinton administration, especially concerning the Middle East and the Gulf, were also highlighted.

Crisis Management (11/18/95) L
Dr. Muhammad Rashad Al-Hamalawi
Researcher, Commerce Department, Crisis Research Unit
Ain Shams University
Cairo, Egypt.
Dr. Al-Hamalawi defined "crisis" and distinguished it from previous terminology such as "struggle," "incident" and "accident." He discussed crisis measures and consequences,

and suggested that the study of crises occurs in the context of economics, politics, sociology, history and administration. He also proposed preventive strategies such as psychological preparation and communication, illuminating the theoretical as well as the practical aspects of this subject. He concluded with the different stages of a crisis, and some proposed management strategies.

Crisis Management (3/16–20/96) W
Dr. Muhammad Rashad Al-Hamalawi
This workshop outlined major methodologies of crisis management in addition to the main concepts and terminology. Different stages of crisis management were analyzed in the pre- and the post-crisis context. The importance of "alarm systems" and capabilities to forecast potential crises were stressed. Three categories of crisis were outlined: economic crisis (witnessed by capital investment companies); social crisis (terrorism and violence); and political crisis (such as the second Gulf War).

Negotiation Techniques (5/4–8/96) W
Dr. El-Sayed Elewa
Techniques of negotiation require understanding of many complex issues: the nature of international conflicts, components of the negotiation process, and principles of negotiation. This workshop offered practical examples of different techniques of negotiation. "Bargain strategy" requires a particular behavior and precise assessment of actual and potential threats. This strategy aims to influence other parties' stand by calculating expected reactions and likely resistance. Politicians and academics have called for the establishment of a "General Theory and Methodology for Negotiation."

Leadership (12/20–24/97) W
Dr. Bader Al-Deehani and Dr. Mahmoud Al-Jamal
The concept of leadership has developed in recent years, due to developments in administrative and technical sciences, especially in the fields of information and communications. This workshop examined the modern concept of leadership, focusing on five areas:

Leadership – Theories, norms, and modern trends: theory of leadership, uses of available information on leadership, interaction between different aspects of leadership, and total quality management.

Leadership in Organizations – Leaders in transition, practices of distinguished leaders, a case study of leadership in the World Bank, and skills in interacting with others.

Leadership – Organizational Structure and Effective Decisions: effectiveness of decisions, creative thinking, and different aspects of authority and organizational structure.

Leadership and Administrative Practices: conflict settlements: how to motivate subordinates, create job satisfaction and overcome work-related pressures.

Leadership – Managing Work Groups and Organizational Change: creating an *esprit de corps*, forming effective work groups, and leadership in carrying out changes.

Sixth Annual Conference
Leadership and Management in the Information Age (11/5–7/00) (Publ. 2002) C
The main focus of this conference was on leadership and management techniques for confronting the challenges posed by the free flow of information and rapid development in the fields of science, technology and knowledge.

Conference Papers:
His Majesty King Abdullah II bin Al-Hussain of Jordan, Keynote Address on "Leadership and Nation-Building in the Information Age."
Dr. Warren Bennis, "Leadership and Management: New Roles and Challenges. A Farewell to the Old Leadership."
Dr. Eliot Cohen, "Managing National Security in the Information Age."
Dr. Jay Conger, "Road to Leadership: Charisma or Competence?"
ECSSR: Keynote Address on "His Highness Sheikh Zayed bin Sultan Al Nahyan and Nation-Building."
Dr. William Haseltine, "The Management of the Socio-Economic Implications of Genetic Engineering."
Dr. Edward Lawler III, "Managing Organizational Change in the Information Age."
Mr. Michael Losey, "Management of Human Resources in the Age of Innovation."
Dr. Robert Mundell, "The Management of the National Economy in the Global Economy."
Mr. David Osborne, "Reinventing Government: Visions for the Future."
Admiral William Owens, "Defense Policy Management for the Twenty First Century."
Dr. Ian Wilmut, "Managing Genetic Engineering Research."

Crisis Management (6/9–13/01) W
This workshop examined selected crises to understand how actual participants have dealt with each crisis. The topics included crisis prevention, escalation, de-escalation, termination and post-crisis management. Dr. Richard Shultz and Dr. Robert Pfaltzgraff facilitated the workshop.

Crisis Management (1/18–22/03)
Dr. Ismael Sabri Maqlad
This workshop discussed the causes that lead to the eruption of crises, the methods of handling a crisis, the importance of information in crisis management, the institutions responsible for gathering information and the different sources of information. It examined the factors that influence the possible scenarios of crisis management and reviewed the available capabilities for dealing with crises.

POLITICS IN THE MIDDLE EAST

Religion, Ethnicity and Ideological Trends in Iraq: From Conflict to Integration
(8/24/03) L
Dr. Faleh Abdul Jabar
Lecturer, London Metropolitan University, UK
Iraqi society is known for its social, ethnic and religious divisions. It is divided into

modern and traditional social stratums. Likewise, some groups combine characteristics of both stratums. Applying only one approach will not help in understanding this society.

French Policy toward the Arab World (9/2/02) (ELS 42) L
Mr. Charles Saint-Prot
Director, Middle East Studies, International Academy of Geopolitical Affairs
Sorbonne University, France

French foreign policy towards the Arab world seeks to promote a dialogue between civilizations and maintain an international cultural, political and economic balance. It is based on recognizing the right of the Palestinian people to have a viable state and promoting cooperation.

The Status of a Weak State in an Unstable Region: Lebanon as a Case Study
(9/9/02) (ELS 44) L
Dr. Walid Mubarak
Head, Department of Sociology and Education
Lebanese American University, Lebanon

Lebanon's stability and survival as a viable state does not depend entirely on the actions of the Lebanese people, but on the balance of power in the Middle East region and the interest of other powers to maintain such a balance.

Water Policies in the Middle East (9/30/02) L
Dr. Ali Ihsan Baghish
Center of Water Policies and Strategic and Development Research
Turkey

The demand for water in the Middle East has increased significantly for different reasons: population growth, agricultural expansion, cultural practices and domestic and foreign policies. Co-operation will be the only way to overcome water conflicts in the Middle East.

SCIENCE

Technology and Society: Recent Technological Advances and their Impact on Humankind (4/29/02) L
Dr. Omar Al-Bizri
Head, Department of Technology,
ESCWA Beirut, Lebanon.

The lecturer discussed technology's increasing role in precipitating human progress and development. He underlined the issue of UN reform and reconstruction, particularly in the field of socio-economic development.

Eighth Annual Conference
Biotechnology and the Future of Society: Challenges and Opportunities
(1/11–13/03) (Publ. 2004) C
   The conference discussed the implications and vital role of biotechnology, which will have its impact not only on medicine and agriculture, but on national security and economy as well.

Conference Papers:
Dr. Jamal Sanad Al-Suwaidi, "Welcoming Remarks."
Michio Kaku, "Advances in the Field of Biotechnology."
John Gearhart, "Stem Cell and Cloning Research: Implications for the Future of Humanity."
Jeremy Rifkin, "What Biotechnology Means for the Future of Humanity."
Juan Enriquez-Cabot, "Will Biotechnology be the Driving Force of the 21st Economy."
Christopher Evans, "Investing in the Biotechnology Industry: The Role of dvelopment."
John Pierce, "Biotechnology and the Future of Materials."
Ray A. Goldberg, "Biotechnology and the Agricultural Industry of the Future."
Sue Bailey, "Bioterrorism and National Security."
Glenn McGee, "The Ethical, Legal and Social Implications of Biotechnology."
Gregory Stock, "Biotechnology and the Future of Medicine."
Allan Haberman, "Biotechnology and the Future of the Pharmaceutical Industry."

Eighth Specialized Conference
The International Date Palm Forum: Date Palm Culture in the United Arab Emirates
(9/15–17/02) C
   This conference aimed to highlight the history of date palm culture in the UAE, the Arab region and the world at large, its major role in the environmental progress and social life in the Arabian Gulf region, in addition to identifying the most modern techniques of date palm plantation, production and marketing, and boosting cooperation among countries, and international and regional institutions concerned with these vital issues.

Conference Papers:
Dr. Jamal Sanad Al-Suwaidi, "Welcoming Remarks."
Mr. Abdel Wahab Zayed, "The Date Palm Culture in the United Arab Emirates: Present Situation and Future Potential."
Mr. Hameed Jassim Al-Juburi, "Date Palm Research and Development in the United Arab Emirates."
Mr. Mark Beech, "Archaeobotanical Evidence for Early Date Consumption in the Arabian Gulf."
Mr. Daniel Potts, "Date Palms and Date Consumption in the Gulf Region during the Bronze Age."
Ms. Margareta Tengberg, "The Origins of Date Palm Domestication: The State of Research on the Origins of Phoenix Dactylifera."
Mr. Hassan Shabana, "Date Palm Varieties in the United Arab Emirates."
Mr. Abdel Rahman Musaiger, "The Nutritional and Health Benefits of Date Consumption."

Mr. Helal Hameed Al-Kaabi, "Date Palm Tissue Culture in the United Arab Emirates: Research Activities and Mass Production."

Mr. Mohammed Ouwaine, "Large-Scale Date Palm Propagation Using Tissue Culture Techniques."

Mr. Michel Ferry, "The Date Palm Axillary Productions: Morphogenesis and its Relevance for Propagation."

SECURITY FROM A UAE PERSPECTIVE

Deterrence Essentials: Keys to Controlling an Adversary's Behavior
(1/28–31/95) (EOP3) W
Dr. David Garnham
Professor of Political Science
University of Milwaukee – Wisconsin, USA

Prominent examples of deterrence failures were contrasted with "apparent" deterrence successes in this workshop. The requirements for successful deterrence were: sufficient capabilities to deny or punish aggression, sufficient credibility, and adequate knowledge of preferences to shape successful deterrence strategy. Computer simulation was utilized to expand on the basic deterrence model and illustrate the importance of other concepts including risk aversion, risk acceptance and preference. The workshop examined how deterrence issues impinge on the UAE. Threats were defined, as well as the capabilities needed to address them. National and international options available to the UAE were considered, along with ways in which threats by the UAE and allies can be made more credible. Intelligence concerning the capabilities, intentions and risk-taking propensity of potential adversaries was assessed. Major obstacles to successful deterrence within the Gulf region were pinpointed.

Deterrence Essentials: Applications for the UAE (3/9–13/96) W
Dr. David Garnham
Content similar to that of the previous workshop.

Gulf Security and the UAE (11/27/96) L
Staff Col. Muhammad Ahmad Al-Hamid
Directorate of Operations
GHQ, UAE Armed Forces

This lecture dealt with the crucial strategic topic of Gulf security, with its regional and international implications. The speaker presented the technical and legal clarifications of some strategic security concepts, and discussed the important strategic balance between Iran and the GCC states, as well as the determinants involved in creating this balance.

National Security Essentials: Applications for the UAE (5/17–21/97) (ELS10) W
Dr. David Garnham
Professor of Political Science
University of Milwaukee – Wisconsin, USA

National security objectives involve three main factors: military, political and economic. Workshop participants examined environmental, geopolitical and cultural aspects, as well as less "traditional," yet equally important, factors of national security policy, such as the nature of international politics, territoriality and the dynamics of population distribution. Also examined was the utility of the concept of "national interest." Case studies and examples of decision-making from the US, Japan and the UK were presented. Assessment and deterrence were examined. The nature of internal and external threats, and the impact of background factors like geography, global and regional power balances were analyzed. A deterrence computer simulation assisted participants to define and identify perceived threats along with the capabilities needed to address them, enhancing appreciation of the policy assets and vulnerabilities that specifically apply to the UAE.

UAE Security: Scenarios for the Coming Decade (1/6/98) (ELS16) L
Dr. David Garnham
Professor of Political Science
University of Milwaukee – Wisconsin, USA

International affairs are highly unpredictable and the present international security environment is especially volatile. As the UAE is relatively wealthy and reasonably secure, any changes to the status quo are likely to have a negative impact. Garnham presented an overview of UAE security issues and suggested specific policy initiatives to enhance security. Among them were strengthening the Gulf Co-operation Council, resolving the ambiguous and contentious border disputes that exist in the region, and reducing reliance on expatriate labor.

National Strategy in the Political Philosophy of H.H. Sheikh Zayed bin Sultan Al Nahyan, President of the UAE (1/20/02) L
Dr. Ahmed Jalal Al-Tadmuri
Advisor to H.H. the Chief of the Emiri Court (Studies and Documentation)
Ras Al-Khaimah, UAE

His Highness Sheikh Zayed bin Sultan Al Nahyan realizes that the policies of the superpowers are based on their own interests, without regard for the values or rights of others. Thus, he has sought to achieve Arab unity, as it gives the Arab world the necessary strength in a world ruled by the powerful.

Fundamentals of the Foreign Policy of the United Arab Emirates (1/29/02) L
Dr. Nayef Ali Obeid
Political Affairs Expert, Court of H.H. the Crown Prince of Abu Dhabi

The United Arab Emirates was established on three basic pillars: individual, Arab and Islamic affiliations, and global interaction. From the outset, the UAE committed itself to abide by certain principles that have since governed its domestic and foreign policies.

SECURITY IN THE GULF

The Role of Superpowers in Gulf Security (12/4/94) (ELS15) L
The Hon. Mikhail Gorbachev
Former President of USSR

President Mikhail Gorbachev noted that while the end of the Cold War has produced changes in international relations, the system remains highly unstable. He opined that emerging problems and international crises are directly linked to national and ethnic tensions. Changes have not been directed towards overcoming existing political imbalances, but used to further national goals and interests. Gorbachev encouraged the international community to make greater efforts to rid the world of nuclear arms. He also emphasized Russia's interests in the Gulf region, and urged rational exploitation of the world's natural resources.

The Yemeni War: Causes and Consequences (7/26–27/94) (Publ. 1995) S

This symposium was convened in response to the rapidly deteriorating political situation in Yemen that resulted in civil war in May 1994. The UAE, under its President's leadership, led the search for a peaceful resolution. Participants explored ideas that facilitated a better understanding of events in Yemen and the political forces behind the conflict.

Papers presented:

Dr. Robert Burrowes, "The Yemeni Civil War of 1994: Impact on the UAE and Other Arab Gulf States" – The impact of the Yemeni civil war on the UAE and other Arab Gulf states would depend more on Yemen's changing role in the balance of power on the Arabian peninsula and the changing relationship between the regime in Sanaa and Saudi Arabia than on any other likely outcome to this struggle.

Dr. Paul Dresch, "The Tribal Factor in the Yemeni Crisis" – The development of the conflict was traced through the main tribal conferences and meetings since 1990. Tribalism as a factor in Yemen's political troubles was analyzed.

Ambassador Charles Dunbar, "Internal Politics in Yemen: Recovery or Regression?" – Five possible scenarios for the post-civil war period in Yemen were sketched. Domestic political elements likely to be present and internal political changes which might be expected to influence each scenario were discussed.

Dr. Michael C. Hudson, "Bipolarity, Rational Calculation and War in Yemen" – Were institutional arrangements associated with Yemeni unity and transition to a multiparty system intrinsically inappropriate for attaining legitimacy and stability? Integration and pluralism in Arab politics were examined in assessing Yemen's future and its impact on Gulf security.

Dr. Mark Katz, "External Powers and the Yemeni Civil War" – The paper focused on how the Yemeni civil war affected the interests of such important external powers as the US, the EU, Russia, the GCC, other Arab states and Iran. The circumstances under which external powers might be motivated to intervene in conflict, how they might do so and with what effect were elaborated.

Dr. Jamal S. Al-Suwaidi, "The Future of Yemeni Unity" – This paper concluded the discussions by offering insight on the prospects for unity in Yemen.

First ECSSR Annual Conference
Iran and the Gulf: A Search for Stability (1/8–12/95) (Publ. 1996) C

The conference stressed that creating stability is the ideal way to achieve peace, security and prosperity for the states and societies of the Gulf region. This requires effective cooperation among the Gulf littoral states. Attempting to understand developments in Iran is the correct approach towards achieving this goal.

Conference Papers:

Dr. Hooshang Amirahmadi, "An Evaluation of Iran's First Development Plan and Challenges Facing the Second Plan."

Dr. Bahman Baktiari, "Institutionalizing the Islamic Revolution: The Presidency, the Supreme Leader and the Majlis in the Islamic Republic of Iran."

Dr. James A. Bill, "The Geometry of Instability in the Gulf: The Rectangle of Tension."

Dr. Anthony Cordesman, "The Iranian Military and its Potential Threat to the Gulf."

Dr. Karen Feste, "The Nexus between Domestic Instability and Superpower Intervention in Iran."

Dr. Bahman Fozouni, "Determinants of Iranian Foreign Policy in the Post-Khomeini Era."

Dr. Anwar Gargash, "Iran, the GCC States and the UAE: Prospects and Challenges in the Coming Decade."

Ambassador W. Nathaniel Howell, "Iran's Policy in Northwest Asia: Opportunities, Challenges and Implications."

Dr. Kenneth Katzman, "Iran's Armed Forces: A Growing Politico-Military Threat in the Gulf."

Dr. Geoffrey Kemp, "The Impact of Iranian Foreign Policy on Regional Security: An External Perspective."

Dr. Saleh Al-Mani, "Ideological Dimensions of Saudi-Iranian Relations."

Dr. Mohsen Milani, "Iran's Gulf Policy: From Idealism and Confrontation to Pragmatism and Moderation."

Dr. Roy Mottahedeh, "Shi'ite Political Thought and the Destiny of the Iranian Revolution."

Dr. Mehdi Noorbaksh, "Religion, Politics and Ideological Trends in Contemporary Iran."

Dr. Eliz Sanasarian, "The Social Dynamics: Education, Gender, and Health."

Gulf 2000: Security Issues in the Gulf
(In collaboration with Columbia University) (3/27–29/95) C

This conference addressed crucial issues concerning the Gulf region.

Conference Papers:

Dr. F. Gregory Gause III, "The Political Economy of National Security in the GCC."

Dr. Alden F. Mullins, "The Logic of Nuclear Proliferation."

Mr. Giandomenico Picco, "Political and Economic Cooperative Measures Available to the Gulf States."

Dr. Richard Schofield, "Border Disputes: Past, Present and Future."

Ms. Sarah Walkling, "A Catalogue of Confidence-Building Measures."

Disinformation and Misinformation: Questions for the Gulf (9/18/95) (EOP36) L
Mr. Todd Leventhal
Researcher, United States Information Agency

Disinformation is a deliberate policy pursued by governments to spread falsehood in the hope of manipulating perceptions. Mr. Leventhal, disinformation analyst in the US Information Agency, argued that despite the end of the Cold War, disinformation techniques are still being employed by many former communist states, among others. In the

Gulf region, Iran and Iraq have actively pursued disinformation policies, particularly during the 1991 Gulf War. Remaining aware of the continual use of disinformation is important in order to counteract its effects.

The Changing Situation in Iraq (10/30/95) L
Dr. Stephen Pelletiere
Strategic Studies Institute
US Army War College
In the aftermath of Operation Desert Storm, the disintegration of the Iraqi state was forecast. However, the continued imposition of UN sanctions and the splitting of the country into different protection zones have not seriously threatened the rule of Saddam Hussein and the Ba'athist ruling party. Iraq faces instability in Kurdish areas as does Turkey, despite the relief operations, with no clear solution in sight. However, there are signs of change, characterized by internal disturbances. It is imperative to put Iraqi events in perspective as these will affect the entire Gulf region.

The Gulf Cooperation Council After Muscat (12/9/95) L
Dr. Kenneth Katzman
Researcher, Congressional Research Service
Dr. Katzman came to ECSSR directly from the 16th Annual Gulf Cooperation Council (GCC) Summit in Muscat to analyze the summit's outcome and consequences. He stated that GCC integration was not a finished process and that, particularly in areas such as defense cooperation, there are still serious differences among the GCC member states over how best to ensure Gulf security and proceed with defense integration. The summit however, was able to pass strongly-worded documents on both Iran and Iraq and present a unified front in this respect.

Second ECSSR Annual Conference
Gulf Security in the Twenty-First Century (1/6–8/96) (Publ. 1997) C
Effective cooperation among Gulf countries is crucial for regional stability. This conference offered an analysis of geopolitical, economic and demographic challenges confronting the region. Topics covered were the relationship between economic issues and security; the extent of economic integration among Arab Gulf states on the one hand and the rest of the Gulf countries, US, Russia and European countries on the other; the impact of the de-escalation of the Arab–Israeli conflict on economic and political interaction patterns in the Gulf region; conflict resolution trends in border and regional disputes; relations with the Indian subcontinent and the demographic consequences of the growing expatriate labor force.

Conference Papers:
Dr. Robert Barylski, "The Collapse of the Soviet Union and Gulf Security."
Dr. Imtiaz Bokhari, "South Asia and the Gulf: Geopolitics of Intra-Regional Conflicts."
Dr. Michael Bonine, "Population Growth, the Labor Market and Gulf Security."
Dr. Jill Crystal, "Social Transformation, Changing Expectations and Gulf Security."

Dr. Charles Doran, "Economics and Security in the Gulf."
Dr. John Esposito, "Political Islam and Gulf Security."
Dr. Jerrold Green, "Iran and Gulf Security."
Dr. Rosemary Hollis, "Europe and Gulf Security: A Competitive Business."
Dr. David Long, "Gulf Security in Broad Perspective."
Dr. Phebe Marr, "Iraq Faces the 21st Century: Potential Challenges for GCC States."
Dr. Joseph Moynihan, "Common and Uncommon Security Interests: The Gulf Cooperation Council and the United States."
Hon. James Placke, "The International Oil Market and Gulf Security."
Dr. Glenn Robinson, "The Greater Middle East Co-Prosperity Sphere."
Dr. Richard Schofield, "Boundaries, Territorial Disputes and the GCC States."
Dr. Jamal S. Al-Suwaidi, "The Public Policy Process in the Gulf."
Dr. Mai Yamani, "Health, Education, Gender and Security of the GCC in the 21st Century."

The Relationship Between Population Pressures and International Peace (3/4/97) L
Dr. Adnan Al-Sayed
Professor of Law and Political Administration
Lebanese University

Dr. Al-Sayed analyzed global population distribution in terms of development, natural resources and income. These factors, in addition to conflict and water scarcity, will prompt significant future international migration. While advances in technology will mitigate these factors, the competition for resources among rising populations will ultimately lead to an increase in tensions and armed conflicts and affect international peace and security.

Gulf Security: A National Perspective (I) (4/5–6/97) C

From a variety of Arab and Western perspectives, serious security challenges persistently confront Gulf states through the direct or indirect interaction of political, economic, social and cultural factors. Responsibility for understanding implications that arise from these security challenges rests with leading decision-makers, officials and scholars from the region. This seminal meeting was organized to provide a forum for forthright discussion of internal Gulf issues along with their external dimensions. Conference topics included the impact of international developments on regional and GCC interaction, and the possibility of designing a common GCC security strategy to provide protection to the region's resources and territories.

Conference Papers:
Dr. Muhammad Jabber Al-Ansari, "An Analytical Study of Gulf Security from the Perspective of a Desert Warrior" by H.R.H. General Prince Khaled bin Sultan bin Abdul Aziz Al Saud.
Brigadier Hayei Jumah Al-Hamly, "GCC Defense Policies: Facts, Challenges, Possibilities."
Dr. Abdullah El-Kuwaiz, "Economic Challenges Facing Gulf Countries."

Dr. Saleh Al-Mani, "GCC Relations with Arab Countries."

Dr. Mohammed Al-Rumaihi, "Internal Security Challenges Facing GCC Countries."

H.R.H. General Prince Khaled bin Sultan bin Abdul Aziz Al-Saud (ELS11), "Roundtable Discussion on Gulf Security."

Dr. Jamal S. Al-Suwaidi, "Regional Threats and International Interference in the Gulf Region."

Alliance Durability: Middle Eastern Alignments with Special Focus on the ACC and the GCC (5/3/97) L

Dr. David Priess
Political Science Department
Duke University, USA

David Priess discussed international relations theories on the durability of international coalitions. He looked at prevailing intellectual schools and discussed his own theory based on socio-psychological research and on common identity between different communities. The main premise is that transnational identities lead, at times, to the preservation of coalitions. Moving to the GCC and the Arab Cooperation Council, he indicated the challenging historic moments that threatened both Councils alike. While they led to the disintegration of the Arab Cooperation Council, they solidified the GCC.

Gulf Security Issues from the British Withdrawal to the Invasion and Liberation of Kuwait (5/4/97) L

Prof. Jamal Zakariya Qassim
Professor of Modern History
Faculty of Arts
Ain Shams University, Egypt

During the colonial era, Gulf security was limited to maintaining the Pax Britannica. The establishment of the GCC was intended to overcome threats to its members and to enhance coordination and cooperation among them. Professor Qassim emphasized that the Iraqi invasion of Kuwait posed a serious challenge to the Gulf states by opening the door to the Western military presence in the region. The dependence of the GCC countries on bilateral defensive treaties with the US and other Western powers would not be a sustainable long-term security policy for the region.

Gulf Security: A National Perspective (II)
The Gulf: Future Security and British Policy (4/29–30/98) (Publ. 2000) C

Following the success of the 1997 Abu Dhabi Security Conference, this forum allowed senior GCC representatives to liaise with officials from the Royal United Services Institute (RUSI) in London to discuss regional military threats, obstacles to socio-economic development and potential challenges to political stability. In the light of the long-standing ties between the Gulf and the UK, defense cooperation was emphasized and maintenance of regional political continuity well into next millennium was analyzed. The findings of the Strategic Defense Review and their implications for future British regional policy were discussed.

Conference Papers:

Dr. Jamal S. Al-Suwaidi, ECSSR Director General, Opening Speech.

Rt. Hon George Robertson MP, Secretary of State for Defence, Welcoming Remarks.

H.H. Sheikh Salim Sabah Al-Salim Al-Sabah, "GCC: Trends in Defense Cooperation."

H.E. Brigadier Hamad bin Ali Al-Atiyah, "Gulf Threat Assessment – II."

Mr. Derek Fatchett, MP, "Gulf Security: A Foreign Policy Perspective."

General Sir Charles Guthrie & Prof. Lawrence Freedman, "Future Warfare: Implications for Gulf Defense."

H.H. Sheikh Salman bin Hamad bin Eissa Al Khalifa, "GCC Defense Cooperation with the West: A Bahraini Perspective."

H.E. Mr. Hisham Nazer, "Energy and Stability in the Gulf."

Dr. John Reid (MP), "Gulf Security: UK Policy and Implications of the UK Strategic Defense Review."

H.H. Sheikh Abdul Rahman bin Saud Al-Thani, "Gulf Security: A Gulf Perspective on the UK Role."

Vice Admiral Alan West, Mr. Derek Plumbly, Mr. George Joffe, "Gulf Threat Assessment – I."

The Future of the Gulf Co-operation Council (GCC) (11/24/98) S

This symposium was convened, prior to the 1998 annual GCC summit meeting, to highlight GCC progress to date as well as future domestic, regional and global developments. GCC accomplishments in the areas of political, economic and social importance were examined. Responses to challenges and risks confronting GCC's further development were proposed. The symposium examined the organizational aspects of the Council; its role in solving regional and international crises; the promotion of external economic ties; and environmental degradation and security cooperation, especially in relation to the future of US policy interests and potential changes of priorities in the Arabian Gulf.

Speakers included: Dr. Abdulkhaleq Abdulla, Dr. Mohammad Al-Assoumi, H.E. Ambassador Abdullah Bishara, Dr. Mohammad O.S. Ghubash, Dr. Ebtisam Suhail Al-Kitbi, H.E. Saif bin Hashel Al-Maskari, Dr. Saeed Abdullah Al-Muhairy, H.E. Khalifa Shaheen Al-Murrar, Dr. Fatima S.M. Al-Shamsi and Dr. Jamal S. Al-Suwaidi.

The Concept of Security in the New World Order (4/23/00) L

Mr. Adnan Sha'aban
Retired Brigadier General
Republic of Lebanon

Developments after the Cold War led to a security dynamic characterized by a global imbalance, multi-dimensional differences on all strategic, economic, political and ideological levels, and ensuing catastrophes. Global management is a difficult task, clouded by priority differences over crises between the US and nuclear and demographic powers. The speaker focused on bipolarity and concepts of security, the post-Cold War era, the right to intervene on humanitarian grounds to achieve political and military goals, religion and the media. A search for an emerging power balance may lead to bi-, multi- or unipolar leadership.

The Implications of the Triangular Iranian–Iraqi–Turkish Relations for Gulf Security
(5/23/00) (ELS34) L
Dr. Ahmed Shikara
Hon. Research Fellow, Political Studies Department
University of Auckland, New Zealand

This presentation stressed that Iran, Iraq and Turkey, though interested in pursuing national interests in the Gulf, have yet to formulate a coordinated strategic vision for Gulf security. Any attempt to forge an alliance between the three countries seems premature. These countries prefer to pursue their strategic objectives either unilaterally, or through bilateral interaction, notwithstanding certain areas of concern, particularly the question relating to Iraq's fate in the foreseeable future.

Gulf Defense Conference 2001
Countering the Threats: The GCC Countries and their Defense Policies
(3/19–20/01) C

This conference was organized in cooperation with the General Exhibition Corporation and Jane's, as part of the Gulf Defense Exhibition (IDEX 2001). It has become an annual event of great importance for GCC countries and all countries concerned with the Arab Gulf region. Maintaining a balance between Arab and Western views in selecting speakers was a prime concern. The conference was considered the first of its kind in the region in terms of topics, scope and the high profiles of the speakers. Two main themes were the assessment of threats in the Arabian Gulf region and defense strategies to counter threats.

Conference Papers:
Dr. Paul Beaver, "Iranian Military Capabilities and their Implication on Arabian Gulf Security."
Maj. Gen. Pilot Khaled A.M. Al-Buainain, "Training and Joint Operations among GCC Countries."
Air Chief Marshall Sir Michael Graydon, "The Role of the Western Powers in Maintaining the Security and Stability of the Gulf Region."
Dr. Saleh A. Al-Mani, "Regional Challenges for National Security in Arabian Gulf Countries."
Dr. Eric Morris, "Iraq and Arabian Gulf Security."
Dr. Joseph Moynihan, "Developments in Modern Military Technology and their Effects on the Defense Policies of GCC Countries."
Dr. Neil Patrick, "The Spread of Weapons of Mass Destruction and the Threat they Pose to the Gulf Region."
Staff Colonel Ahmed Al-Sabab, "The Coordination of Defense Policies among GCC Countries and its Role in Establishing Security and Stability in the Gulf Region."
Dr. Joanna Spear, "The Response to the Spread of Weapons of Mass Destruction and the Threat they Pose to the Gulf Region."

Strategic Balance in the Arabian Gulf Region: Realities and Prospects (4/3/01) L
Dr. Fathi Afeefi
Director of the Academic Center for Strategic Studies
Zaqazeeq, Egypt
   The lecture examined the concept of inter-state conflicts in the Arabian Gulf region and the search for a regional order mechanism. The Iraqi perspective on Arabian Gulf security was outlined and the status quo in Iraq was reviewed in the light of regional and international developments.

Islamic Perspective on Terrorism (10/28/01) S
   This symposium examined terrorism and its implications for society. It also discussed different aspects of terrorism and the Islamic perspective on terrorist acts.

Papers presented:
Dr. Ali Oqlah Irsan, "Terrorism: Concept, Factions, and Intellectual Roots."
Major General Fouad Mohammed Allam, "The Development of Terrorism."
H.E. Ambassador Dr. Riyad Na'san Agha, "Islamic Perspective on Terrorism."
Mr. Ahmed Omar Hashim, "Islam and its Relation to the Followers of Other Religions."
Prof. Mohammed Saeed Ramadan Bouti, "Islam and the Security of Society."

The Future Relations Between the GCC and the EU (5/21/02) S
   This symposium was organized in association with the Bartelsmann Foundation, the Robert Schuman Center for Advanced Studies and the Center for Applied Policy Research. The symposium was aimed at shedding light on common interests and concerns, exploring fields of cooperation, putting forward an agenda for future activities between the GCC and the EU, and discussing proposed policies.

Papers presented:
Dr. Jamal Sanad Al-Suwaidi, Welcoming Remarks.
Mr. Felix Neugart and Mr. Giacomo Luciani, "Presentation GSD – Paper."
Dr. Jamal Sanad Al-Suwaidi, "Political and Security Dialogue: GCC Perspective."
Dr. Shamlan Youssef Al-Issa, "Good Governance and Human Rights: GCC Perspective."
Ds. Rasha Al-Humoud Al-Sabah, "Human Rights and Education: GCC Perspective."
Dr. Mohammed Saleh Kameshki, "Trade and Investment: GCC Perspective."
Mr. Hassan Al-Marzooqi, "Oil and Gas: GCC Perspective."
Mr. Shehab Mohammed Gargash, "Financial Markets: GCC Perspective."

The Formation of a New Political System in Iraq: The Role of the GCC (6/17/03) L
Mr. James Russell
Senior Lecturer, Naval Postgraduate School
Monterey, California, USA
   The GCC has an opportunity to contribute constructively to the development of a new framework for steering the relations between the Arab Gulf states and to show a skeptical international community that the GCC can effectively contribute to the management of the region's political, economic and military relations.

War Against Iraq: Implications for the Arab Gulf States (2/1/03) S
   This symposium aimed to analyze war in Iraq, the possible political, economic, security, strategic and environmental implications for the region. It discussed the best possible ways for coping with such challenges.

Papers presented:
Dr. Jamal Al-Suwaidi, Keynote on "War on Iraq: Repercussions on Arab Gulf States."
Dr. Saleh Abdel Rahman Al-Mani, "The Impact of War on the Gulf Region."
Dr. Philip H. Gordon,"Strategic Plans for Middle East and Arabian Gulf."
Dr. Shamlan Youssef Al-Issa, "The GCC Role in the Iraq of the Future."
Dr. Andrew Rathmell, "Post-War Gulf Security System: Back to the Future."
Dr. Peter Chalk, "The Influence of War against Iraq on Terrorism."
Dr. Neil Patrick, "The Future of a Foreign Military Presence in the Arabian Gulf Region."
Dr. Giacomo Luciani, "War on Iraq: Repercussions on the Economies of the GCC Countries."
Ms. Ruba Husari,"Iraq, Energy Security and the Future of the International Oil Market."
Ms. Rachel Bronson, "Economic Costs of Iraq's Reconstruction: What Could be Expected on the Part of GCC countries."
Mr. Shehab Mohammed Gargash, "Horizons of Economic Relations Between GCC Countries and Iraq Following the Conflict."

Iraq: Reconstruction and Future Role (9/14–15/03) (Publ. 2004) S
   This focused on the various possible political outcomes of the US-led occupation of Iraq and Iraq's role in the Gulf, particularly regarding Gulf security. The speakers indicated that reconstruction of post-Saddam Iraq is the largest and strategically most important post-conflict challenge that has confronted the United States since WW II.

Papers presented:
Dr. Jamal Sanad Al-Suwaidi , Welcoming Remarks.
Dr. Patrick L. Clawson, "The New Role for Iraq in the Gulf."
Ms. Bathsheba N. Crocker, "The Future of US-Iraq Relations."
Dr. Kenneth Katzman, "Political Scenarios in Post-Saddam Iraq."
Ms. Vera De Ladoucette, "Iraq in a New Map of Oil Supplies: Implications for Other Gulf Oil Producers."

Redefining Defense Logistics for the Next Generation Leadership (6/7–11/03) W
Mr. Philibhert Suresh, Dr. Jordan Samhuri, Ms. Elizabeth Barber
   The participants discussed several issues including supply chain management, contracting and outsourcing in military supply chains, military warehouse management policies, (particularly those related to fighter aircraft), management of personal skills, knowledge management and the importance of leadership in defense logistics.

Gulf Security (1/27/03) L
Dr. Mamdouh Anis
Emirates Center for Strategic Studies and Research (ECSSR)
United Arab Emirates
   The lecturer discussed the importance of a realistic view of the various elements of power and its impact on the national security of nations. He claimed that it is important to define realistic goals and then commence working towards establishing a common system for attaining common prosperity. He underlined the importance of monitoring any developments or new changes within the context of studying the variables of regional and international environment.

The Gulf Co-operation Council: Realities and Challenges (4/7/03) L
Dr. Nayef Ali Obeid
Political Expert, Ministry of Presidential Affairs
H.H. the Crown Prince's Court, Abu Dhabi, UAE
   Through a comparative study of the GCC, the lecturer examined political events and developments, particularly regarding the formation of regional organizations. He focused on the UN's role and relationship with other regional organizations, then highlighted the factors and issues of perennial interest to GCC states.

Ninth Specialized Conference
Gulf Defence Conference 2003
Gaining an Edge: Future Challenges and Requirements
for the Armed Forces of the GCC (3/17–18/03) C
   The conference examined the present and future regional and global security challenges, issues of crises management, training, infrastructure, in addition to military procurements required to prepare the GCC forces for dealing with such challenges.

Conference Papers:
Mr. Khaled Abdullah Mubarak Al-Buainain, Keynote Speaker, "Gaining an Edge: Future
   Challenges and Requirements for the Armed Forces of the GCC."
H.E. Sheikh Nahyan Bin Zayed Al Nahyan, Welcoming Remarks.
H.R.H. Prince Faisal Ibn Al-Hussein," Enhancing the Regional Security Environment in a
   Changing World."
Mr. Andrew Stewart, "Future Global Challenges, Prospects and Threats."
Mr. Paul Beaver, "The Iraqi Crisis and Gulf Security: Risks and Challenges Facing the GCC
   Armed Forces."
Mr. Christopher Ledger, "Crisis Management and the Response to Chemical, Biological
   and Radiological Attack."
Mr. David Wood, "Training the GCC Armed Forces to Meet the Future Challenges."
Mr. Mark Vincent, "Protecting Human Health and Environment: Rebuilding the
   Infrastructure."
Mr. David Waters,"Policy, Planning and Procurement to Achieve Interoperable GCC
   Armed Forces."

Ninth Annual Conference
The Gulf: Challenges of the Future (1/11–13/04) (Publ. 2005) C
This conference highlighted several issues related to the Gulf region and the future challenges, including: changing security measures, the wider implications of globalization, investment in knowledge-based developmental economic activities, the massive impact and the far-reaching influence of the media, the issue of Gulf security and regional developments.

Conference Papers:
H.H. General Sheikh Mohammed Bin Zayed Al Nahyan, Crown Prince of Abu Dhabi, Deputy Supreme Commander of the UAE Armed Forces, and President of the ECSSR, Keynote Address, "The Gulf: Challenges of the Future."
Dr. Jamal Sanad Al-Suwaidi, Welcoming Remarks.
H.E. Sheikh Hamad Bin Jassim Bin Jabr Al-Thani, "Positioning the GCC Countries in the Global Economy: Challenges and Policy Options."
Mr. Mahmoud Sariolghalam, "Iran's Emerging Regional Security Doctrine: Domestic Sources and the Role of International Constraints."
Mr. Jerrold D. Green, "Iran's Regional Policies: A Western Perspective."
Mr. Geoffrey Kemp, "The Impact of Iran's Nuclear Program on Gulf Security."
Ms. Muneera Ahmad Fakhro, "The Changing Role of Women in the Gulf Region."
Ms. Badria Abdullah Al-Awadhi, "Women in the Gulf and Globalization: Challenges and Opportunities."
Mr. Saleh Abdel Rahman Al-Mani, "The Future of Cooperation Among Gulf States: Prospects and Challenges."
Mr. Abdel Redha Ali Assiri, "The Role of the GCC in Promoting Regional Coexistence."
H.H. Sheikh Abdullah Bin Zayed Al Nahyan, "The Position of the Gulf Within the New World Order."
H.R.H. Prince Turki Al-Faisal Bin Abdul Aziz, "The Impact of the New Iraq on the GCC."
Mr. Faleh Abdel Jabbar, "Post-Conflict Iraq and the Gulf: Ambivalent Consequences."
Mr. Kamel Mubdir Al Kilani, "Iraqi Economy: Aspirations and Challenges."
Mr. Frederick D. Barton, "Defining Success in Iraq and Its Implications for the Gulf."
Mr. Shamlan Youssef Al-Issa, "The Political Impact of Globalization on the Gulf States."
Gen. Anthony Zinni (Ret.), "Impact of US Policy on Gulf Security: The Military Viewpoint."
Mr. Benjamin R. Barber, "The Challenges of Democratization in the Non-Western World."
Mr. John Major, "Multinational Corporations and State Sovereignty: Redefining Government Responsibilities in a Global Economy."
Mr. Gareth Evans, "Shifting Security Parameters in the 21st Century."
Mr. Mohammed Ali Abtahi, "Iran and International Relations: Impact on Political Stability in the Gulf."
Prof. Bassam Tibi, "Political Innovation in the Gulf: Society and State in a Changing World."
Mr. Jamal Ahmad Khashoggi, "The Evolving Role of Media in the Gulf: Privatization, Competition, Censorship."

International Interests in the Gulf Region (3/15–16/04) (Publ. 2004) S

This symposium deliberated on the strategic interests of major world powers in the Gulf region, particularly after the invasion of Iraq. The participants at the seminar included UAE researchers and experts as well as an elite group of scholars from Arab countries, Europe and the US.

Conflict Resolution in the Post-Cold War World:
Implications for Iraq (2/23/04) (ELS 53) L
Gen. Sir Michael Rose
Non-executive Director, Control Risks Group, UK

US goals in the Middle East are regional stability and access to Gulf oil. It seeks to achieve these goals by establishing liberal democracies, strengthening economic ties and maintaining US military presence in the Arabian Gulf. In addition, safeguarding Israel remains its major goal. As regards Iraq, a way out for the Coalition Provisional Authority would be to give the responsibility for the transition of power to the UN, which should hand over governance of Iraq to Iraqis after elections.

Gulf Security and Regional Watercourse Management:
Implications for the United Arab Emirates (3/28/04) (ELS 57) L
Dr. Bertrand Charrier
Vice-President, Green Cross International, Geneva, Switzerland

The development and management of sustainable water resources are major challenges for the future, especially for the Arabian Gulf region. A water crisis will affect everything, including health, environment, economy, human rights, poverty, politics, culture and conflicts. As water defies political boundaries, any crisis will go beyond the scope of countries and individual sectors, and cannot be dealt with in isolation.

The Repercussions from the Afghan and Iraq Wars for the Arab Gulf Region
(4/4/04) L
Dr. Ahmad Shikara
Instructor of Research Methodology, ECSSR

Since the 9/11 attacks, the pace accelerated for events resulting from the US-led global war on terror. This lecture focused on the important repercussions of these developments on the Arabian Gulf region, especially on its geo-strategic, security, economic (oil) and other related dimensions.

Australia's Strategic Involvement in the Middle East (5/4/04) (ELS 56) L
Prof. David Horner
Professor of Australian Defense History, Strategic and Defense Studies Centre

Australia has several contributions to offer to the Gulf States in the field of military collaboration. In addition to the increasing volume of Australian trade with the Gulf, Australian interests and strategic involvements in this region are expected to continue, and will actually expand in the coming years.

Meeting Iran's Nuclear Challenge (12/7/04) (ELS 60) L
Dr. Gary Samore
Director of Studies and Senior Fellow for Non-Proliferation, International Institute for Strategic Studies (IISS) London, UK
Since Iran's clandestine fuel cycle (uranium enrichment and reprocessing) programs were publicly revealed in August 2002, diplomatic efforts to curb Iran's ambitions to possess nuclear weapons have yielded mixed results. An agreement was reached to suspend uranium enrichment in November 2004. However, Iran prefers to complete its program, which would provide it with the ability to possess nuclear weapons within a few years.

Iraq's National Elections: Implications for Gulf Security (1/4/05) (ELS 61) L
Dr. Kenneth Katzman
Analyst, Congressional Research Service, US Congress
This lecture analyzed the implications of Iraqi elections scheduled for January 30, 2005, especially the consequences of a rejection of the polls and their outcome by Sunni Arabs. If this were to occur, the insurgency in Iraq may carry on or even worsen. The Bush Administration is facing another crucial dilemma: Will it use the elections and the formation of an elected government as a basis for ending the US presence in Iraq?

SECURITY AND TECHNOLOGY

The Revolution in Military Affairs: Non-Lethal Technologies (2/6/95) L
Dr. Joseph Moynihan
Researcher, Emirates Center for Strategic Studies and Research (ECSSR) Abu Dhabi, UAE
This presentation defined Non-Lethal Technologies (NLT) and described their niche within current defense strategy and technology. Dr. Moynihan gave a background summary of the purposes that futurists predict for NLTs, and outlined why he believes there will most likely be an exponential growth in the use of NLTs. The lecture concluded with a discussion of the operational utility of NLTs in specific scenarios, and the capabilities and limitations associated with this important defense program.

Modernization in US Tactical Aviation: Choices and Constraints (2/14/95) L
Dr. Serge Herzog
European and American Defense Policy Analyst
This lecture presented an overview of the modernization of US military tactical fighter aircraft. It examined the reasons why such forces are modernized and explained the set of assumptions guiding modernization options. The modernization plans of the Bush and Clinton administrations were compared in order to highlight the future direction of tactical aviation, both in terms of platforms and associated ordnance. Several problem areas and current trends impeding a sound modernization strategy were identified.

Strategic Uses of Civilian Satellite Imagery (7/30/96) L
Dr. Andrew Rathmell
Deputy Director, International Center for Security Analysis
King's College, London, United Kingdom
   In 1990, Iraq used civilian satellite imagery (CSI) to plan its invasion of Kuwait. A year later, the West European Union decided to establish its own Satellite Center to monitor European arms control agreements. The exploitation of CSI for strategic purposes has peaked. CSI is of proven value in monitoring environmental crises and conducting environmental surveys. Space surveillance can even assist in locating concentrations of deep groundwater as demonstrated in the UAE.

Space-Based Surveillance (11/9 –10/97) (EOP29)W
Dr. Andrew Rathmell and Dr. Bhupendra Jasani
   Uses of civilian satellite imagery (CSI) are environmental as well as strategic (e.g. detection of deep ground water). This workshop reviewed developments in space-based intelligence gathering, international security, space surveillance systems and commercial CSI. Commercial satellites were recognized as increasing in military importance.

Civil Remote Sensing Satellites and National Security (1/10/98) L
Dr. Bhupendra Jasani
Professor, Department of War Studies
King's College, London, United Kingdom
   A spying eye in the sky is not a new idea, but the use of commercial remote sensing data for enhancing national security, monitoring international arms treaties and collecting information as a confidence-building measure is novel. Commercial satellites have improved greatly and many more countries have image processing capacities so that data can be used widely. The lecturer proposed an arrangement, similar to the Western European Union Satellite Center, for the benefit of regional Middle East security.

Artificial Intelligence and Defense Intelligence Systems: A National Architecture
(1/21/98) L
Dr. Anthony Contri and Dr. Angus Reynolds
Researchers, PROTEIS Corporation
Albuquerque, New Mexico, USA
   This lecture explored both the potential and problems associated with new multi-source artificial intelligence gathering, reduction, analysis, collation and distribution, particularly in relation to existent US systems. Its applications for intelligence, counter-espionage, internal security and population control as well as border interaction were examined, in addition to directed automatic data mining, gaming simulations and electronic decision reports.

Air Missile Defense, Counterproliferation and Security Policy Planning: Implications for Collaboration Between the UAE, US and the GCC Countries
(3/29–31/98) (Publ. 1999) W
   This workshop studied key developments in missile defense with particular reference

to national, regional and international implications for future strategic initiatives. The goal was to lay the groundwork for better multilateral cooperation. Participants included:

Dr. Jacquelyn Davis, Institute for Foreign Policy Analysis (IFPA).

Lieutenant General Carl Franklin, Commander, US Air Force.

Dr. Robert Joseph, Director, Center for Counterproliferation Research, National Defense University, Washington, DC, USA.

Dr. David Martin, Deputy for Strategic Relations, Ballistic Missile Defense Organization, USA.

Dr. Thomas Morgan, US Department of Defense.

Mr. Richard Ritter, US Department of Defense.

Ms. Alina Romanowski, Deputy US Assistant Secretary of Defense for Near Eastern and South Asian Affairs.

Dr. Jamal S. Al-Suwaidi, Director General, ECSSR.

Mr. David Tanks, Senior Staff, IFPA.

General Anthony Zinni, Commander-in-Chief, US Central Command.

War in the Information Age (3/21–24/99) W

Thomas G. Mahnken, Andrew T. Parasiliti and Timothy D. Hoyat

A growing number of defense experts in the US and elsewhere argue that we are in the midst of a Revolution in Military Affairs (RMA) that will radically alter the way future wars are fought. They point to similar periods in history, during which the emergence of new combat methods transformed warfare within a relatively short period of time. US armed forces have invested substantial resources to develop innovative technology, concepts and organizations. US interest in the emerging RMA has implications not only for the US, but for its friends and allies as well. This workshop examined the concept of RMA in the context of past transformations of warfare. It explored the roots of RMA in the Gulf War and focused on the current debate in the US. It assessed the future impact of RMA on global and regional balances of power, alliance structures, service roles and missions, as well as concepts and doctrines.

Open Sources and Gulf Security (6/5–7/99) W

Dr Andrew Rathmell and Dr. Bhupendra Jasani

The workshop provided an in-depth introduction to the use of open sources in Gulf security and the role of Commercial Satellite Imagery in promoting transparency and confidence-building, available intelligence information, the impact of Earth Observation Revolution on open source intelligence, and the principles of remote sensing and current methods for using imagery to monitor security-related sites. The strategic significance for the UAE and the Gulf region was emphasized. Security cooperation and the construction of an intra-regional cooperative security system was particularly stressed.

Defense Globalization: Next Steps for a 21st Century Industry (11/3/01) L

Dr. Robert H. Trice Jr.

Vice President of Business Development

Lockheed Martin Corporation

The lecturer described current trends in global defense spending, defense procurement and research expenditures in the world. He also discussed the general trend towards the globalization of industrial economies and its implications for the ways in which nations advance their security interests.

Information Security and Modern Technology (5/17–21/03) W
Mr. Rami Nu'man Jaghoub

This workshop examined several important issues concerning information security within the context of modern technologies, such as the major concepts of information security, confidentiality and security of information on computers, the types of information security systems, information coding systems, password management and backup management.

SECURITY AND WEAPONS OF MASS DESTRUCTION

The Future Face of Terrorism (4/15/96) L
Dr. Douglas Menarchik
Professor, George C. Marshall European Center for Security Studies

Over the last 25 years, international terrorism has become an abiding factor in world politics. Since 1968, analysts have collected data on terrorism and they agree on its general future trends. "Super-terrorism" or the use of WMD poses a tremendous threat in the increasingly vulnerable state system, impacting on other forms of ethnic, nationalistic and anarchic terrorism to which the Middle East will remain vulnerable for the foreseeable future. Terrorism may also mix with other global threats, especially drug-trafficking and organized crime. Combating this threat requires international cooperation and the strengthening of existing mechanisms.

Chemical and Biological Weapons in the Gulf: Lessons from Iraq (7/29/96) L
Dr. Andrew Rathmell
Deputy Director, International Center for Security Analysis
King's College, London, United Kingdom

The issue of weapons proliferation in the Middle East has shifted to the top of the international agenda as a threat to regional stability and the ability of Western powers to intervene in the area. Iraq and Iran are the main concerns. Although Iraq did not use chemical, biological or poison gases against the coalition forces in the Gulf War, it did use some of these weapons against its own internal opposition. The speaker reviewed the different dimensions of chemical weapons in the Gulf and possible deterrence methods.

Protection against Nuclear, Biological and Chemical (NBC) Threats (9/1 – 3/96) W
This workshop was conducted by experts from GIAT Industries.

Control of weapons of mass destruction (WMD) is now one of most important factors influencing international relations. The increasing efforts of many countries to acquire nuclear weapons precipitated the Nuclear Non-Proliferation Treaty in 1968. Most countries joined the pact, but the success achieved by the international community on nuclear arms control stimulated many countries to develop other programs for producing WMD.

Attempts to sign additional international agreements prohibiting the use of such weapons have not yet dissuaded many countries from seeking their acquisition. The Middle East is one of the regions at the center of international concern. Due to the region's vital strategic and economic importance, efforts are underway to make it free of WMD.

The Strategic Implications of Chemical and Biological Weapons for Gulf Security
(6/15/99) (ELS24) L
Dr. Kamal A. Beyoghlow
Professor of International Relations and National Security
Marine Corps Command and Staff College
Virginia, USA
Chemical and biological weapons can be formidable instruments of power in the hands of regional actors, including Iraq, Iran, Israel, Pakistan and India, if reinforced with nuclear weapons. The lecture dealt with the properties of these weapons, their nature, the potential for regional proliferation and their impact. It is likely that such weapons will develop and become destabilizing factors in the Gulf region. A nuclear, biological and chemical weapon-free zone in the Gulf could reduce regional tensions.

WMD Nonproliferation/Export Control and Border Security (10/20–24/01) W
This workshop focused on effective, non-intrusive controls over exports in order to control the proliferation of Weapons of Mass Destruction. H.E. Ambassador Marcelle M. Wahba, John Schlosser, Grace Curcetti, Matthew Borman, Gerald Backen, Karen Nies-Vogel, David Flynn, Anstr Davidson, Stephen Leacy, William Carter and John Malandra took part.

The Nuclear Balance in South Asia (5/21/03) (ELS 52) L
Dr. Chris Smith
Executive Director, Centre for South Asia Studies
King's College, London, UK
It can be said that Indian fears have abounded after developing its nuclear potential. India has attained overwhelming superiority over Pakistan in conventional weapons. Pakistan has tried to offset Indian superiority in conventional weapons by possessing a nuclear capability, thus leaving India uncertain about the possible implications of a conventional war.

SOCIAL/POLITICAL DEVELOPMENT AND THE UAE

Social Challenges in the United Arab Emirates (11/23/96) L
Dr. Mohammad Al-Mansour
Deputy Director for Student Affairs
UAE University
Dr. Mohammed Al-Mansour discussed social development in the UAE, focusing in particular on education, demographic composition, social and economic consciousness. Following a theoretical introduction about the phases of development that the UAE has

undergone, he emphasized the need for further development of human resources in order for the UAE to carry out its responsibilities effectively. He pointed out that effective management and the improvement of human resources are more important than maximum use of such resources.

Regional Challenges Facing the United Arab Emirates (11/24/96) L
H.E. Khalifa Shaheen Al-Murrar
UAE Ambassador to Iran

The prevailing regional variables in the Gulf and the Middle East have created three categories of challenges for the UAE. The first is the area of security in the Gulf, of which regional security is the foremost. The ability to manage this issue effectively is determined by the country's ability to establish diplomatic relations with countries that have a direct impact on the region. The second challenge is the development of the Middle East peace process and the implications of its success or failure for the Gulf. The last major challenge deals with the need for deeper cooperation among the GCC member states.

International Challenges Facing the United Arab Emirates (11/24/96) L
Dr. Abdulla Juma Al-Hajj
Cultural Advisor, UAE Embassy
Washington, DC, USA

The speaker called for a careful monitoring of the structural changes which international organizations have recently undergone on the political, economic and strategic levels. He focused on the emergence of new international actors in the aftermath of the Cold War and the increasing number of economic struggles between the current world powers. He discussed how instability in today's world greatly affects the Gulf region, especially since the decisions made by world powers continue to play a major role in many regional struggles.

Political Union and Political Integration: An Assessment of the UAE Model
(11/25/96) L
Dr. Mohammad O.S. Ghubash
Professor of Political Science
UAE University

Dr. Ghubash presented an analysis of how the UAE Federation's leaders have dealt with the problems that have emerged during its short history. He also discussed the most significant challenges facing the UAE, particularly its demographic composition, and some of the Federation's most important achievements, such as successful social integration among the UAE citizens.

A Modern Reading of the History of the UAE (12/15/98) L

Dr. Mohammed Moursy Abdullah
Director, Centre for Documentation and Research
Cultural Foundation, Abu Dhabi, UAE

Dr. Moursy discussed the historical development of the Emirates since the invasion of the Portuguese. He has consulted Dutch, Arabic and Portuguese sources to document the commercial and Islamic heritage of the country. He paid tribute to Sheikh Zayed's strong interest in preserving both the architectural tradition and the documentary evidence of this development.

Health Development in the United Arab Emirates in a Global Perspective (3/2/99) (ELS23) L

Dr. Hans Rosling
Professor, International Health Studies
Karolinska Institute, Sweden

The UAE has seen dramatic improvement in the health of its citizens in recent decades. This rapid health transition has led to infectious diseases being replaced by non-communicable diseases like diabetes and heart illnesses. These are more costly to care for and cause high levels of disability. A demographic transition will lead to an increased proportion of elderly people. The result is an increase in the future cost of health service in the UAE. The lecture focused on ways to reduce the cost of care and to prevent non-communicable diseases.

The UAE Population Structure: Its Present and Future (5/21/00) L

Dr. Matar Ahmad Abdullah
Head of the Statistical Division Planning Department, Abu Dhabi, UAE

This lecture dealt with the problem of the UAE population structure. It sought to identify the composition of the UAE population, and growth and change factors affecting the demographic structure since the oil boom, which have led to an imbalance in the UAE population. The analysis was based on census figures from 1968–1995. Dr. Matar Abdullah predicted future trends in the UAE population structure and suggested solutions to minimize the worsening population situation.

National Security Challenges for the UAE: Population (6/6/00) L

Dr. Jamal S. Al-Suwaidi
Director General, The Emirates Center for Strategic Studies and Research
Abu Dhabi, UAE

H.E. Dr. Jamal S. Al-Suwaidi spoke of the UAE's demographic composition and the factors that led to the influx of foreign labor to meet the state's development policies following the discovery of oil. After examining the statistics and data, the political, economic, social and security implications of the current demographic imbalance for UAE society were emphasized. There is a need to find practical and effective solutions to this problem by adopting a national strategy with clear objectives and means within a suitable timeframe.

Arab Development Reform: Washington's Greater Middle East Initiative and Arab Human Development Report (5/30/04) L

Dr. Nader Fergani
Director, Almishkat Center for Research
Giza, Egypt

This lecture concentrated on highlighting the Arab Human Development Report as an original vision for renaissance in the Arab world. It reviewed the options available to the Arab world and emphasized that its present situation cannot continue indefinitely. The impasse was a result of the limited response of Arab regimes to the external change embodied by the "American Greater Middle East Initiative," including European amendments, and the "Second Original Alternative," which is based on internal reforms through innovative community efforts made by dynamic forces within in the Arab world.

US FOREIGN POLICY

The Role of the Pentagon in US Foreign Policy Decision-Making (4/16/94) S

The Hon. Caspar Weinberger
Chairman of Forbes Magazine and former US Secretary of Defense

The Pentagon plays a leading role in foreign policy primarily because the pursuit of strategic interests has a major military component. However, it assumes that role in coordination with other governmental institutions. The Gulf War was not just a military victory. An important US foreign policy feature that aggression cannot be allowed to stand was also illustrated. Part of President Bush's concept of a New World Order is based on the rule of law and UN principles. It was a remarkable victory in a short period for the 31-nation coalition, considering the command and control difficulties. US interest in Gulf oil was not the only cause of intervention. The need to establish a system whereby states violating international norms do not go unpunished is equally important. The Iranian weapons program, coupled with policies unchanged since the days of Khomeini, makes it a dangerous neighbor. The symposium concluded that a significant downgrading of military capabilities would be a mistake for the US.

US Foreign Policy: The Domestic Political Dimension (10/3/95) L

Mr. Stephen Dachi
Deputy Director, Office of North African, Near Eastern and South Asian Affairs, USIA

This presentation covered domestic political changes in the US as it entered the 1996 presidential campaign. It focused specifically on the internal dynamics of domestic politics, including the role of Congress, political parties, the media, lobbies and non-governmental organizations. The upcoming presidential elections were viewed as unlikely to prompt a serious debate on US foreign policy as America's domestic problems were predicted to dominate the presidential debate.

A New Conservative Internationalist Foreign Policy (10/17/95) L
Dr. Edwin J. Feulner
President, Heritage Foundation
According to Dr. Feulner, the US should not and cannot be the world's policeman in the post-Cold War environment. It has neither the ability nor the resources to right all the wrongs in the world. Where vital interests are concerned, however, the US can and should function as a volunteer fireman to extinguish those flames that threaten its national interests. This is especially true in the Arabian Gulf, which contains two-thirds of the world's oil reserves and is a crucial pillar of global economic stability. The US must maintain a strong military deterrent in the Gulf to guard against renewed aggression from Iraq or Iran.

US Foreign Policy in the Gulf: Recent Developments (11/7/95) L
Ambassador Richard Murphy
Senior Fellow, Council on Foreign Relations
Ambassador Roscoe Suddharth
President, Middle East Institute
While the predominant US role in assuring Gulf security will continue for the next several years, there are also increasing disagreements between the US and the GCC states over their relationship. The US has discarded the concept of the "balance of power" in the Gulf while the GCC states continue to think in these terms. From an American point of view, it now becomes important to start viewing the Gulf region as a true subset of the greater Middle East system.

The 1996 US Elections and the Electoral Shift (4/13/96) L
Dr. Edmund Ghareeb
UAE Embassy, Washington, DC, USA
There has been a transformation of the American body politic in the past five years. The end of the Cold War and the structural insecurities of an economy that is undergoing a transformation from an industrial to a technological base has significantly altered the way in which Americans regard the world and their place in it. This lecture focused on the success of the Republicans in addressing this sea change in the American electorate and on the ability of the Democrats to regroup after the devastating Congressional polls of 1994.

An Analysis of the American Elections (11/9/96) L
Dr. Peter Gubser
President of American Near East Refugee Aid
This presentation looked at the 1996 US election for the presidency, Senate and House of Representatives. It reviewed possible reasons for the ensuing election results, with an emphasis on the themes of peace and prosperity. The speaker also discussed aspects of the American and global economies, the need to reduce unemployment, the budget deficit and the role of candidates in the context of some pertinent social issues. Finally, he discussed the future economic, political and social implications of the election results.

Prospective Policies of the New US Administration in the Gulf and Middle East
(11/10/96) L
Ambassador Roscoe Suddharth
President, Middle East Institute

Based on his experience as ambassador to a number of Arab countries, as an official in the State Department and as the President of the Middle East Institute, the speaker explained his view of future US policies towards the Middle East over the short to medium term, with reference to the rapidly unfolding events in the region, especially on the Palestinian-Israeli peace process and the situation in the Arab Gulf region. The focused discussion after the lecture revealed the speaker's intimate knowledge of the Gulf and the Middle East situation.

US Policy in the Gulf Region (2/25/97) (ELS4) L
Mr. Lincoln Bloomfield
Armitage Institution, USA

Mr. Bloomfield noted that US security policy in the Gulf has been characterized by two elements: a practical approach to current problems, and a vision of its impact on regional stability. As the Gulf will continue to be an extremely important security area, the Pentagon will continue to have considerable influence in Gulf affairs. He concluded that the second Clinton Administration was likely to be more forceful internationally and would deal with current problems, but was not focusing on a long-term policy for the region.

The US and the Middle East: Common Interests or Absolute Hegemony?
(11/17/97) L
Dr. Tawfiq Y. Hesso
Resident Researcher, Middle East Institute
Washington, DC, USA

The US has strategic interests in the Arabian Gulf and the Middle East. The stability of the region and strong relations with its states are of paramount importance. US policy has three objectives: preserving the security of Israel, maintaining access to Gulf oil and securing regional stability. This policy went through three phases: Cold War phase, post-liberation of Kuwait phase, and a third phase based on the idea that the Middle East will remain unstable in the near future, and that alternative oil sources exist.

US–Iran Relations: Issues and Implications (5/4/98) L
Prof. Farhad Kazami
New York University, USA

Recent developments in Iranian internal politics were reviewed, particularly factors leading to the landslide victory of President Khatami and the base of the opposition groups. The US containment policy in relation to terrorism, weapons of mass destruction and peace initiative issues was examined. While there is room for some guarded optimism, Dr. Kazami pointed out that there have been no real breakthroughs in these areas.

US Elections 1998: Implications for US Foreign Policy (11/11/98) (ELS20) L
Dr. Peter Gubser
President of American Near East Refugee Aid
   The lecture reviewed the general political situation in the US and the major issues debated by candidates during the 1998 Congressional elections, in addition to polls held for state and local government offices. It presented an analysis of the mid-term election together with its outcomes and implications for US policies. The state of the economy, trade and investment, the end of the Cold War, the current isolationist trend in foreign policy and the Lewinsky case were explored as factors relevant to the campaigns.

US–Iran: From Containment to Engagement (2/2/99) L
Prof. Ahmed Ghoreishi
Naval Postgraduate School
Monterey, California, USA
   The status of US–Iran relations following the election of Mohammed Khatami to the Iranian presidency was explored. Khatami has called for the expansion of cultural and sports exchanges between Iran and the US to break the "wall of distrust" between the two countries. Iran and the US, despite differences, have common interests. The US should test Iran by modifying its containment policy rather than trying to economically weaken and politically isolate it. The promotion of rapprochement through such a modification would foster US strategic and economic interests.

The Emergent Arab-American Political Constituency (6/8/99) L
Dr. James Zogby
President, Arab American Institute
Washington, DC, USA
   Arab-Americans can point to several important gains in ending their political exclusion: a community that identifies itself as Arab-American, an electoral base, as well as national and local institutions to address community concerns. US policy toward the Middle East is a function of both national interests and politics, and the ability to yield electoral political power through money and votes is the key to US elections. The American-Jewish community has worked for 70 years to shape US foreign policy in support of Israel. Arab-Americans are now trying to create a counterweight.

The 2000 American Elections (2/6/00) L
Mr. John Zogby
President and Executive Director
Zogby International
   An analysis of the presidential, House and New York Senate elections offered a better understanding of the history, personalities, the process and the numbers behind these polls. The 2000 elections were especially critical in view of the policies of President Bill Clinton, and the importance of US foreign policy, particularly towards the Middle East. With the House of Representatives controlled by a Republican majority of 223 to 211, a swing of only a few seats could mean a Democratic majority.

The State of Middle East Debate: Changing Public Opinion, Emerging Partisan Split and the Position of the Presidential Candidates of 2000 (2/6/00) L

Dr. James Zogby
President, Arab American Institute
Washington, DC, USA

Dr. James Zogby asserted that there has been a noticeable shift in America's attitude towards the Middle East over the last 25 years. The lecture assessed changes in public opinion and US policy towards the Middle East and the way in which such changes are reflected in the position of candidates and the platforms of the political parties. Dr. Zogby called for a public debate on Middle East issues and noted the failure of the American media to promote such a debate.

US Perspectives on the Middle East (3/11/00) L

Ambassador Richard Murphy
Senior Fellow, Council on Foreign Relations
Ambassador Roscoe Suddharth
President, Middle East Institute

Current issues and key developments in the Middle East were presented from a US standpoint: the uncertain situation in Iraq, the popular mandate won by President Khatami's reformist faction in Iran and its implications, and the perils that beset the Arab-Israeli peace negotiations. Attention was focused on global economic issues affecting the Middle East. US presidential candidates and their differing stands on Middle East issues were also assessed.

Sailing without an Anchor: Contemporary Determinants of US Policy in the Gulf (6/11/00) (ELS33) L

Dr. Clive Jones
Senior Lecturer, Institute for Politics and International Studies
University of Leeds, United Kingdom

The aftermath of the Cold War has brought US foreign policy under scrutiny. US policy towards the Gulf lacks unity of purpose and clarity of thought. Its strategy of "Dual Containment" is struggling to adjust to changing alliance patterns. Though the US has the capability to project its power and influence in the region, doubts remain over its political will. With the demise of Dual Containment and the changing bilateral relations in the Gulf, US policy is in danger of "sailing without an anchor."

US Foreign Policy Following the Year 2000 Election (11/12/00) L

Dr. Peter Gubser
President of American Near East Refugee Aid

The US elections of 2000 focused on domestic issues. This presentation discussed possible trends in foreign policy. Would the US subjugate economic interests to foreign policy? What would relations be with other powers? Would the US respect prior agreements or work unilaterally? Would defense expenditure continue to fall? How would the US deal with the energy issue? What would US policies be with regard to Iraq, Iran, energy supply and price? Dr. Gubser concluded that radical policy changes were rare, but the President enjoys great power and could change foreign policy.

The US and Iran: Analyzing the Structural Impediments to Rapprochement
(1/23/01) (ELS32) L
Dr. Robert Snyder
Associate Professor, Southwestern University
Texas, USA

Dr. Snyder analyzed the enmity existing between the US and Iran for almost twenty-five years and examined the possibilities of reconciliation. The answer lies in analyzing structural factors. As stated in his book *The US and Third World Revolutionary States: Understanding the Breakdown in Relations*, the collapse of relations is attributable both to revolutionary domestic policies pursued by Iran and to the rigid containment policy followed by the US. It was suggested that Iran should pursue more liberal domestic policies detached from theocracy while the US should ease its containment policies.

The Religious Dimension in US Policy towards the Palestinian Question (9/11/01) L
Dr. Yousef Al-Hasan
Minister Plenipotentiary, Foreign Ministry, UAE

The speaker examined the roots of Western bias in favor of Israel, explaining the role of the Christian fundamentalist movement in influencing policies on Palestine.

US Policy towards Iraq in the Aftermath of September 11 (3/26/02) (ELS 39) L
Dr. Gregory Gause
Director of Middle East Studies Program
University of Vermont, USA

Since the attacks of September 11, 2001, the Bush administration has reoriented American foreign policy toward the fight against terrorism. The Bush administration is also very determined to address the situation in Iraq.

US Intelligence since September 11: Closing the Gaps (7/27/03) (ELS 48) L
Ms. Ellen Laipson
President and CEO, Henry L. Stimson Center
Washington, USA

To improve intelligence performance regarding terrorist threats, it is important to function at operational and strategic levels. To introduce workforce changes, it is essential to appoint persons with appropriate skills to undertake the required tasks. It is also important to promote collaboration between intelligence institutions and organizations.

The anticipated US War against Iraq: Regional Strategic Implications
(2/18/03) (ELS 50) L
Dr. Ahmed Shikara
Lecturer in Research Methodology
ECSSR, UAE

The political forces favoring a peaceful resolution to the US-Iraqi standoff have mustered public opinion worldwide, thus leading to salient divisions not only in Europe, but also in the UN Security Council as well. Any US-Iraqi military confrontation will have important strategic, political and economic consequences for the Middle East and the Arab Gulf region.

Recent Developments in US–Iran Relations: Impact on the Gulf Region (6/28/03) L
Dr. Flynt Leverett
Visiting Fellow, Saban Center for Middle East Studies
Washington, USA
   Domestic Iranian politics have dramatically changed in recent years and most Iranians are now showing strong support for a diplomatic opening with the United States. A wide-scale debate is going on in the US regarding the best possible ways of making use of the successive changes in Iran.

The US War on Terrorism: Impact on US–Arab Relations (6/30/03) (ELS 49) L
Mr. James H. Noyes
Research Fellow
Hoover Institution, Stanford University, USA
   The September 11th attacks had an immediate negative impact on US-Arab relations. It might appear that US-Arab relations are constantly shrinking, but it is possible to correct the path of these relations, and to agree ways and means of joint collaboration, provided that both parties undertake a more realistic assessment of the common threats and capabilities.

Prospects for a US–Middle East Partnership (7/7/03)
H.E. Marcelle M. Wahba
Former US Ambassador to the UAE
   The Middle East Partnership Initiative (MEPI) seeks to promote US relations with the governments and the peoples of the region. The Middle East Free Trade Area (MEFTA) aims to establish a free trade zone in the region within ten years, while the Partnership for Learning (P4L) program is based on academic cooperation and exchange programs that aim to promote better understanding between the USA and the Muslim world.

US Foreign Policy toward the Middle East after September 11th (4/9/02) L
Dr. Geoffrey Kemp
Director, Regional Strategic Programs, Nixon Center
Washington, DC, USA
   The attacks on September 11, 2001 resulted in the reshaping of US relations with the Middle East, pressure from the US administration to change Saddam Hussein's regime in Iraq, the re-consideration of complex US relations with Iran and a new US policy regarding the Arab–Israeli conflict.

Arab–US Relations from an Arab Perspective: Constants and Variables (4/16/02) L
Dr. Ragheed Al-Sulh
Specialist in International and Regional Relations
Oxford University, United Kingdom
   The collapse of the Soviet Union, the occupation of Kuwait, the Palestinian *Intifada* and the attacks of September 11, 2001 in the United States affected US strategic goals and interests in the Arab world, for example its oil interests and support for Israel.

US Policy toward Political Islam (4/22/02) (ELS 45) L
Dr. Graham Fuller
Senior Political Consultant, RAND
Washington, DC, USA

Virtually all Muslims pursue values of political freedom, but they see US policies as an obstruction of the freedoms they need in order to develop the personal and national capacities for democratic values. The US should start a dialogue with Muslim *ulama*, Muslim scholars and the representatives of moderate political powers in order to support democratization in the region.

US Policy toward the Arab–Israeli Conflict: Examining the Changes (5/20/02) L
Dr. Hisham Sharabi
Honorary Professor, Georgetown University
Director of the Palestinian Center for Political Studies
Washington, DC, USA

The lecture examines the role of the Jewish lobby in decision-making and policy-making in the United States, in particular the Conference of Presidents of Major American Jewish Organizations and the American–Israeli Public Affairs Committee.

International Terrorism and US Foreign Policy (5/26–28/02) W
Dr. Richard Shultz

This workshop covered the following topics: how the United States government assessed the issue of international terrorism before the September 11th events; describing the Al-Qaeda network which carried out the attacks; the US military campaign in Afghanistan; and what the next phase of the Bush Administration's global war against terrorism will be as compared to the Clinton Administration's policy.

The War on Terrorism and its Implications for Political Developments in the Middle East (6/3/02) L
Ambassador Edward Walker
Head, Middle East Institute
Washington, DC, USA

Americans sympathize with people without a state, but they are horrified by the images of civilians killed by suicide bombings. Similarly, they find it hard to sympathize with scenes of occupation, including tanks heading towards houses. However, in the wake of the attacks of 11 September, Americans understand the situation of the Israelis.

Islam and the West after September 11: Civilizational Dialogue or Conflict?
(6/3/02) (ELS 40) L
Prof. John L. Esposito
Director of the Center for Muslim–Christian Understanding
Georgetown University
Washington DC, USA

The approach of some US government officials to condemn anti-Americanism fails to address real issues and grievances. The war against terrorism should not justify an erosion of important values in the US or become a green light for authoritarian Muslim regimes to increase repression.

The Role of the Gulf Region in the Formation of US National Security Policy
(6/6/04) (ELS 58) L
Dr. Lawrence Korb
Senior Fellow, Center For American Progress

No region of the world is more important to US security than the Arabian Gulf, being a region that controls a great portion of the world's confirmed oil reserves. Consequently, the US cannot afford to allow any hostile power or radical group to control all or part of the region. To prevent such events, the US maintains the capability to apply military power throughout the Arabian Gulf region, through the maintenance of bases and forces in the region and adjacent areas.

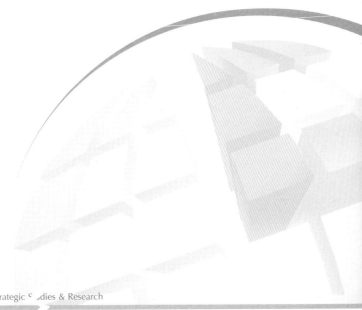

Central to the objectives of the Emirates Center for Strategic Studies and Research (ECSSR) is the promotion of professional research and scientific inquiry. In order to serve the communities of academics, policy practitioners and interested readers, the Center publishes objective analyses of issues affecting the UAE and Gulf region, covering the fields of politics, economics, sociology and strategic studies.

ECSSR has thus developed a comprehensive plan to become a principal source in the region for specialized scholarly books. The foremost of these are Arabic and English volumes, which are collections of original papers presented at conferences and symposia sponsored by the Center throughout the year. These books focus on contemporary issues of vital importance to the Gulf region.

Such volumes include *The Yemeni War: Causes and Consequences* and *Iran and the Gulf: A Search for Stability*, which won the 1997 First Prize for the Best Book in Humanities and Social Sciences at the Sharjah Book Fair (UAE), both were edited by Dr. Jamal S. Al-Suwaidi, Director General of the ECSSR. In addition, the Center has published *Gulf Energy and the World: Challenges and Threats*; *Gulf Security in the Twenty-First Century*; *The Information Revolution and the Arab World: Its Impact on State and Society*; and *Strategic Positioning in the Oil Industry: Trends and Options*.

Among the Center's recent books are: *Iraq: Reconstruction and Future Role*; *International Interests in the Gulf Region*; *Arab Media in the Information Age*; *With United Strength: H.H. Sheikh Zayid Bin Sultan Al Nahyan, The Leader and the Nation*; and *The Three Occupied UAE Islands: The Tunbs and Abu Musa*.

The Center also publishes two monograph series in English: *The Emirates Occasional Papers* and the *Emirates Lecture Series*.

Publications

(March 1994–June 2006)

English Publications

Books

The Emirates Occasional Papers (EOP) ISSN 1682-1246

Emirates Lecture Series (ELS) ISSN 1682-1238

The English publications are categorized below by subject.

ARAB/ISRAELI PEACE PROCESS

Inter-Arab Relations in the Post-Peace Era

Ann M. Lesch EOP1 (1995)

Changes in inter-Arab relations that might occur as a result of a diplomatic resolution of the Arab–Israeli conflict are examined in this study. It addresses both regional and sub-regional levels, the former comprising the GCC states (Bahrain, Kuwait, Oman, Qatar, Saudi Arabia and the UAE), Iran, and the Levant (Syria, Lebanon, Jordan, Palestine and Israel). Possible policy changes are assessed in the wider context of the post-Cold War era as well as in the aftermath of the Gulf crisis. Finally, Lesch examines the impact of varying roles by Iraq and neighboring Iran on regional and sub-regional relations. Some attention is paid to the possible impact of Arab–Israeli peace on internal politics in key Arab countries.

Israel at Peace with the Arab World
Mark Tessler EOP2 (1995)

Tessler examines three interrelated topics. Firstly, and most importantly, he discusses the position that Israel is likely to seek to define for itself in the Middle East if its conflict with the Arab world is resolved. Specifically, he assesses the strategic, economic, political and ideological factors that will determine Israel's interests in the Middle East, speculates on the kinds of alliances and relationships Israel is likely to seek in pursuit of these interests, and considers the probable character of selected bilateral relationships that are likely to emerge as a result. Secondly, Tessler assesses the likely impact on Israel's ties with key actors outside the region, particularly the US, of its peaceful and deepening involvement in Middle Eastern international relations. Thirdly, he considers the ways that peace will affect political dynamics inside Israel, including those relating to the formulation and conduct of foreign policy. In particular, he explores how the competition between moderates and hard-liners, a key dimension of present-day politics, might be transformed by a resolution of the Arab–Israeli conflict.

Political Legitimacy of the Minorities: Israeli Arabs and the 1996 Knesset Elections
P.R. Kumaraswamy EOP20 (1998)

The treatment of Arab minorities has been a controversial and contentious issue in Israel. Both prior to its founding and in its aftermath, the Arabs in Israel were seen primarily as a "problem" to be tackled and a "security threat" to be contained. The Arabs in erstwhile Palestine lost their majority status overnight and involuntarily acquired Israeli citizenship. They thus became an ethnic, national, linguistic, religious and cultural minority in a predominantly Jewish country.

Was there a systematic policy of discrimination against the Arabs? The first section of this paper discusses the electoral system within which the Arab population operates. The second section discusses the politicization of the Arab sector and the relative importance and performance of the Arab electorate in Israeli elections. The third section focuses on the process of legitimization of the Arab electorates and Arab-oriented parties under the Rabin-led Labor government. The last section analyzes the role of the Arab voters in the closely contested 1996 elections, especially for the post of Prime Minister, and represents a tentative projection for the future.

Competing Trade Agendas in the Arab–Israeli Peace Process
J.W. Wright EOP23 (1998)

Most analyses of the Arab–Israeli peace process and the negotiations that surround it have been political. This analysis challenges the notion that politicians drive the negotiations. Using theoretical underpinnings drawn from work written by a diverse group of economists, this paper investigates the roles that competing trade agendas have in the Arab–Israeli peace process.

Moreover, it endeavors to paint a portrait of a process that is directed by people who control distributive policies and who regulate the influence of money in both economics and politics. Such a view identifies the financial and fiscal interests of individuals, corporations, politicians and political parties as the driving forces behind the Arab–Israeli negotiations, as opposed to identifying leaders with real ambitions for building sustainable peace in the region. It further asserts that Israel's core conglomerates and powerful American and European partners are skeptical of the gains to be made from retooling their war-oriented systems into production structures that can effectively compete in a peacetime economy.

The Palestinian Economy and the Oslo Process: Decline and Fragmentation
Sara Roy EOP24 (1998)

The foundations for a viable, self-sustaining Palestinian economy have not emerged since the start of the Oslo peace process. Economic conditions in the Gaza Strip and West Bank have deteriorated markedly, leaving the Palestinian economy weaker now than it was in 1967, when measured against the advances made by other states in the region. The reasons for Palestinian economic decline are many but turn on one key issue: Israeli closure policy. Closure restricts the movement of labor and goods, and distorts rational economic activity. Now a permanent feature of the local economy, closure has resulted in the physical and economic separation of the West Bank and Gaza Strip and their separation from Israel, high unemployment, permanent unemployment for a growing segment of the labor force, a doubling of poverty levels, increasing child labor, constrained trade relations and a growing need for relief and social assistance among Palestinians. Closure has devastated Palestinian economic growth and reform, and has made it increasingly difficult for people to meet their basic needs. If closure continues to be enforced, the economic and political changes promised by the Oslo agreements and now so desperately needed in the West Bank and Gaza will not be possible.

Israel and the Decline of the Peace Process, 1996–2003
Hassan Barrari EOP51 (2003)

The deterioration of the Palestinian–Israeli peace process since 1996 can be attributed to domestic variables in Israel, such as the fragmented political system, internal contests and the balance of power. The factional power base, ideology and personalities of leaders like Netanyahu, Barak and Sharon have played a crucial role, as well as Israeli responses to Palestinian actions.

Palestinian Relations with the Arab World: From Exile and Revolution to Homeland and Self-Rule
Khalil Shikaki ELS6 (1997)

The Oslo agreement, the subsequent Israeli–Palestinian accords and their implementation in Gaza and Jericho brought to a conclusion a dual process of transformation in the Palestinian national movement, and put an end to some of its problems. The center of gravity shifted from outside to inside, from exile to homeland and from revolutionary vehicle for socio-political change to a national authority or state.

In the past, the nature of exile had shaped these relations in such a way as to make the Palestinians vulnerable to pressures from Arab regimes and to the consequences of Arab division. The movement to the inside will reduce vulnerability, intervention and containment. The nature of emerging Arab-Palestinian relations will depend on the needs and requirements of the new era — the self-rule transition to statehood. This means establishing relations based on a common political, social and cultural heritage.

US Policy in the Middle East and the Arab–Israeli Conflict
Shibley Telhami ELS7 (1997)

The debate over US foreign policy in the Middle East is generally waged between those who argue that America's actions are driven by strategic interests and those who believe that policy decisions are determined by domestic pro-Israeli political considerations. Telhami argues that the tension between these two components helped to shape US policy during the Gulf War, and that since the Gulf conflict the domestic component has reigned supreme. From this perspective, Telhami reviews and examines US policy towards the Arab–Israeli conflict, the Arabian Gulf, and social and political movements in the Middle East.

The Israeli Political System: Antecedents, Institutions and Trends
Peter Gubser ELS27 (2000)

The Israeli political system with its deeply-rooted traditions, its current complexities and emerging political patterns, is analyzed from three different perspectives: the historical background, the principal institutions and contemporary electoral trends. The interaction between the chief state institutions and their respective powers are sketched, while emerging trends in the country are viewed through the prism of the crucial 1999 prime ministerial and Knesset elections that propelled Ehud Barak and his One Israel party to power with a convincing mandate for Middle East peace.

The Israeli political system has its roots in ancient religious law, Ottoman law and British Mandate legislation. While it has no formal written constitution, it has a "Basic Law" that lays down essential guidelines for political functioning. The Israeli parliament, or Knesset, is the supreme body, with its membership divided among political parties that are elected in accordance with a system of proportional representation.

The traditional split between left and right, represented by Labor (currently One Israel) and Likud respectively, is very much in evidence. However, these major parties have been declining in strength and more small parties are gaining ground in the Knesset, giving rise to unstable coalition governments. The religious-secular divide is becoming more pronounced, while ethnic divisions between Jews of Middle Eastern and European origin, especially Russian Jews, is a cause for concern.

ASIAN/ARAB RELATIONS

The Balance of Power in South Asia
ISBN: 0-86372-267-9 (hb) 0-86372-282-2 (pb) (2000)

The nuclear tests conducted by India and Pakistan in May 1998 have had far-reaching implications not only for South Asia, but for the Arab Gulf region. On the surface, the tests merely confirmed the existing nuclear capabilities in the two countries, but the deeper impact has been to raise tension between India and Pakistan, tilt the strategic balance of power in South Asia and adversely affect international arms control regimes, thus indirectly undermining the national security of states already committed to nuclear non-proliferation.

Events leading up to the nuclear tests and their aftermath point to a three-cornered

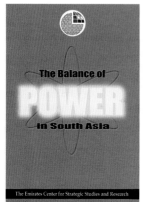

nuclear interaction involving China, India and Pakistan. China's strategy of hemming in Indian power and influence is likely to be complicated by New Delhi's overt nuclear status. Pakistan's nuclear capability has not altered the fundamental reality of India's conventional military superiority, which may continue to be the dominant strategic factor on the subcontinent. It is argued that the risks of war may have been heightened rather than negated by mutual nuclear deterrence, and the overt nuclear status of India and Pakistan has undeniably raised the stakes in any future conflict on the subcontinent.

Papers in this volume address the rationale behind the nuclear tests and their wider implications for South Asia, while offering a Gulf perspective on these developments. In addition to the issue of geographic proximity and the high number of South Asians working in the region, a major concern is that of the proliferation of weapons of mass destruction (WMD) in other countries in the Middle East. In this context, it becomes imperative to consider ways to establish the region as a WMD-free zone.

Emerging Powers: The Cases of China, India, Iran, Iraq and Israel
Amin Saikal EOP12 (1997)

The broad objective of Amin Saikal's paper is to look at examples of both strong and weak states in the zone stretching from East Asia to the Middle East, focusing primarily on China, India, Iran, Iraq and Israel, and to do so with a view to investigating which direction these states are likely to take into the next century, especially in the context of the changes which have come to beset states and the present statist international system. His aim is not to provide a detailed account of the internal and external dynamics affecting each of these states, but to focus on the question of how nationalist, aggressive, expansionist, or for that matter, inward-looking each might be in the coming decades.

The Changing Balance of Power in Asia
Anoushiravan Ehteshami EOP16 (1998)

This paper argues that from the fallen edifice of the Cold War have emerged four major Asian powers of considerable potential and influence, each possessing varying types of assets. These four land-based continental powers (China, India, Iran and Russia) are well placed to shape this vast continent's destiny in the next millennium. Each of the four actors has stepped onto the Asian scene anew, each having been affected very differently by the region's changing geography and by the passing of bipolarity.

These four actors have the power to shape Asia's political map in the next millennium. Each has been a party to Asia's fluid and dynamic inter-state system for some time. Now each is busy mustering the assets (geopolitical, economic, military, industrial, technological, territorial, human, natural or mineral) needed for ensuring its own survival and prosperity in today's highly dynamic multipolar international system.

Asian-Pacific Security and the ASEAN Regional Forum: Lessons for the GCC
K.S. Balakrishnan EOP25 (1998)

This study deals with two major issues: the evolving context of Asian-Pacific security and the role of the ASEAN Regional Forum (ARF) as a security dialogue mechanism. While the latter has been heralded as a forum that is pan-regional in scope, there is continuing concern that its mandate should extend beyond confidence-building measures to address substantive security issues affecting the region. A particular issue is whether the ARF can mitigate or prevent conflict in a region in which there are still unresolved territorial disputes and military insecurity.

Consequently, the search for a viable, all-encompassing pan-regional security apparatus is an ongoing theme and endeavor in the Asia-Pacific, although economically the region has enjoyed the fastest growth rate in the world in the last decade. A prevailing sense of uncertainty exists and a major worry is the role of the US, which some fear exercises a unipolar presence not necessarily healthy in the long run for the region. Nonetheless, the US is regarded as a key actor that will deter the rise of "new hegemons" and reduce the risk of militarism. The paper concludes by drawing comparisons from the Asian-Pacific experiences for the Gulf.

The GCC and the Development of ASEAN
Julius Caesar Parreñas EOP26 (1998)

The Association of South East Asian Nations (ASEAN) is a grouping of originally five, now nine, resource-rich and mostly economically dynamic countries that lie strategically between the Pacific and Indian Oceans, astride sea-lanes that are vital to the economic and military security of several Northeast Asian countries. As a grouping that exerts strong influence in the Asia-Pacific Economic Cooperation (APEC) and forms the core of the ASEAN Regional Forum (ARF), ASEAN is emerging as a key player in the security and economic development of the Western Pacific region. Due to these factors, ASEAN's stability and continued development are essential to the future stability and prosperity of the whole Asia-Pacific area.

In some respects, a linkage exists between the security and economic development of ASEAN and the Arab Gulf. Oil from the Arab Gulf is a very important factor in the economy of ASEAN countries. It is also important to the economic security of Japan, and the fact that this commerce passes through sea-lanes in Southeast Asia accounts significantly for the latter's importance to Tokyo. This, in turn, is an essential consideration in the US strategy in Asia, as its relationship with Japan continues to be the cornerstone of its policy. While non-oil trade between the Gulf states and ASEAN is not substantial, the Gulf is important to many ASEAN countries as a major destination of overseas workers, whose remittances play a large role in their economy.

Enhancing Peace and Cooperation in West Asia: An Indian Perspective
Jasjit Singh EOP27 (1998)

India has a long and deep-rooted relationship with the region often referred to as West Asia, the area covered from the Suez Canal eastward to Pakistan. Over the past 50 years, in spite of some negative developments, these bonds have been reinforced by geopolitical and geoeconomic factors. This study reviews the challenges and opportunities in the post-Cold War era and explores the potential for cooperation in promoting peace and stability in the region and beyond. Some of the challenges include a revolution of rising expectations, energy security, regional conflicts, narcotics trafficking and the proliferation of light weapons. Moreover, Singh argues that economic imperatives hold opportunities for cooperation as well as prospects for competition that could produce friction and conflict. Consequently, peace is a precondition for development as both old and new conflicts have to be managed.

Asia and the Gulf: Prospects for Cooperation
Veluthevar Kanaga Rajan EOP28 (1998)

Asia, especially East Asia, has seen unprecedented economic transformation in recent decades, and the momentum is likely to continue despite occasional blips and turbulence. Indeed, the economic focus has shifted from the Atlantic to the Pacific. A booming Asia poses both opportunities and challenges for the Arab Gulf states, which already depend on Asia for approximately 52 per cent of their total trade. Much of Asia's increased demand for energy will be met by the countries of the Arab Gulf. A major challenge in this regard is to safeguard the security and safety of navigation in the vital sea-lanes through which an increasing number of tankers will travel. However, energy need not be the only basis of cooperation. Generally, the East Asian economies have become competitive through effective use of information technology and skill development.

Institutional linkage between ASEAN and the GCC offers a good basis for a quick start at the political level, thus paving the way for more broad-based cooperation involving economic, security and cultural dimensions. Political will and determination are required to give impetus to this effort.

The Security Environment of Central Asia
S. Frederick Starr ELS22 (1999)

The global attention that has focused on the energy resources of Central Asia has tended to obscure the real security issues affecting this vital region. According to this analysis, the eight new states to the east and west of the Caspian Sea face major challenges as fledgling sovereignties seeking to carve out new national identities and sustain their legitimacy while shedding their legacy as former Soviet states. The involvement of diverse nations in the exploitation and export of Caspian oil offers the best hope of stability in the region, although the fear that a single external power might gain monopolistic control over these coveted resources is an issue of major concern. Any economic or social breakdown in the region is likely to create a dangerous power vacuum, since the states are surrounded by three current nuclear powers and another aspiring nuclear power. These Central Asian states share several characteristics with the Gulf states and, like them, are exploring avenues for intra-regional cooperation and integration. The Gulf states are therefore poised to play a unique role in the development of the strategic Central Asian region with which its destinies have historically been linked.

The Future of Pakistan in the Aftermath of the Events of September 11, 2001 and the US-led War in Afghanistan
Maqsudul Hasan Nuri ELS41 (2003)

After the US decision to take action against the Taliban, Pakistan rapidly realigned its foreign policy and joined the US-led anti-terrorist coalition. This decision brought some immediate gains for the Musharraf government. However, some long-term problems are casting their shadows, such as the deteriorating economy, the India–Pakistan military standoff and terrorism from Taliban and Al-Qaeda groups.

Nuclear Weapons in South Asia
Chris Smith ELS52 (2004)

This paper explores issues relating to the nuclearization of South Asia following the acquisition of nuclear weapons by both India and Pakistan. It is divided into six parts: the history of nuclearization in South Asia; the weapons tests that took place in May 1998; nuclear stockpiles and delivery systems on both sides; emerging nuclear doctrines; nuclear stability and the threat of nuclear war; and South Asia's nuclear future.

The nuclearization of the conflict between India and Pakistan was precipitated by the Indian decision to undertake nuclear tests, after which Pakistan had little option but to proceed with its test program. Paradoxically, the events that followed have added little to India's security vis-à-vis Pakistan and the gains against China are dubious at best. Pakistan's nuclear doctrine is deeply destabilizing even if logical in the context of conventional inferiority. India's decision has therefore led to a net loss of security, which decision-makers may come to regret in the future.

DEMOCRACY AND POLITICAL DIALOGUE

Arab Perceptions of the Euro-Mediterranean Partnership
Mohammad El-Sayed Selim EOP42 (2001)

Although most Arab countries have endorsed in principle the European Union's proposal for an Euro-Mediterranean Partnership (EMP), they also harbor serious reservations about its conceptual and security aspects, and its future impact on their economies and on the peace process in the Middle East. The main concern is that the Euro-Mediterranean Free Trade Zone and its related rules of socio-economic conduct would expose fragile Arab industries to strong external competition and destroy indigenous enterprise.

As long as the EU continues to follow a one sided approach, with differential treatment for Israeli and Arab partners, the Arabs will continue to be ambivalent partners in the Barcelona process. This is evident from the cases of Tunisia and Morocco, which have signed partnership agreements with the EU, but are now expressing serious doubts about the viability of the process. Further, the EU's concept of politico-security cooperation is geared toward conflict prevention, crisis management and the introduction of CBMs, rather than on conflict resolution and the establishment of a balanced strategic system in the Mediterranean.

The EU's responses to these Arab perceptions and misgivings will decide the future success of the EMP. It may be concluded that if the EU persists in its self-centered approach to Euro-Mediterranean cooperation, the EMP project is unlikely to materialize. This is particularly applicable to the economic partnership, which must be based on technology transfer and infrastructure support rather than trade liberalization, and security partnership, which should focus on conflict resolution and strategic balance rather than on maintaining the status quo.

Britain and the Middle East: Into the 21st Century
The Rt. Hon. Malcolm Rifkind ELS1 (1997)

In a major policy address, the Right Honorable Malcolm Rifkind, British Secretary of State for Foreign and Commonwealth Affairs, stated that his country's relations with the Middle East would continue to be centered around three major issues: peace, prosperity and progress. Regarding peace, Secretary Rifkind described Britain's objectives in the Middle East as defending its friends and allies, eliminating weapons of mass destruction, preserving the territorial integrity of all states, including Iraq, and promoting the Arab–Israeli peace process. Britain also plays an integral role in promoting prosperity in the region and he reaffirmed that Britain would continue to push for increased trade access and investment between the Middle East and the European Union. Finally, he noted that increased educational exchange and extended methods of consultation and participation would undoubtedly lead to a more prosperous future.

Five Wars in the Former Yugoslavia: 1991–98
The Rt. Hon. Lord David Owen ELS19 (1998)

The break-up of Yugoslavia was the consequence of the collapse of Communism in 1989. The vacuum left by the authoritarian unifying forces was filled by nationalist leaders, and control of the state moved from one central authority to the Presidents of the different Yugoslav republics. At the outset, in 1990, the US wanted to maintain the unity of the Yugoslav state, but was not prepared to take any action that would have stopped this process, e.g., preventing Croatia and Slovenia from declaring their independence. Lord Owen describes the results of the US desire to be seen as a leader throughout the five wars in former Yugoslavia between 1991 and 1998 and its unwillingness to accept the risks and responsibilities that arise from the exercise of global leadership. He urges the formulation of intergovernmental cooperation among European states in order to support common European foreign and security policies with military clout.

Patterns of Order and Changes in International Relations: Major Wars and their Aftermath
Kiichi Fujiwara ELS36 (2001)

The neo-realist school maintains that as long as the world is comprised of sovereign states, the main structure of international relations will be the same. Another school of thought states that the process of globalization and the interdependence of nations have challenged the isolated autonomy of sovereign states. This lecture adds another factor to the equation, namely, the entry of non-Western actors and powers.

French Policy Toward the Arab World
Charles Saint-Prot ELS42 (2003)

French policy towards the Middle East and the Gulf region is embedded in the context of a long-standing French interest and historical relations between France and the Arab world. France's Arab policy is based on a balance between states, a political philosophy of independence and equality, and a strategic choice that is based on and favors the principle of multipolarity.

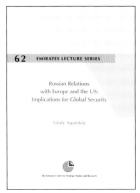

Russian Relations with Europe and the US: Implications for Global Security
Prof. Vitaly V. Naumkin ELS62 (2005)

In recent years, relations between Russia and the West have entered a controversial phase, characterized by rapprochement as well as disagreements on a number of issues, signaling the emergence of a "new rivalry." The West has accused Moscow of pursuing a policy of "managed instability" in those areas of the Commonwealth of Independent States (CIS) where insurgents are active, including Georgia, Azerbaijan and Moldova. It has been alleged that Moscow uses this instability to prevent a consolidation of these states, thus preserving Russia's military presence. The EU is continuing in its effort to build a strategic partnership with Russia in order to safeguard international security. Some Russian analysts contend that the period of the US-dominated world is drawing to a close and that Russia has to decide who its main strategic ally is – Europe or America. However, on questions of strategic stability, combating transnational terrorism and the proliferation of WMD, the US is still Russia's principal partner.

DEVELOPMENT

Sociopolitical Security and Communicable Disease
Martin Schönteich EOP55 (2004)

Communicable diseases can detrimentally affect state capacity and political stability, as well as social, economic and state security. In short, epidemics have the potential to impact upon virtually every aspect of human development and well-being.

Communicable disease epidemics can combine with population pressures and trends to create more volatile social and political situations. This combination can produce heightened competition for limited resources and foster more intense rivalries among groups in countries marked by inter-group conflict. Communicable disease on an epidemic scale can also detrimentally affect the capacity of governments, especially their capacity to deliver basic social services.

The massive demographic and social changes HIV/AIDS in particular is likely to bring about in the most affected regions of the world may influence crime patterns and the state's ability to respond to crime. In contrast to most communicable diseases, which impact most heavily on the elderly and the very young, HIV/AIDS takes its greatest toll among young adults.

The combination of extreme poverty, malnutrition, lack of infrastructure, and the weaknesses of government institutions and political leaders have made Africa particularly vulnerable. However, a similar combination of some of or all these factors is increasing the likelihood of full-blown epidemics in parts of Eastern Europe and East Asia, including strategic nuclear powers like the Russian Federation, China and India.

ECONOMY/TRADE

An Institutional Approach to Economic Policy Reform in the Gulf States
Julia Devlin EOP13 (1998)

In the Gulf States today, economic activity is characterized by abundant energy resources, large public sectors, small trade-oriented private sectors and cultural norms shaped by Islamic belief and practice. In the early 1990s, governments throughout the region began introducing fiscal consolidation measures. They are now beginning to focus more intensely on long-term structural issues, such as the need for financial market deepening, labor market reform and privatization. Devlin explores the potential gains from a microeconomic policy framework targeting entrepreneurial ventures in small and medium-sized enterprises using Islamic institutions, such as mudarabah venture capital. An institutional approach to economic policy reform which targets areas of culturally authentic private and public investment has the potential to enhance the sustainability of current reforms as well as deepen the participation of the private sector in structural reform efforts.

Investment Prospects in a Sample of Arab Stock Exchanges
Kamal Naser EOP17 (1998)

In the last few years, policy makers in most Arab countries have recognized the role of the private sector in shaping their economies. Furthermore, as long-term economic growth is dependent on the provision of funds to finance domestic capital formation, these countries are undergoing a process of economic reform to diversify their economies and to privatize public assets. As effective privatization programs should be backed by well-prepared and fully-equipped stock markets, governments in the Arab countries are paying attention to domestic capital markets as a way of enhancing the supply of money. This study assesses changes in the economic conditions in Bahrain, Egypt, Jordan, Kuwait, Morocco, Oman, Qatar, Saudi Arabia, Tunisia and the UAE and the performance of their stock markets over the past eight years.

The Changing Composition and Direction of GCC Trade
Rodney Wilson EOP18 (1998)

Trade diplomacy has been much neglected in the Gulf. Yet, with power being increasingly a matter of economic muscle as well as military strength, and following the globalization of economic activity, new responses are needed from the GCC states. Wilson examines the changing trade patterns of the GCC, including export and import trends, the development of entrepôt trade and trade in commercial services. Trade between the GCC states is analyzed and issues of Arab regional integration are considered. The GCC's commercial relations with Asia are discussed, as well as the stalled dialogue with the European Union. Finally, trade prospects are reviewed. Although there has been some successful export diversification, the GCC countries have not yet developed a trade strategy or used their considerable bargaining power effectively outside the OPEC arena.

Challenges of Global Capital Markets to Information-Shy Regimes: The Case of Tunisia
Clement M. Henry EOP19 (1998)

The evolution of the global economy since the end of the Cold War poses special challenges to the Middle East and North Africa (MENA). Official development assistance has diminished, whereas private capital flows to developing countries have dramatically increased. Little of the new private capital goes to MENA. The region received only US$6.9 billion in 1996, barely more than its quota of official development assistance. Most of the MENA countries are now in need of infusions of external private capital, yet seem to be at a major disadvantage in competition with other regions, notably East Asia, Europe, Central Asia and Latin America.

Many reasons can be given for MENA's economic plight. Arguably, the region may now be at a disadvantage precisely because of its earlier affluence. However, other factors may also be at work. In this paper, political factors are examined, using Tunisia as the case study. It suggests that political structures may be inhibiting economic growth and reform by constraining information flows and thereby deterring private investment. An attempt is made to specify relationships between flows of information and investment flows. Other facts may also inhibit investment flows, but the free flow of information is becoming a requisite in the globalizing economy for certain forms of foreign and local investment.

Food Safety and Quality Standards: Private Sector Strategies and Imperatives
Lokman Zaibet EOP43 (2001)

The private sector in Arab countries is widely expected to achieve a rate of growth and contribution to the national economy higher than current levels. To attain this goal, private companies must maintain their competitiveness and market position in export markets. Until recently, exports in most Arab countries have received substantial support from national governments. However, current trends indicate that levels of government backing will decline and private companies will increasingly lead fresh initiatives.

Among the factors expected to play an important role in the new millennium are food safety and quality standards, which represent both a competitive requirement and a competitive advantage. Internationally, the momentum clearly seems to be in the direction of food quality and safety adoption, and the emergence of certification as a necessary condition to do global business. There is a growing awareness and interest in food standards adopted in the EU, the US and other parts of the world.

The adoption of such standards has been a relatively slow process in many Arab countries, despite considerable efforts in this direction by national governments. This study investigates the different aspects of food safety and quality standards, and underlines the importance of quality improvement strategies for food companies in the Arab world that aspire to do international business. Finally, the study develops a strategic framework to improve the overall competitiveness of the Arab food sector in the global market.

Reforming Intellectual Property Rights Regimes in Developing Countries: Implications and Policies

Tarik H. Alami and Maya Z. Kanaan EOP44 (2001)

The Uruguay Round has produced the most fundamental reform of the world trading system since the establishment of the General Agreement on Tariffs and Trade (GATT) in 1947. It testified to a wider and deeper commitment to trade liberalization. The Uruguay Round went far beyond previous rounds in involving developing countries in multinational trading systems, and in covering new aspects of trade such as Trade-Related Intellectual Property Rights (TRIPS).

The TRIPS agreement means that developing countries will no longer be able to rely on other countries' intellectual property rights (IPRs). Developing countries are likely to suffer short-term losses from the TRIPS agreement, losses mitigated by the long phase-in period allowed under the Uruguay Round. In the long run, however, these countries should gain from stimulated local research and development efforts, from accelerated rates of technical change and the development of their own knowledge-based industries. This study provides an overview of the various intellectual property rights regimes and discusses how the amendment of intellectual property laws and enforcement procedures might affect economic activity in developing countries. Public policies related to IPR protection are also proposed, which could be used to maximize the benefits and minimize the costs of intellectual property rights.

The Role of Industrial and Development Finance Institutions in the GCC States: Dimensions and Policies

Ali Abdulrazzaq, Kamal Naser and Peter Sadler EOP45 (2002)

The study discusses the industrial sector in the GCC states and identifies the challenges facing diversification strategies in their economies. The extensive restructuring and reform being experienced by the financial sector worldwide is reflected in the GCC financial sector too. Many countries have established industrial and development finance institutions (IDFIs) that provide credit and financial support to the industrial sector. Project and capital financing is the major activity of all IDFIs in the region, for the primary purpose of achieving a number of developmental objectives. Lending is the most important source of financing, with restrictive conditions attached to the use of local production factors.

The future roles of IDFIs will be affected by macroeconomic changes in the GCC region, especially the anticipated decline in public sector resources, changes in the financial sector and the industrial development strategies of countries. The IDFIs will not only be faced with threats of privatization and more difficult access to subsidized public funds, but they may also experience greater competition in their markets from a number of sources. The IDFIs will have to adapt to new realities and identify their markets, services, customers and appropriate lending policies.

Customer Information Exchange, Ethical Frameworks and Gender in the Arab Business World

Ali Shamali and Kenneth Wild EOP46 (2002)

Individuals use different ethical frameworks to evaluate customer information exchanges by companies in the Arab business world. This study examines gender-based differences in the use of ethical frameworks.

The study found that the outcomes of a customer information exchange influenced women's ethical evaluations of the exchange, their inferences about the particular company and its customer relations, and their decisions to do business with the company in future. Men were less likely to be influenced by the outcomes of the customer information exchange.

Women in general were more likely to have a care-based ethical framework, which takes into account the consequences of actions, and men were more likely to have a justice-based ethical framework, which is based upon particular principles. Arab female managers and non-managerial staff agreed that outcomes were relevant to decision-making regarding continued business with a company. However, Arab female managers, like their male peers, agreed that the outcome of a customer information exchange was irrelevant to two issues, namely the likelihood that a company would provide good service and the right of a company to sell customer information to marketing companies.

Gulf Banking and the WTO's General Agreement on Trade in Services
Victor Murinde and Cillian Ryan EOP49 (2003)

The banking sector in Gulf economies involves high-skilled and high-income activities that may enable diversification. This study analyzes its strengths and weaknesses, and the positive and negative implications of membership of the World Trade Organization and the General Agreement on Trade in Services (GATS). It broadly favors the liberalization of GCC banking systems in accordance with the GATS.

GATT and the Impact on the GCC Countries
Mohammed Saleem ELS2 (1997)

This paper gives a short exposition of the General Agreement on Tariffs and Trade (GATT), its origins and its objectives, the basic principles on which its edifice stands, and looks at its achievements and potential problem areas. After a brief overview of the principal results of the Uruguay Round, Saleem highlights the importance of GATT and outlines its impact not only on the world business community in general, but on the UAE and GCC countries in particular.

Implications of WTO Membership for the Global Economy
Lawrence Klein ELS9 (1998)

This paper presents an historical analysis of free trade that covers the two eras of liberal international economic regimes: the Pax Britannica of free trade and the classical Gold Standard of the mid-to-late nineteenth century, and the Pax Americana of the Bretton Woods system from 1945 to 1971. Klein discusses how the 1990s constitute a transition period that differs in many respects from the working of the world economy of the 1970s. He then discusses the WTO, its role in monitoring the functioning of the world trade system and the implementation of the decisions taken during the GATT Uruguay Round. Klein concludes with an analysis of intensified globalism, further regional economic alliances and rapid technical change particularly with reference to their impact on the UAE economy.

Labor Markets and Policy in the GCC: Micro Diagnostics and Macro Profiles
Sulayman Al-Qudsi ELS12 (1998)

Dr. Al-Qudsi diagnoses the structure of labor markets in the GCC countries based on data drawn from the Oman census of 1993, assessing micro forces underpinning macro profiles and their policy drivers. Based on lessons derived from this micro analysis, he critiques the consistency of demographic and labor market policies in achieving the long-term mainstay development goal of "nationalizing" domestic labor markets; he also discusses emerging labor regulations in the context of budget imbalances and requisite policy reforms. The micro-macro framework of analysis utilized in this paper provides valuable insights that can aid policy makers in designing consistent and effective policy measures.

The Crisis in Southeast Asia: Origins and Outcomes
Richard Robison ELS21 (1999)

Asia's dramatic economic and financial meltdown appears to confirm the view that the world is witnessing the end of "Asian capitalism" and moving into a global era of free markets. Among neo-classical economists and within the IMF it is generally proposed that because the crisis was caused by excessive governmental intervention in market mechanisms, recovery necessarily requires structural changes to end these market-distorting systems. Critics of this position argue that fundamentally sound economic systems were unraveled as a consequence of hasty and imprudent deregulation of financial systems. Hence, the solution lies in proper regulation of capital markets. In this lecture, Robison proposes that the origins and outcomes of the crisis are best understood in terms of the impact of structural changes upon the contest between coalitions of power and interest to define the rules that govern economic activity. In any event, these coalitions may well survive the assault of this crisis.

The Arab Gulf Economies: Challenges and Prospects
Ibrahim M. Oweiss ELS26 (2000)

The Arab Gulf economies of Bahrain, Kuwait, Oman, Qatar, Saudi Arabia and the UAE share obvious common denominators but in reality have experienced fluctuations in growth stemming mainly from exogenous factors. There are promising prospects for these economies in the coming decades, provided certain favorable variables prevail; but if negative trends predominate there could be cause for concern. What seems likely is a mixed scenario, determined by the resultant impact of opposing forces.

The study begins with a general overview of the Gulf economies, taking into account the region's reliance on oil revenues. A statistical estimate of the price elasticity of demand for oil is made, given the fluctuations in oil prices from peaks in 1974 and 1979 to low levels in the mid-1980s and in early 1999. Analysis of macro-economic data over a 20-year period pinpoints the sources of regional economic growth, while a detailed econometric study identifies the oil price determinants during the years 1983–1998.

From the empirical results of this study and an examination of the region's endogenous factors, such as population growth and human productivity, and other exogenous factors, such as globalization and economic blocs, the prospects for the coming decades are sketched and some practical recommendations are offered that could speed up the process of Arab monetary integration and boost the UAE's national economic growth.

Money Laundering: An International Issue
Michael R. McDonald ELS30 (2001)

The global explosion of crime committed by organized groups over the past two decades has lent urgency to the need for anti-money laundering initiatives as part of a concerted campaign to combat international crime. This study outlines the evolution of anti-money laundering initiatives as an international tool to combat organized crime in several arenas, including narcotics trafficking, terrorism, arms dealing, kidnapping, disabling of government programs through extortion and corruption, and the penetration by criminal groups of legitimate financial systems. It reviews the legislative and regulatory programs implemented by various nations in their efforts to fight organized crime. Other aspects discussed include the "extraterritorial reach" of the US money laundering laws, the principal alternative remittance systems used by international drug traffickers to launder billions of dollars in drug proceeds, and some identified money laundering schemes actively used in the world of international finance.

For effective anti-money laundering initiatives, it is imperative to pass laws prohibiting the laundering of the proceeds of crime and the concealment of assets acquired through international criminal activity, and also to enact strict regulatory requirements for financial institutions to report suspected criminal activity as well as extraordinary and dubious financial transactions. Additionally, the development and structuring of a national Financial Investigation (or Intelligence) Unit (FIU) is an essential element for success. The FIU will undertake the task of monitoring reports and financial intelligence while managing financial information consistent with the country's privacy and regulatory protocols. At the regulatory level, the study suggests several practical measures that will enable financial institutions to protect themselves from penetration and utilization by criminal organizations for money laundering purposes. Particular emphasis is placed on the Financial Action Task Force's list of recommendations for the development of sound anti-money laundering programs.

The Gulf – EU Trade Relationship: Challenges and Opportunities
Rodney Wilson ELS37 (2002)

This paper reviews the trade and financial relations between the European Union and the Gulf Cooperation Council (GCC) states during the 1980s and 1990s. It examines how far economic relations have depended on oil price developments, and explores to what extent changing policies can affect future relations. Although much of the past and current emphasis has been on trade liberalization, the relationship arguably needs to be seen in a broader context. There are, for example, very specific educational, skills and training needs in the GCC states in which there is already much European involvement, although not at EU level. There is also considerable financial interdependence between individual European states and companies and Gulf governments. The 1989 Cooperation Agreement sets out to strengthen the relationship between the EU and the GCC and to ensure that the exchanges are covered on an inter-regional rather than a country-by-country basis. Overall the preconditions are beginning to be put in place for more successful EU–GCC relations, especially since the new mandate was introduced in July 2001. There is a need for broader discourse, but this should not be at the expense of tackling current problems.

The Iraqi Economy: Present State and Future Challenges
Muhammad-Ali Zainy ELS54 (2004)
The key challenge facing Iraq is providing stability and internal security as the bedrock for the support and maintenance of all other measures only addressing the problems of foreign debts and war reparations will alleviate Iraq's financial burdens and give it the opportunity to revive the economy and project it on a path of sustainable growth. To succeed, two key policy ingredients will have to be embracing a market economy, and diversifying the Iraqi economy and adopting measures for achieving self-sustained economic growth.

EDUCATION, MEDIA AND THE INFORMATION AGE

The Information Revolution and the Arab World: Its Impact on State and Society
ISBN: 1-86064-247-0 (hb) 1-86064-209-8 (pb) (1998)
The papers in this volume were among those presented at the ECSSR Third Annual Conference in 1997. This conference brought together leading academics as well as government and business representatives from around the globe in an exploration of the frontiers of the information and communications revolution. As a result, this volume offers an innovative, stimulating and provocative analysis of a variety of issues which have profound and enduring political, social and economic effects on nations, corporations and individuals. The spectrum of topics addressed includes the implications for national development of global telecommunications trends and policies, the growth in information technology and its impact on finance, business, the media, human resource development, cultural imperialism and the widening of the North–South information gap, and the spread of direct broadcast satellite television services in GCC states.

Education and the Arab World: Challenges of the Next Millennium
ISBN: 0-86372-255-5 (hb) 0-86372-270-9 (pb) (1999)
What kind of world should we strive for in the next century? What roles will education and training play in creating such a world? With rapid technological advances and the arrival of the information age, education systems as well as labor markets have undergone tremendous changes, affecting not only curricula and teaching methodology, but also the nature of skills and competencies required of graduates and new entrants to a changing workforce in the twenty-first century. This volume is unique in that it engages in cross-national and cross-cultural studies ranging from Australia to Japan, Canada and the UAE. It explores central concepts in educa-

tion, such as Total Quality Management and Just-in-Time Learning, and provides an economist's view of how and in what form education and training influence growth. While the models for effective education may differ, it is undeniable that education is crucial for individual development, economic growth, national productivity and a strong civil society.

Arabizing the Internet
Jon W. Anderson EOP30 (1998)

The Internet is a complex web of technologies and applications, not all of which are interrelated or develop at the same rate. Widely viewed as the first wave of an Age of Information, it is constantly being reshaped by new users. Advocates of the Internet see a structure of decentralized communication as the model of a new, universal culture and social organization of information that will sweep cultural differences aside. Such reflections on the cultural future of the Internet are as much a part of the phenomenon as its technological and organizational features. The Internet is not one thing but several: a physical infrastructure, the software and protocols that make it work, the tasks and values that the software and protocols implement, a social organization of regulation and communities of use, and a cultural context that includes reflection upon communication, information and knowledge. As the Internet spreads, alternative local and regional models emerge. Overseas Arabs brought Arab culture and politics to the Internet while it was developing in academic and research settings. However, it is commerce and telecommunications developments that now bring the Internet to Arab countries. The Arabization of the Internet draws on the competing priorities and visions of relations between local orders and globalization.

The Media and the Gulf War: An Eyewitness Account
Peter Arnett ELS3 (1997)

Peter Arnett, CNN senior reporter in Baghdad during the Gulf War, gives an overview of developments in the mass media since the Vietnam War, and how they have enriched his experience as a reporter. Some have described the Gulf War as the "CNN War." Indeed, many world leaders, including President Bush, watched the Gulf conflict unfold on CNN. Arnett explains how he evaded censorship both in Baghdad and in Washington in order to deliver authentic and unprejudiced reports. He also speaks about his meeting with Saddam Hussein and how it was so bitterly received in the United States.

Education for and in the 21st Century
The Hon. Jerzy Wiatr ELS5 (1997)

The twentieth century produced enormous changes in the field of education, including the expansion of educational systems to regions of the world and sectors of society previously left without access to formal education, the expansion and changing role of higher education from a general system to a more specialized one, the internationalization of information and educational systems, the increased access to available information, and the widespread use of new technologies of data gathering and data processing. Wiatr points out that such changes have directly contributed to the creation of a more open and dynamic society, but have also produced negative consequences. He believes that too much information has resulted in school curricula being overloaded, while specialization has resulted in the narrowing of intellectual perspectives. It has become clear to education theorists and practitioners that more than cosmetic changes are required. Wiatr suggests that education should focus on personality building rather than on the simple assimilation of factual information for regurgitation in examinations. He also suggests that it should be more general and more international, with a stronger emphasis placed on student and teacher mobility.

The Psychology and Politics of Parent Involvement
Daniel Safran ELS8 (1997)
Education is never a neutral commodity. In every society, the content, process and context of education are intrinsically related to the character and future of that society. If democratic societies cherish the values of individualism, egalitarianism and participatory government, schools must be modeled on inclusion and partnership. Safran states that the task of creating educational partnerships is as challenging as it is essential. He suggests that what is required is a new way of thinking about the goals of parent involvement and new approaches to training teachers if educational partnerships are to be successful.

The Arab World and Space Research: Where Do We Stand?
Farouk El-Baz ELS14 (1998)
Advances in space exploration have raised the levels of science and technology in countries with viable space programs, and most tangible benefits remain in these countries. Dr. El-Baz reviews the available satellite imaging systems and their data, and outlines a proposal for the planning, launch and operation of "Desertsat," an imaging satellite to be dedicated to photographing arid lands, particularly in the Arab world. He gives examples of practical uses of space images in solving problems, particularly those relating to a better understanding of the origin and evolution of the Arab deserts in the hope that this information will lead to more widespread use of satellite images in development plans in the Arab world.

Mass Education, the New Media and their Implications for Political and Religious Authority
Dale F. Eickelman ELS18 (1998)
Recent shifts in religious consciousness throughout the Muslim world have increasingly blurred the line between religion and politics. The growing fragmentation of political and religious authority associated in part with the rise of mass education, the inexorable growth of multiple channels of communication, and intensified migration and travel has added multiple voices and views to the political arena and expanded the sense of what is political. This lecture comparatively assesses the prospect for Islamic liberalism (and its opponents) in the Middle East. It also comments on the different kinds of accommodation which many seek between their Muslim identity and the transformative power of the economic and political forces at play in the late twentieth century.

Arab Satellite Television and Politics in the Middle East
Mohamed Zayani EOP54 (2004)
The new media scene of muliple satellite TV stations stands in marked contrast with a long tradition of state-controlled television. The political implications of the new media net-

works are not all that clear. In many instances, although several of the emerging channels are private, private ownership has not necessarily guaranteed the diversity of content. In fact, broadcasting has switched from a public to a private monopoly with a relatively narrow margin of freedom.

There is no doubt that ideology and national agendas still form an important force in satellite channels in general and news broadcasting in particular. However, one should not fail to note the emergence of a more critical tendency in television, not only on the part of the news practitioners, but also on the part of the viewers. In many ways, satellite broadcasting has also brought about a pan-Arab consciousness.

While in the past, public life as projected by TV was dominated by representations of state power and authority, the new public sphere that is emerging is more heterogeneous and less authoritative. The political effects of the media cannot be studied in isolation, but have to be understood within the larger socio-cultural setting of the region. There is a lack of public dissent, acceptance of some censorship and a socio-cultural disposition of media to play down controversy and dissent, but also a balance between cooptation and coercion by governments. Satellite TV is not only creating a community of participants, but also fostering a mediated communication between the representations of different forces in society.

Arab Media in the Information Age
ISBN: 9948-00-819-7 (hb) 9948-00-818-9 (pb) (2006)

In recent years, the Arab media has achieved both qualitative and quantitative progress. This has been achieved by means of Arab satellite stations, Arabic websites on the Internet, and transnational Arab newspapers and magazines. Nevertheless, the Arab media scene still exhibits structural imbalances and weaknesses that need to be highlighted with a view to addressing and overcoming them. This book makes a contribution towards understanding the current realities of the Arab media and enhancing its future effectiveness by assessing its performance and content; exploring its societal functions; examining its influence in shaping Arab public opinion and the western perspective of Arabs, in addition to studying the experience of the newly established Arab news channels. The book also seeks to address issues such as media independence and credibility, and the impact of commercial interests and political influence on the media. Furthermore, it presents comparative studies on the western media experience, examines the role of the media during wartime and under occupation, and highlights the growing importance of the Internet in Arab societies. A noteworthy feature of this ECSSR 10th Annual Conference book is that it compiles the presentations made by a diverse and elite group of Arab and foreign media personalities, researchers and academics.

ENERGY

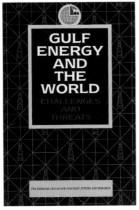

Gulf Energy and the World:
Challenges and Threats
ISBN: 1-86064-210-1(hb) 1-86064-211-X (pb) (1997)

The objective of this volume is to provide energy trend assessments and analyses of the future relationship of oil and gas to the world economy, and to offer policy recommendations for the Gulf region. Currently, the Gulf oil-producing countries are faced with manifold challenges to their pre-eminent position among the world's key providers of energy resources. The downward trend in the real price of oil since the early 1980s has forced the Gulf economies to undergo a series of significant adjustments. This book provides an historical overview of the Gulf's role in world energy and outlines several factors underlying the price trend. Conservation measures in consumer countries, weak economic performance in industrialized nations, and new oil- and gas-producing ventures outside OPEC are among the issues considered. Also examined are the energy-related strategic planning agendas of OPEC countries and the short-term energy market choices and constraints facing these nations.

Given the sizable oil reserves available in the Gulf, the rising energy demand in Asia, and the growing energy needs of the Gulf itself, the Gulf region will continue to play a crucial role in the world energy market. In this context, some of the potential threats to the Gulf position in the world oil market are discussed, including the development of energy efficient technologies, the competition between gas exporters in the Gulf and the production potential of the former Soviet Union. In light of the different issues raised and the finite nature of the energy resources available in the Gulf, this book concludes by underlining the urgent need for economic diversification in the Gulf states.

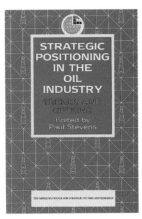

Strategic Positioning in the Oil Industry:
Trends and Options
Paul Stevens (ed.)
ISBN: 1-86064-362-0 (hb) 1-86064-366-3 (pb) (1998)

This volume presents papers drawn from ECSSR's Second Annual Energy Conference in 1996. It highlights and investigates the changes which are occurring in the demand structure for oil, changes that will have far-reaching consequences for oil producers, refiners and distributors who wish to perform in a competitive market. Written principally by leading practitioners, the essays represent current thinking on how and in which direction the oil industry, particularly in the Gulf region, is developing. Readers will find trenchant analyses of vertical integration as a strategy for oil security; refining and petroleum product specifications in Asia; privatization initiatives in the Gulf's energy sectors; downstream integration of national oil companies; and options and opportunities for Gulf oil companies in the Asian market. It represents a valuable collection of information and argument and also offers a rare insight into the beliefs and perceptions of those participating in today's international oil industry.

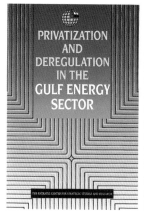

Privatization and Deregulation in the Gulf Energy Sector
ISBN: 1-86064-410-4 (hb) 1-86064-411-2 (pb) (1999)

ECSSR's Third Annual Energy Conference in 1997 united leading practitioners and scholars in an effort to explore the important micro and macro issues related to the privatization and deregulation of the energy sector. Topics included oil production and refining, gas and electricity production and modes of transmission and distribution. This collection of papers from that conference assesses the arguments for and against deregulation of the energy sector and highlights the political, legal, institutional and resource requirements for successful implementation of a privatization program, drawing on international experience. Indeed, privatization is spreading globally after its small and uncertain beginnings in Britain in the early 1980s. Today, states of the GCC are actively examining the privatization of a number of key industries and infrastructure projects. The route to prosperous and effective privatization programs lies in the ability of GCC states to learn from both the successes and the mistakes of others.

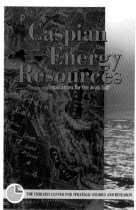

Caspian Energy Resources:
Implications for the Arab Gulf
ISBN: 0-86372-268-7 (hb) 0-86372-278-4 (pb) (2000)

This volume discusses the various dimensions of Caspian oil, ranging from its attractions, the rationale and scope for foreign investment, the complexities of the region's legal environment, contentious pipeline issues, regional political trends and the economic impact of Caspian energy on oil producers from the Arab Gulf countries and the world market. The potentially rich energy resources of the Caspian region have proved to be a tantalizing magnet for nations, oil companies and investors, and this prospective oil bonanza has prompted intense media coverage. As nations continually seek new supplies to replace depleted barrels of oil, Caspian oil assumes significance because of its high quality and export potential. How far will this potential be realized, and to what extent will these resources become a substitute for Gulf oil?

Given the limited opportunities available to exploit Caspian oil, studies suggest that there is little prospect of serious competition to Gulf oil and that the market control of the Arab Gulf producers may be relatively unaffected in the short or medium term. However, Caspian oil will be a significant addition to non-OPEC output and may eventually threaten the predominant position of Gulf oil, unless oil producers in the region adopt more market-oriented economic investment and pricing policies.

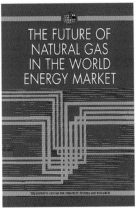

The Future of Natural Gas in the World Energy Market

ISBN: 1-86064-722-7 (hb) 1-86064-723-5 (pb) (2001)

The global trend to replace traditional fossil fuels like coal and oil with clean burning natural gas has been spurred on largely by heightened environmental concerns and international commitments to comply with noxious emission limits. The physical and combustion characteristics of natural gas are able to respond to these environmental concerns, thus providing highly industrialized nations in particular with a means to meet the requirements of international environmental agreements. The use of natural gas also includes the important advantage of high efficiency in gas-to-electricity conversion, a factor central to developing nations. Both factors have created a new demand sector for natural gas, which is reflected in the substantial growth of internationally traded gas over the last decade.

This volume reflects the insight of gas industry experts who gathered at the ECSSR's Fifth Annual Energy Conference in 1999. It covers topics ranging from the commercial opportunities and constraints relating to natural gas exploitation (and its implications for the global oil industry) to the emerging gas technologies that are likely to chart its future development. The book also assesses the impact of government regulation and liberalization on the industry from Canadian and European perspectives, as well as the regional developments in the Asian market, thus presenting a broad vision of past and future trends in the natural gas industry.

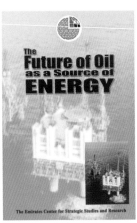

The Future of Oil as a Source of Energy

ISBN: 9948-00-010-2 (hb) 9948-00-009-9 (pb) (2003)

Despite the projected increase in energy demand due to population growth, environmental concerns and anti-emission policies are likely to reduce oil's share in the energy market over time. A combination of conversion technologies and energy sources like natural gas, renewable energy and hydrogen now has the potential to form more than niche markets in certain parts of the globe. Nevertheless, oil will probably continue to be the energy source of choice for most regions of the world.

Oil at the Turn of the Twenty-First Century: Interplay of Market Forces and Politics
Hooshang Amirahmadi EOP5 (1998)

Amirahmadi conducts an objective analysis of different trends prevailing in oil markets and studies various factors affecting both the supply and demand sides of oil economics, including market and regulatory measures. In doing so, he relies on assumptions and projections made by the IEA and other organizations and examines current views on the future of oil politics, OPEC's authority and the impact of the environmental movement. He concludes that the future holds uncertainty for oil producers and consumers alike, including governments and oil companies. He discusses the implications of this uncertainty for policy development and suggests that in the absence of new approaches emphasizing cooperation and coordination, politics may cause distortion in the working of oil market mechanisms.

Investment and Finance in the Energy Sectors of Developing Countries
Hossein Razavi EOP22 (1998)

The World Bank's projection of world economic growth indicates that while industrial countries are expected to experience a growth rate of 2.4 per cent per annum for the next 15 to 20 years, developing countries are likely to see a growth rate of 5.4 per cent per annum. The substantial difference between the two growth paths has significant impact on energy consumption, energy investments and financial requirements for energy projects. For example, the investment needs of the power sector in developing countries is expected to be around US$130 billion per year, more than twice the projected power investments in industrial countries. Also, the biggest increases in demand for oil and gas are occurring in the developing world, which is where most of the world's proven oil and gas reserves are located. Thus, international energy companies, investors, contractors and consulting firms are shifting their attention from Europe and North America to developing countries, which are likely to offer more business opportunities in the energy sector in the future. Although numerous energy projects are initiated, many of these projects do not reach the implementation stage because of difficulties in mobilizing financial resources. The difficulties are due to the presence of various types of political and commercial risks in developing countries. As a result, structuring finance packages for energy projects in developing countries has become a complex discipline that involves innovative combinations of multilateral, bilateral and commercial funds. This paper provides a global projection of energy investments in the developing countries, and then describes emerging methods of financing oil, power and natural gas projects.

The Arab Oil Weapon: A One-Shot Edition?
Paul Aarts EOP34 (1999)

Oil is a multipurpose fluid and its production and consumption have a long history. Oil as a political weapon, however, only entered the fray after World War II. Aarts argues that apart from the "unique" circumstances of late 1973 (when the oil weapon indeed scored a home run) both preceding and subsequent attempts to use oil as a political and economic weapon have not succeeded. He argues that there is a "new oil order," with the Saudi–American condominium as its linchpin. Though the shape of things to come had been apparent for quite some time, the outcome of the 1991 Gulf War, so successful for the West, gave fresh impetus to a radically different configuration of the oil market. As long as the Pax Americana is a political reality (in which ironically the US itself is using oil as a political weapon) and as long as there is a buyer's market, it seems unthinkable that the oil exporters can ever again use oil as a weapon. In hindsight, the success of late 1973 and early 1974 looks very much to have been a one-shot edition, leaving the Arab world saddled with a permanent feeling of nostalgia.

Outlook for LNG Exports:
The Qatari and Egyptian Experiences
Hussein Abdallah EOP35 (1999)

Energy is an international industry. Natural gas is only one of several major sources of energy. This leads to inter- as well as intra-fuel competition. Hence, a comprehensive analysis of the prospects for liquefied natural gas has to be undertaken within the context of the world energy scenario.

This study covers four sections, the first of which deals with world energy demand, supply and prices over the foreseeable future. World demand for energy is expected to grow at an annual rate of 2.3 per cent, in comparison to growth rates of 2.1 per cent and 3.2 per cent for oil and gas respectively. The second section analyzes the development of gas production, consumption and reserves over the past quarter of a century. The positive properties of gas as a clean and highly efficient fuel enhance its attractiveness in a world which is increasingly dominated by concerns of energy conservation and environmental protection.

The third section provides a comprehensive analysis of the Qatari experience in liquefying and exporting natural gas. The analysis involves extensive calculation of costs and revenues of two LNG projects, the first of which came on stream early in 1997, and a second which was scheduled to start production during 1999. Useful lessons are derived from the Qatari experience, which can be used in determining the technical and economic feasibility of a planned Egyptian LNG project. The fourth section analyzes the role of energy in the Egyptian economy, where oil and gas account for 92 per cent of domestic energy consumption, and 10 per cent of GDP. This is followed by estimates of future energy needs through 2017. The section concludes by offering a number of strategic recommendations for building a comprehensive energy policy.

Turkey and Caspian Energy
Gareth M. Winrow EOP37 (1999)

This study provides an overview of Turkey's policies toward the Caspian region. Interest in consuming Caspian oil and gas and in transporting this energy to outside markets has led Ankara to concentrate on developing relations with Azerbaijan, Georgia, Kazakhstan and Turkmenistan. Ties with Iran and Russia are also important as Turkish officials are eager to promote stability in the Caspian so as to enhance the prospects for the construction of oil and gas pipelines across the region to Turkey. Many in Ankara, though, still perceive Russia as a potential destabilizing element.

Turkey needs to import more oil and gas to satisfy its rising energy needs. Azerbaijani and Kazakh oil as well as Turkmen, Russian and Iranian gas may help to meet Turkey's pressing energy requirements. The decision-making process in Turkey relating to Caspian energy issues is complex and bureaucratic. Various groups and individuals are involved, including leading politicians, several ministries and state agencies, construction companies and also the Turkish armed forces. Consequently, it is difficult to establish a coordinated and consistent energy policy.

The prospects for the realization of the Tengiz-Baku-Ceyhan main export oil pipeline to transport Azerbaijani and Kazakh crude to Turkey and the world market is analyzed. Its construction may be impeded because of problems in securing throughput guarantees, and because international energy companies are interested in alternative routes. In such a situation, Turkey may seek to place greater controls on the passage of tanker traffic through the Bosphorus. The possibilities of Turkey importing more Russian, Iranian and Turkmen gas are also examined. While future developments are difficult to predict, it seems clear that the pipeline to Ceyhan is perceived by Ankara as a necessity, in the context of the country's increasing need to consume Caspian oil and gas.

Energy Statistics:
IEA Methodology and Models
John Denman, Mieke Reece and Sohbet Karbuz ELS31 (2001)

Rising global demand for adequate and reliable energy supplies makes the availability of energy statistics indispensable for formulating national energy policy and ensuring that the energy market functions effectively. An unregulated energy market does not automatically produce reliable, objective and timely statistical data that will ensure its transparency, since no single enterprise can bear the costs of maintaining a complex data system. It is therefore incumbent on state authorities to collect, verify and disseminate energy market statistics.

This study highlights the key role and methodology of the International Energy Agency (IEA) in the field of energy statistics. The Statistics Division of the IEA plays a predominant role, as it collects, verifies, and publishes information on energy from both OECD member countries and non-member countries. Data gathering from member countries is undertaken through established reporting systems. For non-member countries and international organizations, the customary mode for data collection is through bilateral exchange, cooperation agreements or personal contacts. An important task for the Statistics Division is to disseminate data, which is done through publications, electronic data and the Internet.

The underlying reasons for gathering energy data and the means of collection are examined, with the UK and the US serving as case studies. The authors outline the legislation relating to the collection of energy statistics, which indicates the level of government intervention in economic affairs. A corresponding issue is the degree of statistical confidentiality.

The classification of data is examined in detail for all products and all flows (or uses) of the energy. The treatment and verification process for data received by OECD member and non-member countries is also demonstrated. Finally, guidelines are provided regarding the construction of a commodity balance, the conventions of an energy balance, as well as the IEA energy balance format, which facilitates both cross-fuel and cross-country comparisons.

Blood or Gold: Politics, Economics and Energy Security
Michael Lynch EOP47 (2002)

There are two typical views of energy security and oil crises, with distinct analytical approaches and policy recommendations, which can be classified as "geopolitics" and "economics." The geopolitical approach links imports to vulnerability or at least influence, and maintains that reduced oil imports improve security. One major weakness of this approach is the focus on petroleum trade balances among regions and countries as the critical variable, ignoring the fact that oil is a fungible commodity. If necessary, almost any amount of crude oil can be replaced fairly quickly in the event of a single-nation embargo.

Economists often directly contradict the geopolitical view, presuming that all trade is done for money, and that specific trade flows are irrelevant because oil is a fungible commodity and any disruptions will be resolved by markets. Energy security, according to this view, need only concern itself with the ability of the market to allocate supply efficiently during a disruption.

Although consumers often treat short-term price fluctuations as "crises," they really represent normal cyclical behavior for a cartelized commodity. Oil crises are political events, but the primary damage is economic, through the mechanism of oil price change. Even when supply and consumption are relatively balanced, hoarding can create or exacerbate price increases. A major element that causes hoarding (and price changes in a more general sense) is uncertainty about supply, which is typically worse due to political interference in the market, whether intentional (as in 1973) or an exogenous event (as in 1979).

Future oil crises, while far milder than 1979, can be expected to exceed the experience of 1990 in terms of price increase and related economic damage. Hoarding appears to be the most likely danger, but other things, including policy mistakes, remain a concern. The passage of time reduces the number of policymakers with experience of oil crises, and raises the likelihood of bad policy choices during future supply disruptions.

However, the primary current energy security threat is that of hoarding, given the significant probability of supply disruptions which are just large enough to cause price spikes, and which would be greatly worsened by the wrong inventory behavior. This is pertinent to policy-makers because hoarding is rational behavior during a period of supply uncertainty. Since the political element of supply disruptions creates or magnifies uncertainty about supply and encourages hoarding, political intervention to reduce hoarding seems particularly appropriate.

Asian Energy Markets:
Dynamics and Trends
ISBN: 9948-00-570-8 (hb) 9948-00-569-4 (pb) (2004)

Energy has become a crucial determinant shaping the security environment of Asia. The continent's phenomenal growth is projected to raise oil and gas consumption to dramatic new levels. As major Asian nations become net energy importers, this thirst for oil will determine world energy export patterns and shape regional geopolitics. With the Arabian Gulf supplying the major proportion of Asian energy needs, Gulf – Asia links will emerge as a key factor in the global energy scenario. Energy security concerns will dominate Asian economic policy and strategic decision-making and spur Asian investment in oil exploration, oil refining and development of alternative energy sources.

What are the economic and strategic implications of Asia's growing dependence on Gulf oil? How far can Asian countries counter such dependence by improving energy efficiency and developing new sources? What are the energy transitions that Asian nations are undergoing? What kind of structural reforms are needed in the Asian energy markets? What are the implications of Asian energy consumption trends and current economic reforms for the Arabian Gulf producers? What will the impact of Asian markets be on the global energy scenario? These and related issues were examined by energy experts at the Seventh Annual Energy Conference held in Abu Dhabi from January 13–14, 2002. This volume of conference presentations discusses wide-ranging issues relating to the Asian energy sector including supply security, consumption trends, privatization moves, energy diversification, energy self-sufficiency and foreign investment.

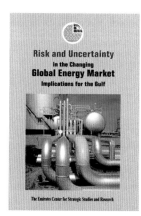

Risk and Uncertainty in the Changing Global Energy Market: Implications for the Gulf
ISBN: 9948-00-573-2 (hb) 9948-00-572-4 (pb) (2004)

The complex dynamics of the world energy market make it virtually impossible to map clearly the contours of the emerging global scenario. However, realistic trend evaluation, risk assessment, change management strategies and provision for eventualities are imperatives for nations, organizations and companies that have a major stake in the energy industry. Uncertainties may originate from many quarters—geopolitical factors, market forces, energy security issues, environmental and safety concerns. These risk factors call for careful analysis and effective solutions.

ECSSR's Eighth Annual Energy Conference, held in Abu Dhabi from October 19–20, 2002 assembled a panel of energy experts to identify and assess the major risks and uncertainties affecting the global energy market.

The conference presentations contained in this book shed light on issues such as geopolitical and military risks, supply disruptions, accidents and contingencies, infrastructure constraints, price fluctuations, market uncertainties and technical challenges. For both energy producers and consumers there are valuable guidelines on minimizing foreseeable risks through techniques such as energy supply diversification, import reduction moves, developing alternative energy sources, building strategic links with suppliers, signing regional cooperation agreements, maintaining oil stockpiling, implementing pricing strategies, enhancing energy conservation, increasing energy efficiency and countering speculative trading.

The Future Financing of the Iraqi Oil Industry
Dr. Ali Hussain ELS55 (2004)

Iraq has enormous reserves of oil and gas, which can be exploited at very low cost. Iraq also has an experienced work force to support the reconstruction and development of its oil industry. However, due to very high international debt and the need to pay war compensations, Iraq may not be able to finance the development of its oil industry. The decision as to whether Iraq should welcome foreign investment in this industry is one that a new elected Iraqi government will have to take.

Gulf Oil in the Aftermath of the Iraq War: Strategies and Policies
ISBN: 9948-00-753-0 (hb) 9948-00-752-2 (pb) (2005)

A founding OPEC member with an established oil sector and vast untapped oil reserves, Iraq has always been a major player in the global oil industry. However, its oil sector has never realized its full potential as it was hindered by UN sanctions in the 1990s and later by infrastructural damage following the US-led invasion of 2003. The disruption in Iraqi oil supply and the prospect of its resumption carries both short and long-term implications for Iraq, the Arabian Gulf, OPEC and the world oil market. Although OPEC did stabilize supply and prices in the immediate aftermath of the invasion, such geopolitical upheavals create major challenges in market management. What are the prospects for a quick revival of the Iraqi oil industry? How will the return of Iraqi oil supplies to the world market affect Gulf producers? What are the resulting quota and supply adjustments that OPEC will have to consider? How will OPEC and Non-OPEC relations develop in the future? What strategic investments should Gulf oil producers make to safeguard their global position in the emerging oil scenario? Such key issues were debated by the industry experts who gathered at the ECSSR Ninth Annual Energy Conference entitled Gulf Oil in the Aftermath of the Iraq War: Strategies and Policies from October 19–20, 2003 in Abu Dhabi, UAE. The conference presentations compiled in this book collectively offer valuable insight on all these vital energy concerns.

The Gulf Oil and Gas Sector: Potential and Constraints
ISBN: 9948-00-809-X (hb) 9948-00-808-1 (pb) (2006)

With world demand for oil projected to reach unprecedented levels led by Asian economic powers such as China and India and geopolitical crises fueling greater uncertainty, issues of global supply security have come to the fore. All these factors have led to a steep rise in petroleum prices. In this energy scenario, where does the Gulf oil and gas sector stand? How can it meet its long-term strategic requirements while satisfying the energy needs of the global economy? This was the main focus of the ECSSR Tenth Annual Energy Conference on The Gulf Oil and Gas Sector:

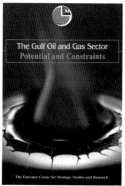

Potential and Constraints, held in Abu Dhabi, from September 26–27, 2004. The important energy issues covered here include future prospects of OPEC, the impact of world oil prices on global growth, the strategic objectives of the Gulf energy sector, the influence of markets and technology on regional reserves, the emerging partnerships between national and international oil companies, the imperatives for attracting Gulf energy investment and new developments in gas technology and regional gas trade. Regional case studies outline possible scenarios for the future of Iraqi oil, highlight policy options for Saudi Arabia as a swing producer and focus on the Norwegian experience of economic diversification.

GLOBALIZATION

Globalization and Regionalization: New Trends in World Politics
Richard Higgott ELS13 (1998)

Four common interpretations of globalization are in circulation: a specific epoch, the confluence of a range of specific phenomena, the so-called triumph of "American values" and a technological and social revolution. Higgott demonstrates the limitations of these views and argues that globalization represents a fundamental shift in the behavior of the modern world economy, with ensuing implications for contemporary world politics. He discusses the growth of economic integration and that of institutional economic cooperation as the two major trends of regionalization, and examines their relationship with globalization. Higgott argues that the management of the global and regional orders cannot be undertaken separately, and new forms of governance are needed.

INTERNATIONAL LAW

Sources of International Law: Scope and Application
Christoph Schreuer ELS28 (2000)

International law is not derived from static sets of rules or mutually exclusive sources, but is the manifestation of a complex decision-making process in which different forms of legal authority interact. The cornerstone of international law is the consent of states. This may be explicit, as in the case of signed international treaties, or it may be implicit, as in the case of customary international law. Law-making through multilateral treaties is a protracted process involving consent, ratification and often reservations by state governments. The interpretation and application can be complex because of different language versions. Customary law, on the other hand, is difficult to prove conclusively. Increasingly, the decisions of courts, tribunals and international organizations, as well as scholarly writings, are becoming non-traditional sources of international law and its interpretation.

These traditional sources and tools with their shortcomings are inadequate, especially in dealing with new areas that do not fit the traditional mold, such as human rights, international criminal law and international economic law, all of which transcend state barriers. International investment law is one obvious field where legal principles such as "sanctity of contract" conflicted with "state sovereignty." Alternative sources, such as customary law and bilateral treaties, were inconclusive and had to contend with socialist ideologies and nationalist decolonization doctrines. Obviously, fresh thinking and new legal techniques are necessary to meet the challenges of the modern world.

The UN, the US, the EU and Iraq:
Multiple Challenges for International Law?
David M. Malone ELS51 (2004)

The medium and long-term outlook for the United Nations Security Council is more uncertain than it has seemed at any time since the end of the Cold War opened up an era of unprecedented optimism over the Council's future role. The question mark is thus the most important item in the title of this paper, which seeks to address the Council's influence over international politics and law in recent years.

The text is in two parts. Part one seeks to situate the Council in the post-Cold War political context, moving on to examine the changing approach of the US to multilateralism in general and the UN in particular. It also examines the recent fascination with the notion of "US Empire," and examines how other governments, notably European ones, have reacted to US power within the Council. Part two moves from this consideration of the actors on the Council to examining how they have responded to the new challenges before it.

Evolution of International Environmental Negotiations:
From Stockholm to Rio de Janeiro
Marc Gedopt ELS29 (2001)

International environmental negotiations shifted gradually from being a peripheral issue of international politics to becoming a core issue. Negotiations evolved primarily from concern for local problems encountered by the industrialized world. Later, it expanded to include trans-boundary issues and thereafter began to focus on emerging global issues, firmly establishing the link between environment and development. The two UN Conferences on the Environment in Stockholm (1972) and Rio de Janeiro (1992) may be viewed as the two poles in this evolution. The policy instruments used in this period reflect the transformation, ranging from actions to remedy existing problems to preventive action and the increasing use of economic instruments.

In terms of content, international environmental conventions are more political instruments than clear legal instruments with well-defined obligations for the parties. Their political nature is also indicated by an absence of strong compliance regimes. Most of these treaties are process-oriented, with the creation of institutions that allow the issue to be kept under periodic review by the international community. Mechanisms like national reporting are also used to allow for national and international scrutiny.

Nation states are the major actors in environmental negotiations. It is important to understand the rationale behind the respective positions of these nations, or groups of nations, especially the US, the developing countries and the EU. Moreover, international environmental negotiations are characterized by the active presence and significant role of non-state actors such as non-governmental organizations, the business community and the scientific community.

An analysis of the provisions of the UN Framework Convention on Climate Change and its Kyoto Protocol provides an illustrative case study. The Convention is in a preliminary stage, with a very ambiguous commitment and no compliance regime, but an elaborate institutional framework. The aim of the Kyoto Protocol is to clarify the commitment and create new economic mechanisms. However, it remains very cautious on compliance. The Sixth Conference of the Parties to the Convention held from November 13–25, 2000, demonstrated the difficulties in resolving the outstanding issues needed to implement the Kyoto Protocol.

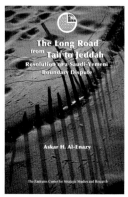

The Long Road from Taif to Jeddah: Resolution of a Saudi-Yemeni Boundary Dispute

ISBN: 9948-00-721-2 (pb) (2005)

Competing territorial and boundary claims have historically ignited intense disputes between countries. The boundary dispute between Saudi Arabia and Yemen during the past seventy years has been no exception. The disputed area, covering both land and sea, constitutes strategically and economically important territory between the two largest states in the Arabian Peninsula and the issue has periodically threatened regional peace and stability. This book is perhaps the first systematic study of the resolution of this dispute. It provides an assessment of various aspects of the dispute and legal attempts to resolve them, also with reference to the principles of international law. Special attention is given to the Treaty of Taif in 1934 and subsequent developments until the Treaty of Jeddah in 2000, which incorporated the Treaty of Taif and established a maritime and land boundary between Saudi Arabia and Yemen. The book provides both an important legal analysis of the Saudi-Yemeni boundary dispute and a valuable case study of dispute resolution.

Border Disputes and their Resolution According to International Law: The Qatar–Bahrain Case.

Giovanni Distefano ELS59 (2005)

The key element of the territorial and maritime dispute between Bahrain and Qatar was the need to determine sovereignty over the area of Zubarah, the Hawar Islands and Janan Island. On the matter of sovereignty over Zubarah, the ICJ ruled in Qatar's favor, relying on an international treaty signed in 1913 between the Ottoman Empire and Great Britain. The territorial dispute over the Hawar Islands was the most bitterly fought of the entire case. Qatar invoked the principle of contiguity to prove its claim, while the basis of Bahrain's argument rested on a decision made by Great Britain on July 11, 1939, that awarded sovereignty to Bahrain. Based on this decision, the ICJ ruled that the islands belonged to Bahrain. Ultimately a territorial dispute, which gravely embittered the relations between two friendly states, has been successfully settled.

ISLAM/POLITICS

Islam, Western Democracy and the Third Industrial Revolution: Conflict or Convergence?
Ali A. Mazrui ELS17 (1998)
The word "globalization" is new but the process itself has been going on for centuries, beginning with cultural globalization promoted by universalist religions, of which the most ambitious have been Christianity and Islam. Mazrui traces the historical development of Islam and Christianity, comparing them in order to determine if there are links between religious doctrine and democratic theory, between liberal democracy and the rise of capitalism, or between religious pluralism and political pluralism. He stresses that although Muslims are often criticized for not producing the best, they are seldom congratulated for having standards of behavior which have averted the worst seen in the West. He also discusses the potential impact of the information revolution on the globalization of Islam. Will it include a momentous movement of religious reform? Will the Internet, cyberspace and the third industrial revolution do to Islam what printing and the first industrial revolution did to Christianity?

Liberalism and the Contestation of Islamic Sovereignty
Amr Sabet EOP52 (2003)
Some Muslim scholars, reacting to a general crisis in the Muslim world, have come to project Western historical experience on revelation under the rubric of "liberal Islam," while overlooking God's plans for history. The process of emulating and adapting to the values of another force will not be the source of salvation. As the power of such a force runs its course, so will its values. "Liberals" fail to show how liberal democratic values may necessarily lead to positive outcomes for Islam and Muslims.

Islam and the West after September 11: Civilizational Dialogue or Conflict?
John L. Esposito ELS40 (2002)
The approach of some US government officials to condemn anti-Americanism fails to address real issues and grievances. The war against terrorism should not justify an erosion of important values in the US or become a green light to authoritarian Muslim regimes to increase repression.

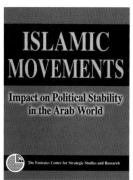

Islamic Movements:
Impact on Political Stability of the Arab World
ISBN: 9948-00-546-5 (hb) 9948-00-545-7 (pb) (2003)

Islamic movements have maintained a strong presence in the political and social life of the Arab world since the last century, through the active pursuit of the Islamization of their particular state or society. The strength of the movements has led to clashes and prolonged confrontations with some Arab regimes, which has greatly affected political and social stability in these states.

This book consists of important studies by several specialists on Islamic movements. The analyses focus on the conditions that led to their emergence and the relationships between their thinking and praxis in particular political and social contexts. The studies also discuss the radical and moderate orientations of these movements, highlighting the reasons behind such approaches and their impact on the current situation in the Arab world.

Islamic Approaches to Conflict Resolution and Peace
Abdul Aziz Said, Nathan C. Funk and Ayse S. Kadayifci EOP48 (2002)

Within the Muslim community, the call for peace has manifested and will undoubtedly continue to manifest itself in diverse ways. This reflects continuous efforts to interpret and apply foundational Islamic values in specific historical, social and cultural situations. Islamic conceptions of peace have often been misrepresented, misunderstood or simply ignored. There are indeed differences between prevailing Western and Islamic conceptions of peace. These differences constitute a basis for an ongoing dialogue on the topic.

Beneath different interpretations of Islam, there is an underlying unity of intention that gives coherence to various approaches to peace. Approaches to peace in Islam can be categorized in five paradigms. Many Muslims have, at one time or another, subscribed to views that incorporate aspects of more than one paradigm.

The paradigm of power politics exalts state authority, views peace simply as an absence of war and emphasizes the political necessities created by threatening environments. The Islamic world order approach sees peace as a condition defined by the presence of such core Islamic values as order, justice, equity, cultural coexistence (as in the Iranian "Dialogue of Civilizations" initiative), and ecological stability. Practitioners of Islamic approaches to conflict resolution adhere to a restorative conception of peace that encompasses notions of just compensation for losses, renunciation of retribution and forgiveness. Though it is not widely recognized, an Islamic paradigm for nonviolence does in fact exist, and some of the most notable recent applications of this paradigm have occurred in South Asia and Southeast Asia. Peace is understood as the presence of social justice, which must be sought by just means. The last approach to peace, the Islamic equivalent of a transformational, spiritually centered paradigm, defines peace as a condition of harmony attained through the transformation of human consciousness.

The dominant Western approach to peace finds the substance of peace in political pluralism, individual rights and, in practice — if not in precept — consumerism. In contrast, Islamic precepts permit a view of peace based on communal solidarity, social justice, faith and cultural pluralism. The differences between Western and Islamic approaches to conflict resolution reflect some of the differences between Western and Islamic perspectives on peace. While the strongest Western approach to conflict resolution is to conceptualize and solve problems, the Islamic approach emphasizes the mending and maintenance of social relationships. Muslims see conflict and competition between individuals and groups as a threat to social unity, stability and welfare, and are often somewhat less optimistic about conflict than the advocates of new Western approaches.

Research and dialogue on conceptions of peace and peacemaking provide an alternative to the solipsism of culture-bound thinking. They can promote a deeper understanding of cross-cultural differences and a greater appreciation of the shared values and goals that will be needed if true coexistence — and perhaps even intercultural complementarity — is to be achieved.

MANAGEMENT ISSUES

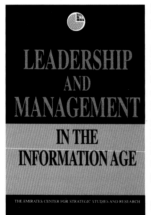

Leadership and Management in the Information Age
ISBN: 1-86064-776-6 (hb) 1-86064-777-4 (pb) (2002)

A key aspect of the world economy, as shaped by the information revolution and the forces of globalization, is the role of leaders and managers as motivators, planners and administrators. The traditional roles are at variance with new global dynamics. Increasingly, leaders are finding themselves compelled to take decisions in a rapidly changing environment, characterized by vast flows of information and highly competitive markets. They are also being called upon to transform the human resources at their disposal and to make full use of individual capacity in their organizations.

This volume contains papers presented by leading thinkers and pioneers in the fields of leadership and management at the ECSSR Sixth Annual Conference in 2000. It demonstrates dynamic views on the topics of successful leadership, management of organizational change in the public and private spheres, transformation in human resources, effective management of genetic engineering and biotechnology advancements, the future of the national economy and the nature of defense and national security in a changed global environment.

Human Resource Development in a Knowledge-Based Economy

ISBN: 9948-00-412-4 (hb) 9948-00-413-2 (pb) (2003)

This volume contains papers presented at the ECSSR's Seventh Annual Conference in 2002. Unconventional parameters characterize the knowledge-based economy of the twenty-first century. With the individual as the cornerstone of the new economic order, personal skills, innovation and creativity are not merely factors of production, but sources of wealth and imperatives for economic growth. In the global war for knowledge and talent, human resource development becomes a crucial strategy for nations and organizations to gain competitive advantage.

Studies in International Conflict and Crisis Management
David Garnham ELS25 (2000)

War is an abiding affliction affecting human society and during the twentieth century, warfare between nation states has claimed some 30 million battle deaths, principally during the two world wars. Although evidence suggests that the world has become somewhat more secure in the post-Cold War era, interstate conflict remains very much an immutable feature of international politics. Garnham examines the nature of international conflict and pinpoints the common causes behind interstate wars. Factors that increase the likelihood that an international crisis will escalate to warfare are analyzed and particular attention is devoted to the conditions that predispose pairs of nation states to fight. The effectiveness of various strategies of crisis management are assessed with a view to avoiding future warfare. Of particular relevance are case studies of the major crises of the twentieth century, including World War I (1914–18), the Korean War (1950–53), the Suez Crisis (1956), the Cuban Missile Crisis (1962), the Gulf of Tonkin Crisis (1964) and the Gulf War (1990–91). Crises reflect the gravity of underlying conflicts, so it is imperative that these are resolved before conflict occurs. Judicious crisis decision-making such as minimizing groupthink, misperceptions and risk acceptance will improve the chances of avoiding war. The settlement of outstanding territorial disputes is an important factor in minimizing the likelihood of conflict.

POLITICS IN THE MIDDLE EAST

The Position of a Weak State in an Unstable Region: The Case of Lebanon
Walid E. Moubarak ELS44 (2003)

Lebanon's stability largely depends on other powers' interest in preserving a regional balance of power. Various factors ensure that there will be no solution in the near future to the instability experienced by Lebanon, including the presence of Palestinian refugees, the ongoing proxy conflict between Israel and Syria in southern Lebanon and the alliance of the various major groups in Lebanon with outside powers.

Iraq: Upcoming Elections and Possible Future Scenarios
Kenneth Katzman ELS61 (2005)

Doubts have been raised about how Iraq will evolve politically after the planned January 30, 2005 national election. A useful tool for evaluating Iraq's future is to examine alternative post-election scenarios and possibilities. One such scenario is that of a "puppet government" that has a questionable legitimacy, ruling within limited areas of the country, with the backing of a superpower. Another possible outcome is described by the "strongman model," which would take the form of a one-man or one-party rule, which is heavily dependent on repressive security measures to preserve order. Some observers have referred to a "failed state" in Iraq as being more threatening to US interests than a strong state. In the failed state model, every major Iraqi faction could be fighting against virtually every other faction, as well as against the central government. A further model which could emerge after the election is a "power sharing" compromise among the major factions.

SCIENCE

The Date Palm:
From Traditional Resource to Green Wealth
ISBN: 9948-00-551-1 (hb) 9948-00-551-3 (pb) (2003)

The date palm has come of age. Cultivated for millennia in the arid regions of the world, the importance of the date palm is being rediscovered. Its value as the sustaining pillar of market gardens in marginal agricultural communities cannot be overemphasized. Modern science and technology is also investigating the undisputed usefulness of the date palm in changing arid microclimates, increasing the potential for crop diversity and arresting desertification.

As a tree that has emerged from ancient history into the modern world, the date palm is eliciting a great deal of interest in fields as diverse as biotechnology and international marketing. To explore the potential of the date palm and all aspects of its industry, The Emirates Center for Strategic Studies and Research hosted the International Date Palm Forum in Abu Dhabi, on September 15–17, 2002. This book represents a collection of expert papers on the full range of topics pertaining to the date palm, from its archaeology, cultivation and traditional uses, to international marketing and biotech applications in modern propagation methods and disease control. It provides a thorough overview for any reader wanting to gain insight into this industry, from its ancient roots to its modern day practices.

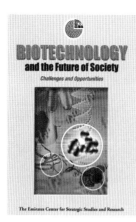

Biotechnology and the Future of Society: Challenges and Opportunities

ISBN: 9948-00-509-0 (hb) 9948-00-508-2 (pb) (2004)

Breakthroughs in biotechnology are redefining the very concept of life, transforming society and presenting unprecedented opportunities and challenges: Will human genome sequencing help to treat genetic diseases and indefinitely prolong life? Will stem cell therapy and tissue engineering allow routine regeneration and replacement of diseased organs? Can new diagnostic tests revolutionize medicine and healthcare? Will genetic engineering allow parents to design perfect babies? Can nature's workshop inspire superior bio-materials that transform industries? Will genetically modified super crops feed a hungry world?

With biotechnology set to be the driving force of the twenty-first century, mastery of the life sciences will be the key to wealth generation and economic ascendancy. Can the Arab World regain its past supremacy in these fields? Can it benefit from the biotech revolution while avoiding its perils? Such implications were debated by experts at the ECSSR Eighth Annual Conference titled *Biotechnology and the Future of Society: Challenges and Opportunities*, held from January 11–13, 2003 in Abu Dhabi, United Arab Emirates. This volume of conference presentations explores the broad impact of the biotech revolution, highlighting trends in healthcare and molecular medicine, the genetic revolution in agriculture, the future of materials production, new drug discovery technologies and national security issues, including the threat of bio-terrorism. It also examines the complex ethical, legal and social issues raised by the biotech revolution that need to be resolved by governments and decision-makers.

SECURITY FROM A UAE PERSPECTIVE

Deterrence Essentials: Keys to Controlling an Adversary's Behavior
David Garnham EOP3 (1995)

This paper examines the challenges of conventional deterrence. It emphasizes the knowledge and capabilities required for the successful implementation of strategies, such as deterrence by punishment, by denial and by appeasement. Intelligence requirements, including knowledge of adversary preferences and personalities of decision-makers, are also addressed. Examples of conflicts, such as the Japanese attack on Pearl Harbor, NATO's stance towards the former Soviet Union, and the Gulf War of 1990–91, are cited to illustrate the dynamics of deterrence success and failure.

National Security Essentials: Application for the U.A.E.
David Garnham ELS10 (1998)

Garnham discusses the fundamental concepts of national security analysis. To illustrate the process by which states interact and develop security agendas, he draws on a wide variety of classic works including those of Machiavelli, Hobbes, Morgenthau, Waltz and Jervis. The paper considers the relevance of geopolitics, particularly the role of geography, culture and history, and their impact on formulating and implementing national security plans. Garnham also analyzes the problems involved in communicating and implementing security decisions.

UAE Security: Proposals for the Coming Decade
David Garnham ELS16 (1998)

International affairs are highly unpredictable, and international security is especially volatile. The UAE is wealthy and reasonably secure, so any changes to the current status quo are likely to have a negative impact. Garnham presents an overview of UAE security issues and suggests specific policy initiatives to enhance security, among them strengthening the GCC, resolving the ambiguous and contentious border disputes which exist in the region, and reducing reliance on expatriate labor.

Diplomacy and Defense Policy of the United Arab Emirates
William Rugh ELS38 (2002)

Since the establishment of the United Arab Emirates in 1971, the country's foreign and defense policies have largely been formulated by the late Sheikh Zayed bin Sultan Al Nahyan (may Alla have mercy on him). From the beginning, Sheikh Zayed identified four objectives, namely the establishment of good relations with his immediate neighbors, peaceful settlement of disputes, solidarity with the Arab and Islamic worlds, and fruitful cooperation with all nations.

Despite major challenges to foreign policy, such as the two Gulf wars and the dispute with Iran over the occupation of the three UAE islands in the Gulf, Sheikh Zayed was able to adhere to the UAE's foreign policy objectives, and steer its defense policy accordingly. This approach ensured that by 2001 the UAE, which in 1971 had been a weak fledgling state facing hostile neighbors and almost no friends, had established strong alliances in the Gulf and the Arab world, strategic ties with the United States and the West, and a position of widespread respect and influence.

SECURITY IN THE GULF

The Yemeni War of 1994: Causes and Consequences
Jamal S. Al-Suwaidi (ed.)
ISBN: 0-86356-300-7 (hb) (1995)

On May 22, 1990, a long-standing Yemeni national dream became a reality when North and South Yemen were united in the Republic of Yemen. The process of political integra-

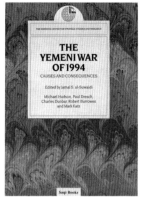

tion was violently disrupted four years later, however, and civil war broke out. This book is an examination of the 1994 civil war by five international area experts. Events leading to the conflict are viewed from both Northern and Southern perspectives. The South's fear of Islamic fundamentalism emanating from the North is contrasted with Northern concerns over a Southern push to advance social progress at the expense of traditionalism. A major chapter focuses on the tribes and tribal organizations and contemporary political develop-ments in Yemen. Tribalism as a system and whether it played a role in the 1994 civil war is discussed in detail. The regional implications of the civil war are also examined. In assessing the consequences for the Arabian peninsula, particular attention is paid to Yemen's capacity to influence events in the region, its relationship with Saudi Arabia and other GCC states, and the functioning of a balance-of-power system in the area.

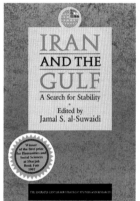

Iran and the Gulf: A Search for Stability

H.E. Dr. Jamal S. Al-Suwaidi (ed.)

ISBN: 1-86064-143-1 (hb) 1-86064-144-X (pb) (1996)

This volume presents the research and analyses of internationally recognized scholars concerning the internal and external dynamics which affect and often determine the policies of the Islamic Republic of Iran. Following an introduction designed to provide an analytical and contextual backdrop, the volume takes a detailed look at the Iranian polity, its evolution before and after the revolution, and the role of ideology. The next section addresses Iranian foreign policy with respect to the Arab Gulf states, and discusses this policy as a function of domestic dynamics and as a response to regional and international events and constraints. The third section discusses Iran's military capabilities and includes reasoned judgments concerning the Islamic Republic's intentions and aspirations in the military realm. The book concludes with a discussion of the evolving relationship between the GCC states and Iran with particular focus on the security dynamics that attend that relationship for the foreseeable future. This timely and comprehensive work acknowledges Iran's important and immutable role in Gulf affairs, and particularly in Gulf security issues. It also acknowledges the important evolution in Iranian foreign policy which has occurred since the Revolution of 1979, and particularly since the death of the Iranian revolutionary leader Ayatollah Ruhollah Khomeini.

Iran and the Gulf won First Prize for the Best Book in Humanities and Social Sciences at the 16th Annual Sharjah Book Fair, 1997.

Gulf Security in the Twenty-First Century
David E. Long, Christian Koch (eds)
ISBN: 1-86064-316-7 (hb) 1-86064-365-5 (pb) (1997)

The nexus between regional instability and the preservation of global security is nowhere more evident than in the Gulf. Events since the 1990–91 Gulf War continue to confirm the fragile interaction among states in the region and their susceptibility to external forces. This book brings together some of the foremost area experts to explore the most pressing issues, including military threats to the region, obstacles to economic development and socio-economic harmonization, and challenges to political stability.

In particular, the work examines Iran's often enigmatic foreign policy vis-à-vis its Gulf neighbors, Iraq's resurgent military threat, choices and constraints confronting US Middle East policy, and Europe's inability to identify and pursue a united policy to safeguard its economic interests in the area. These topics are further illuminated with an analysis of Russia's historical attempt at balancing foreign policy objectives in the Gulf with its enduring interests in Central Asia. The potentially explosive issues of religious radicalism and the challenges of democratic pluralism are discussed in an effort to ascertain the potential of political Islam to disturb or enhance regional security. Similarly, the problems inhibiting the settlement of territorial disputes in and around the Gulf are brought into focus to illustrate lingering historical tensions among neighboring states. To complete the book's topical coverage, several contributors shed light on the region's unfettered dependence on foreign labor, growing demographic pressures, associated social and economic transformations, and challenges to responsive public policy.

The Gulf: Future Security and British Policy
ISBN: 0-86372-260-1 (hb) 0-86372-272-5 (pb) (2000)

The Arabian Gulf region has increasingly become the focus of international concern since the Gulf War of 1991 which clearly demonstrated the link between regional stability and global security. An effective Gulf security framework hinges, to a great extent, on the integration of national and regional policies with the defense policies of allied countries. The end of the Cold War has afforded the opportunity for the Gulf region to develop a more stable security paradigm that is not constrained by the imperatives of a bipolar system. Against this backdrop, the book examines the foundation and scope for closer security ties between the UK and the GCC countries.

This volume includes a number of specialized papers presented by prominent military officials and experts from the GCC countries and Britain in a conference held jointly by ECSSR and the Royal United Services Institute for Defense Studies (RUSI) in London, 1998. It thus offers a unique opportunity to access professional experience in the field of security and stresses the need to develop a greater range of consultative mechanisms. In highlighting both immediate and potential threats to Gulf security and effective national and regional measures to counter these, the book aspires to provide a deeper understanding of the security issues that will define the shape of the GCC–UK relationship in the twenty-first century.

The Iranian Revolution and Political Change in the Arab World
Karen A. Feste EOP4 (1996)

The Iranian Revolution has been the paramount catalyst challenging the political order of the Middle East in recent times. Feste explores whether the emergence of political Islam is the key to understanding the power struggle in the Middle East. Focusing on the link between civil unrest and government response throughout the Arab world, do events leading up to and following the revolution in Iran render a model that explains political change in the Middle East? Examining the factors that converged to create the 1979 revolution in Iran, what does the interaction between domestic and international pressures underpinning social and political change in the region suggest? Employing aggregate measures based on cross-national, longitudinal event data, Feste tests the correlation between public dissent and government sanctions across three distinct phases in Middle East political history in order to discern patterns of political change associated with temporal, geographical and leadership traits.

Resolving the Security Dilemma in the Gulf Region
Bjørn Møller EOP9 (1997)

This paper begins with an analysis of the concept of "region," which is more ambiguous than one might think. This is followed by an analysis of the Gulf region's structural features and outstanding problems, both of which bode ill for stability. The region is fundamentally multipolar and "open-ended," the internal balance of power is changing rapidly, the involvement of external powers is unpredictable, most of the states in the region are internally unstable, and there are several outstanding territorial and other problems that might trigger a war. The author further looks at one particularly disturbing aspect of these problems, namely regional arms acquisitions, which exhibit most of the characteristics associated with a full-fledged arms race.

As a possible solution to these problems, the author looks at the concepts of common and cooperative security that are based on a realization that states cannot achieve lasting security at the expense of each other. While acknowledging that these concepts are profoundly political, the author nevertheless focuses on the military implications, the concept of defensive restructuring of the armed forces. Ideally, each state in a region should be capable of defending itself against the others, but incapable of attacking its neighbors. As a way to achieve this goal, the author argues in favor of a combination of indigenous efforts at strengthening defensive capabilities, a region-wide arms control process and an "arms transfer restraint regime."

Water Scarcity and Security Concerns in the Middle East
Mary E. Morris EOP14 (1998)

Water is the most precious resource in the Middle East, with water ownership, management and use among the most difficult and serious problems. The basic issue is two-dimensional; increasing scarcity of water exacerbates inter-state disputes while at the same time governments face increasing internal demands from various sectors. Geographic reality and issues of politics, culture, religion and tradition complicate an already difficult situation. Competition for non-saline water factors into many regional political controversies as well.

As regional domestic, agricultural and industrial water demands grow, finite supplies are pushed to the limit, contributing to a variety of environmental distresses and increasing the potential for regional tensions. Morris argues that the resolution of existing and potential water conflicts will depend on three critical factors: the management of population growth and distribution, interstate cooperation on international water systems, and the reduction of regional political tensions that impede cooperative efforts. While water conflicts may not cause wars, they may prevent an enduring peace and put at risk a secure future for the inhabitants of the Middle East.

International Aid, Regional Politics, and the Kurdish Issue in Iraq after the Gulf War
Denise Natali EOP31 (1999)

The intra-Kurdish conflicts that brought down the first Iraqi Kurdish government in 1994 and which cause continual fighting among Kurds are a function of transformation in the political context. These transformations are not necessarily explained as part of tribal politics. Rather, the post-Gulf War climate witnessed structural changes caused by massive refugee flows, international and internal sanctions, and the rise of the lucrative petroleum smuggling market. Iraqi Kurdistan became a *de facto* autonomous region and the Kurds became tied to the international relief and security communities. There was no longer one official state apparatus, but various political centers employing different strategies to appeal to Kurdish elites. External policies favored or appeared to favor some political parties over others depending on the regional alliances they maintained. Lacking an institutionalized political-economic system, the Kurdish government could not withstand the internal instability that shook its fragile foundation. Given the instrumental behavior of political elites, Kurdish leaders profited from this situation by aggrandizing their own power, rather than instilling a sense of Kurdish unity in the government.

Network-Building, Ethnicity and Violence in Turkey
Hamit Bozarslan EOP33 (1999)

In a 1996 car accident near the Turkish town of Susurluk, a radical-right militant was killed together with his second wife and a high-ranking member of the police. Sedat Bucak, a deputy and head of a Kurdish tribe survived. The testimonies of the passengers revealed that they were part of a "gang" composed of members of the security forces, politicians and radical-right militants.

This data has prompted new perspectives on the comprehension of Turkish political life and the state coercion and civil violence which have dominated it for the past decades. They also shed new light on the country's ethnic relations, disclosing the link between ethnicity and violence and, at the same time, revealing the limits of ethnicity as the sole criterion of network-building or policy-making.

This monograph explores the network-building process in Turkey. It puts into question "state-based" sociology. Bozarslan suggests that the reproduction of networks in the Middle East is dependent on the ability to expand and transfer the senses and mechanisms of solidarity from a narrow framework to wider power-structures.

Iraqi Propaganda and Disinformation During the Gulf War: Lessons for the Future
Todd Leventhal EOP36 (1999)

This monograph examines Iraqi disinformation and propaganda from Iraq's invasion of Kuwait in August 1990 through the end of the Gulf War in February 1991. Although these events occurred at the beginning of the 1990s, they remain relevant because the fundamental nature of the Iraqi regime has not changed, and renewed confrontation or conflict remain ever-present possibilities, as is evidenced by the December 1998 US/UK four-day bombing campaign against Iraq. The harsh glare of war throws the actions of states as well as individuals into stark relief. War demands an all-out effort that sweeps away niceties and illuminates what may have previously remained hidden. Policies, practices and people reveal themselves *in extremis*. The Iraqi propaganda and disinformation efforts from their invasion of Kuwait in 1990 to their expulsion in 1991 were extensive, sustained, professional and, in many respects, quite effective. This is not to say that some of Saddam Hussein's propaganda stunts did not backfire. Moreover, misconceptions about what really transpired in several key events still linger, despite the passage of time. Leventhal examines these areas so that countries which may need to counter future Iraqi propaganda and disinformation will have a complete picture of the gambits they may face in the future and the methods necessary to counter them effectively.

Iran, between the Gulf and the Caspian Basin: Strategic and Economic Implications
Shireen T. Hunter EOP38 (2000)

With its strategic and sensitive location between the Gulf and the Caspian Sea, Iran has the undeniable potential to become a major regional player, both in political and economic terms. However, the country has failed to capitalize on this situation and, on the contrary, has suffered considerably from the systemic and geopolitical shifts generated by the collapse of the Soviet Union, primarily because of its failure to adapt to the harsh realities of the post-Cold War scenario. This study analyzes the strengths and weaknesses stemming from Iran's unique location and how the ideological residue of the Islamic Revolution and national policies have resulted in diplomatic and regional isolation. It surveys Tehran's post-Cold War relationships with its neighbors, particularly the Arab Gulf states, the former Soviet Union, Turkey, Pakistan and Afghanistan.

As a country with one of the longest borders with the Soviet Union, the collapse of that country meant the loss of a potential source of financial and technological help. The end of a bipolar world, resulting in the international ascendancy of the West and its enhanced ability to act unilaterally, has caused a corresponding decline in the importance of states like Iran which had more or less hostile relations with the West. The emergence of six new fragile states in place of the former Soviet Union has confronted Iran with potential new economic adversaries and sources of instability in its vicinity.

What are the main causes behind Iran's failure to adapt to the post-Soviet system? Can Iran rectify its past mistakes and counter the negative fallout from the end of the Cold War? Or are its political and economic problems too deeply embedded in its structure to allow it to make the necessary adjustments for a change of direction? Ideological differences within the leadership, together with an ongoing struggle between moderates and hard-liners, has created a complex and fluid domestic situation, despite the gains by the former faction in the Majlis elections of February 2000. According to Hunter, Iran's greatest challenge in the coming years will be to resolve its internal dichotomies and power struggles, improve its deteriorating security environment, and facilitate its eventual reintegration into the international community.

Turkish–Israeli Relations: From the Periphery to the Center
Philip Robins EOP41 (2001)

Israeli–Turkish relations underwent a profound transformation during the 1990s. Since 1996, in particular, the relationship has been widely perceived as exclusively focused on security ties. This aspect of the relationship has adversely affected the regional power balance and undermined stability. This study offers insight on the dynamics of this change, first by tracing the development of Turkish–Israeli relations from the 1980s. Thereafter, an analysis is made of the underlying reasons for the dramatic change in bilateral relations from 1996 onwards and how the two sides have conducted themselves in the aftermath. Finally, the study assesses the prospects for the future development of Turkish–Israeli ties in the light of governmental and personnel changes on both sides. Robins argues that the Israeli–Turkish relationship was a broad-based one that stirred little regional criticism until three defense agreements were signed in 1996. The Turkish military and the Israeli defense establishment have been largely responsible for the transformation in ties. While the Turkish armed forces have been driven by factors relating to domestic identity, the Israelis have the large Turkish arms market uppermost in mind. The study concludes that while the relationship is not unassailable and may be affected by contingencies, it seems likely to endure as part of the Middle East political scenario for years to come.

Iranian Security Policies at the Crossroads?
Peter Jones EOP50 (2003)

The so-called reformers and conservatives in Iran are not unified forces. The struggle between them has also been played out against the backdrop of some consensus positions between most reformers and most conservatives, especially on the need for internal stability. However, a more confrontational phase in the relationship may be emerging. It will be difficult for the reformers to wrest power away from the conservatives.

Round-Table Discussion on Gulf Security
H.R.H. General Khaled bin Sultan bin Abdul Aziz Al-Saud ELS11 (1998)

Situated between East and West, the Gulf region controls important naval and land routes linking Asia, Africa and Europe and thus, historically, has been the locus of conflicting international powers seeking to ensure their own interests by exploiting the Gulf's strategic location. In addition to the Strait of Hormuz being a vital outlet for the transport of oil, a number of islands and smaller bays, which are ideal locations to build military bases, have also added strategic importance to the Gulf states. The author presents proposals which he believes would help GCC members to reach a consensus on core security interests and offers a number of recommendations and guidelines with regard to developing a stable and secure regional and international system.

H.R.H. General Khaled is a graduate of the Royal Military Academy, Sandhurst. During the 1990–91 Gulf War, he was the Commander of the Joint Forces and Theater of Operations.

The New World Order
Mikhail Gorbachev ELS15 (1998)

Since the end of the Cold War, international relations have entered a new dimension; a plethora of complicated issues and unforeseen difficulties have arisen, related foremost to the rise in national, ethnic and racial conflicts in various regions around the globe. This paper argues that a new world order is required if problems associated with the environment, demographics and nuclear proliferation are to be resolved successfully.

Gorbachev proposes that nations work towards a global partnership that can swiftly and adequately react and respond to the requirements of an ever-changing world, as well as strike a balance between the interests of countries and peoples while maintaining stable conditions for the world's general development.

Iran, Iraq and Turkey: Strategic Impact on Gulf Security
Ahmed Shikara ELS34 (2001)

Iran, Iraq and Turkey are key actors in Middle East and Gulf security. Their individual strategies in this respect are affected by the dynamics of their internal politics and by the changeable balance of power between them. A brief overview of the security situation of the three countries reveals that they are strongly, albeit not entirely, focused on internal and cross-border sources of threat. Yet, it is evident that all three countries consider the Gulf in particular as strategically important from a political, security and economic perspective. Despite this, the intricacy of the internal and the regional dynamics that influence the foreign policies of Iran, Iraq and Turkey result in a fluid policy environment with respect to the Middle East. This is compounded by the interests of the international community in the strategic energy value of the Gulf. It is within this variable and complex environment that a viable framework for a system of Middle East and Gulf security needs to be found. Such a system of security is not only important for the Middle East and the Gulf. Since the Gulf has enormous strategic energy implications for the broader international community, stability in the region acquires broader global significance.

Iraq: Reconstruction and Future Role
ISBN: 9948-00-639-9 (hb) 9948-00-638-0 (pb) (2004)

While the legitimacy of the 2003 war in Iraq remains open to question, attention has shifted from the debates in the international arena to developments inside Iraq itself. This volume looks at Iraqi political factions, Iraq–US relations, an evaluation of the reconstruction effort, developments in the oil sector and the potential impact of a predominantly Shia Iraq on its neighbors, particularly the Arab Gulf states.

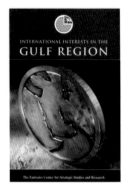

International Interests in the Gulf Region
ISBN: 9948-00-659-3 (hb) 9948-00-658-5 (pb) (2004)

Major powers have long pursued their interests in the Arabian Gulf region, and particularly since the discovery of oil. By virtue of their power and influence in world affairs and in international forums, the interests in the Arabian Gulf region of Russia, France, Germany, the United States and Britain are especially notable. This volume considers the various interests of these states in security, energy, social development, commerce and trade, as well as in the war against international terrorism.

The Gulf: Challenges Of The Future
ISBN: 9948-00-705-0 (hb) 9948-00-704-2 (pb) (2005)

Through history, the Arabian Gulf has always commanded a strategic and positive significance whether as a hub of world trade or as a major supplier of the world's energy. However, since 2001, the entire Middle East, including the Gulf region has come under negative scrutiny as a potential battleground in the unrelenting war against terrorism. After 2003, the region has been exposed to new vulnerabilities stemming from the divisive and deadly war in Iraq. Against this disturbing backdrop, the Gulf region must deal with diverse challenges: the deteriorating regional security environment, the sweeping effects of globalization, the diversification of oil-dependent economies, the transition to knowledge-based economies, burgeoning population levels, rising demand for job-creation, externally induced reform pressures and widening political participation.

Influential policy makers, regional leaders, respected scholars and experienced analysts who gathered at the Ninth Annual Conference of The Emirates Center for Strategic Studies and Research, held from January 11–13, 2004, in Abu Dhabi, focused on the subject of The Gulf: Challenges of the Future. In identifying major hurdles to political, economic and social development, they also pinpointed effective ways to surmount these difficulties through new and existing frameworks. Collectively, these conference presentations offer insight on: shifting security parameters; redefining of government responsibilities; initiating political and social change; evolving media roles and responsibilities; and expanding opportunities for women in the Gulf. Particular sections assess the security situations in Iraq and Iran and their wider implications, while sketching the prospects for greater security cooperation and economic integration in the Gulf region.

Formation of the Iraqi Political System: Role of the GCC
James Russell ELS46 (2003)

Regime change in Baghdad represents the dawn of a new era in the Gulf in which the friction of an unfolding transition process will affect all the countries in the region, if not the entire international community. Although this friction will perhaps be felt most acutely in the Gulf Cooperation Council (GCC) countries, as neighbors of Iraq, it is safe to say that the impact of the coming transition throughout the Gulf will be felt in capitals and financial markets around the world. It remains unclear, of course, just what the effects of the region's transition will be and the impact that a newly reconfigured Iraq will have on this process. All that can really be said is that future relationships and patterns of behavior in the Gulf will be different from what they were in the past.

US–Iran Relations: Looking Back and Looking Ahead
Flynt Leverett ELS47 (2003)

The US–Iran relationship is one of the most important variables affecting the strategic environment of the Arabian Gulf region. Since the war to unseat Saddam Hussein, policy toward Iran has risen rapidly to a prominent place on America's foreign policy agenda. On the Iranian side, the question of the Islamic Republic's relations with the United States has become the most important foreign policy issue for Tehran and a central issue in Iran's internal political drama. The status and future course of US–Iran relations are also very much on the minds of people in the Arab states of the Gulf region. For all of these reasons, it is timely indeed to consider the factors shaping this very important bilateral relationship

US Intelligence after September 11: Closing the Gaps
Ellen Laipson ELS48 (2003)

The terrorist attacks on the United States, the pervasive feeling of national crisis and failed warnings, followed by the Bush Administration's decisions to go to war against Al Qaida and the Taliban in 2001 and against Iraq in 2003, create a compelling new context in which to review US intelligence, its strengths and weaknesses, and the many ideas of how to reform or change the complex set of agencies and offices that comprise it.

The US War on Iraq: Regional Strategic Implications
Ahmad Shikara ELS50 (2004)

The Iraq situation has to be resolved on two important levels. On the domestic level the internal differences and the increasing divisions within Iraq have to be settled peacefully. It is hoped that the new regime will place more emphasis on the idea of national integration and on applying genuine democratic transparent federalism for all sections of the population. On the external level, American involvement in Iraqi affairs may create further problems for Iraq and its neighbors, if not properly managed. To avert this, the new regime needs to construct a united political and constitutional system and not become subservient to the occupying forces of the United States and Britain.

Furthermore, any failure to guarantee Iraqi territorial sovereignty and unity will exacerbate the regional situation. The reordering of the Middle East map according to US interests may generate unforeseen problems in the short or the long term, particularly if handled without any positive input from the regional players.

Conflict Resolution in the Post-Cold War World: Implications for Iraq
Gen. Sir Michael Rose ELS53 (2004)

Although US foreign policy is still based on the desire to secure freedom, justice and democracy for all people – a vision which is shared by most Western nations – following the attacks against US targets on September 11, 2001, President Bush declared that the elimination of international terrorism had become a top priority for America. However, a determination to use military force in order to defend these values and pre-empt attack against America has inevitably altered its relationship with other nations.

Australia's Strategic Involvement in the Middle East: An Overview
Dr. David Horner ELS56 (2004)

It is perhaps not realized that Australia has a very long history of strategic interest and engagement in the Middle East. It is a record of sustained involvement and considerable commitment. Australia comes as a friend and peacemaker, and with no local ambitions. Australia has much to offer the Gulf states in the field of military cooperation. Coupled with Australia's growing trade with the region, it seems likely that Australia's strategic interest and engagement with the region will expand over the following years.

International Terrorism: Drivers, Trends and Prospects
Michael Hough EOP56 (2004)

Some of the main trends in current international terrorism are: the emergence of individuals who do not work for any established terrorist organization and are not sponsored by any state; a growing lethality and tendency towards indiscriminate attacks in public places; and an increasing terrorist use of information technology for purposes of communication, coordination and propaganda. There is a tendency, in some instances, to deny responsibility or less frequently claim responsibility for attacks. Trained people are planted close to their targets for some time, even though amateurs are at times involved. In addition, the attack is launched on the territory of a third party with little or no connection to the dispute in question. Religion became an increasingly important motivation of terrorism in the 1990s, instead of ideological motivations like Marxism. A third of all terrorist groups that are currently active are deemed to be religiously motivated. Ethnic separatism accounted for about 37 percent of all international terrorist acts in the mid-1990s.

In some cases terrorism and crime are linked as a method to obtain funds. A more recent trend points to an increase in suicide bombings, especially in the case of Palestinian groups and Chechnyan rebels. They are often viewed as martyrdom operations, and terror groups realize that it is difficult to prevent suicide attacks. In the wake of the September 11 incidents it has been stated that this may well be an attractive model for future terrorism.

Some of the characteristics of contemporary terrorism are of course likely to continue in the future, for example less restraint, less centralized organization and individuals acting on their own. Similarly, the dominance of religious and ethnic motives, combined with nationalism, seem set to continue. Thus, future trend analysis largely seems to focus on new weapons and new technology, as well as on diversification of targets.

The current focus on al-Qaida often neglects the fact that there are many other groups who are also involved in international terror, whether they have links with al-Qaida or not. It is clear that the September 11 attacks in the US have set a precedent for other al-Qaida operatives and for other terrorist organizations. The demonstrative effect of the September 11 incidents and the increasing trend towards suicide bombings, often viewed as martyrdom operations by the perpetrators, may be some of the most dangerous threats currently posed by international terrorism. In this sense international terrorism has certainly become more "transnational" in nature, with seemingly greater cooperation among certain groups, the wide geographical scope of operations linked to al-Qaida, and the concept of a global jihad, with the US as the prime target.

Gulf Security and Regional Watercourse Management: Implications for the UAE
Bertrand Charrier ELS57 (2005)

Many long-standing water-related disputes remain unresolved, and the growing demand for finite freshwater resources heightens the possibility of conflicts over the issue. Green Cross International and the United Nations Educational, Scientific, and Cultural Organization (UNESCO) joined forces in 2001 by launching a program on "From Potential Conflict to Cooperation Potential: Water for Peace," the aim of which is to promote peace in the use of trans-boundary watercourses. In the Tigris-Euphrates river basin – shared by Turkey, Syria, Iran, Iraq and the mouth of the Gulf – surface and ground water resources are becoming catalysts of tension and conflict. Political decision-makers should tackle this issue by employing trans-boundary water management in order to avoid conflicts over water.

Meeting Iran's Nuclear Challenge
Gary Samore ELS60 (2005)

Although Iran's secret nuclear fuel cycle program began as early as 1985, the full extent of the program was not publicly disclosed until 2002. To avoid referral of its file to the Security Council, Iran reached an agreement with the EU-3 (the United Kingdom, France and Germany) in October 2003 to resolve its past safeguards violations, and accept more intrusive IAEA inspections. In return, the Europeans agreed to counter US efforts to refer Iran to the Security Council. However, by early 2004 an emboldened Iran began to renege on the October 2003 agreement. The EU-3 responded by threatening to refer Iran to the UN Security Council. As a result, a new agreement was reached in November 2004. A key factor in determining the success or failure of EU-3/Iran talks will be whether the US is prepared to endorse and support an agreement between them.

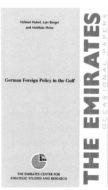

German Foreign Policy in the Gulf
Helmut Hubel, Lars Berger and Matthias Heise EOP58 (2005)

For analytical purposes, German and European policies towards Iran, Iraq and the GCC countries have to be investigated separately. Regarding Iran, the European consensus on the need to engage the Iranian leaderships has enabled Germany to pursue political cooperation and economic ties. Yet, it remains doubtful whether the recent British-French-German initiative concerning international safeguards on Iranís nuclear program will be successful. Concerning the war in Iraq, it is for the first time that the Federal Republic openly disagreed with the US on a matter of war and peace. With regard to the relations with the GCC countries, the strong US military presence will continue to put limits on the level of Germanyís and the EUís influence. On the other hand, the significant impact the Gulfís oil resources have on the global energy market, Germanyís economic well-being will ensure its continuing interest in the region.

The Three Occupied UAE Islands: The Tunbs and Abu Musa
ISBN: 9948-00-765-4 (hb) 9948-00-764-6 (pb) (2006)

Unresolved territorial disputes have historically raised tensions between nations, often leading to regional destabilization and international repercussions. The issue of the three occupied UAE islands – the Greater and Lesser Tunbs and Abu Musa – deserves particular attention because it threatens to undermine regional security and has potential global implications. Given the commanding position of the islands over the major shipping lanes of the Arabian Gulf and their strategic location in the vicinity of important offshore oilfields, the continuing Iranian occupation of these key islands is undoubtedly a matter of international concern.

By documenting the historical record and examining the relevant international precedents, this comprehensive study highlights and reinforces the legal and sovereign rights of the United Arab Emirates over the three islands. The study is supported by extensive and meticulous research based on both primary and secondary sources: declassified British and US archival records and original historical documents, relevant legal studies, memoirs of important personalities, interviews with key players and analysis by political commentators.

In keeping with the UAE's policy of seeking a just and peaceful resolution to this dispute, this book aims to promote a better understanding of its complexities by offering fresh insight on the historical, political, legal, regional and international dimensions of the islands issue for the benefit of policy makers, academics, researchers and decision makers-concerned with the future security and stability of the Gulf region.

SECURITY AND TECHNOLOGY

Air/Missile Defense, Counterproliferation and Security Policy Planning

Jacquelyn Davis, Charles Perry, Jamal S. Al-Suwaidi (eds.)
ISBN: 1-86064-491-0 (hb) 1-86064-492-9 (pb) (1999)

The Arabian Gulf, widely identified as one of the world's most volatile regions, continues to face security challenges emanating from different quarters which need to be addressed by collective security arrangements. This book studies the implications for defense collaboration between the US and GCC countries. It examines regional threat scenarios, studies proliferation trends endangering the area and assesses the effect of these on the regional balance of power. It highlights the options available for countering security threats and discusses issues crucial to enhancing cooperation and collaboration on regional air and missile defense.

While underlining the dangers of the global and regional proliferation of missiles and weapons of mass destruction, the book outlines effective political and military strategies to combat such threats and explores existing and emerging technology and systems that can protect civilian populations, key infrastructure and strategic installations. The benefits and constraints of regional defense collaboration are assessed, covering aspects such as shared early warning systems, integrated battle management, joint command and control systems, collaborative intelligence operations and interoperability requirements.

Information Warfare: Concepts, Boundaries and Employment Strategies
Joseph Moynihan EOP7 (1997)

Joseph Moynihan examines the emerging Information Warfare (IW) capabilities of the United States' defense and security estates and provides a framework for the conceptual boundaries of these much-debated methodologies. The author specifically relates the tactics and techniques of IW to more traditional forms of military employment and notes its current "force multiplier" doctrinal relevance to those who command military forces. Information Warfare processes and procedures are operationally defined in terms of their relevance to the family of products and services known to the warfighter as C4I (Command, Control, Communications, Computer and Intelligence) and the potential usefulness of IW capabilities in terms of the admittedly situational strategy of "control" or compellance (significantly reducing the ability of an opposing force to engage in military activity) is addressed. Moynihan concludes with a section discussing the implications of IW capabilities for national and regional security decision-makers.

Power, Information and War
Dan Caldwell EOP15 (1998)
Caldwell focuses primarily on the application of information in the politico-military arena, although many of the findings are relevant to other areas as well. The study has four central objectives: to demonstrate that information is a vital element of power; to review several historical cases of the strategic use of information; to describe the contemporary information revolution and the capabilities that it makes available to decision-makers; and to suggest ways in which decision-makers can take advantage of information in order to maximize individual, corporate and/or national power.

International Arms Transfers and the Middle East
Ian Anthony and Peter Jones EOP21 (1998)
The end of the Cold War and the relentless pace of technological change are altering the patterns of international arms transfers. For a number of economic and technological reasons, the US is becoming increasingly dominant, particularly with respect to the very highest military capabilities which these technologies promise, though this will not be without dislocations for the Israeli military and society. Other countries such as Iran, Iraq and Saudi Arabia may acquire some additional conventional capabilities, but they are not likely to be decisive in relation to Israel, though they could increase tensions associated with other disputes in the region. Finally, in the absence of progress towards a resolution of the Arab-Israeli and other regional disputes, Israel's increasing technological edge is likely to boost the efforts of some countries to explore asymmetric responses such as acquiring non-conventional weapons or resorting to terrorism.

The Role of Space-based Surveillance in Gulf Security
Bhupendra Jasani and Andrew Rathmell EOP29 (1998)
The rapidly improving quality and availability of commercial satellite imagery will soon enable any state to collect detailed and comprehensive imagery intelligence on its neighbors. If harnessed into multinational bodies such as regional satellite monitoring agencies, this capability can be used positively to promote transparency and confidence-building measures. The Middle East as a whole, and the Gulf in particular, currently lacks an effective confidence-building regime and the means to promote greater transparency. In the Middle East, the multilateral Arms Control and Regional Security talks have stalled, while in the Gulf no stable security system has been established since the end of the 1991 Gulf War. Instead, the US-led policy of dual containment is extending a temporary security umbrella over a fundamentally unstable region. There is a pressing need for enhanced security cooperation and for the construction of a more inclusive, intra-regional cooperative security regime. This must include confidence-building measures and transparency as initial steps. This paper makes the case for the establishment of a Gulf Satellite Center which, run on a multilateral basis and using commercially available imagery and techniques, could have a dramatic effect in improving intra-regional transparency. The satellite center could be modeled on the Western European Union's Satellite Center and would have similar roles, including arms control verification, crisis monitoring and environmental monitoring. It could also assist in border security and maritime policing tasks.

SECURITY AND WEAPONS OF MASS DESTRUCTION

Integrated Middle East Regional Approaches to Unconventional Arms Control and Disarmament
Laura Drake EOP32 (1999)

The topic of biological weapons and the issues of arms control and disarmament are addressed in Middle East regional perspective. The different approaches to unconventional and mixed arms control are considered in terms of how they affect the national interests of regional states, and how they are most likely to appear as increasing rather than diminishing security. The US–USSR nuclear arms control effort during the Cold War is advocated as a process model for the Middle East. It provides a way to disarm the most heavily-armed regional powers of their most dangerous weapons without damaging their respective national interests. The further recommendation to marry the US–USSR arms control negotiation model to the Middle East theater and its long history of negotiated military agreements, beginning with the Arab-Israeli armistice agreements in 1948–49, contains the additional benefit of separating the military requirements of arms control from the political shackles of a declining Middle East peace process.

The Strategic Implications of Biological and Chemical Weapons on Gulf Security
Kamal A. Beyoghlow ELS24 (1999)

The characteristics and complexities surrounding the deployment of chemical and biological weapons are outlined in this study, which assesses the strategic impact of such weapons in undermining Gulf security. In isolation, such weapons are unlikely to tilt the balance of terror in the region, but in conjunction with nuclear weapons capability, these can provide awesome leverage to regional players like Iraq, Iran, Israel, Pakistan and India. The prospect of the regional proliferation of these weapons is also analyzed in the study, which tackles several key issues, including their impact on civilian and military targets. It also details the kind of defensive mechanisms needed for protection against possible covert attacks from non-state actors or groups. While highlighting the growing threat from missile technology and other devices, the study focuses on the need for effective non-proliferation and counter-proliferation measures by the Gulf countries. In the context of global advances in information technology, nuclear, chemical and biological weapons are likely to evolve increasingly as destabilizing factors in the Gulf area. Therefore, confidence-building measures are essential and the study advocates a nuclear, biological and chemical weapon-free zone in the Gulf to reduce regional tensions. It also recommends inter-state cooperation at the GCC level and inter-agency coordination at the domestic level to build a cohesive and collective system of defense against potential nuclear, biological and chemical attacks.

The Peaceful Use of Nuclear Energy: The Contribution of the IAEA
Mohamed ElBaradei ELS43 (2003)

The International Atomic Energy Agency (IAEA) is dedicated to the prevention of nuclear arms proliferation and the sharing of safe nuclear technologies. Its verification mandate relates to the compliance of state parties to the Treaty on the Non-Proliferation of Nuclear Weapons (NPT). The IAEA is now able to provide more credible assurance about the use of declared nuclear material and the absence of undeclared material.

SOCIAL/POLITICAL DEVELOPMENT AND THE UAE

WITH UNITED STRENGTH
H.H. Shaikh Zayid Bin Sultan Al Nahyan
The Leader and the Nation
ISBN: 9948-00-400-0 (hb) 9948-00-401-9 (sd)
(2004)

Visionary statesmen who have created an enduring state edifice through purposeful consensus and persuasion remain a historical rarity. The formation of the United Arab Emirates on December 2, 1971 under the inspiring leadership of its late founding father, Shaikh Zayid Bin Sultan Al Nahyan (may Allah have mercy on him) is a living example of nation building that has earned its founder his rightful place among the outstanding statesmen of all time.

Against the backdrop of the British withdrawal from the Arabian Gulf region, it was His Highness Shaikh Zayid who accomplished the complex task of unifying the erstwhile Trucial States, creating the only thriving federal state in the Middle East. While fulfilling his personal destiny as the chosen leader, His Highness Shaikh Zayid strengthened the nation by uniting disparate tribal groups and sustained it against formidable challenges. He pioneered the modernization of the country and ultimately realized his dream of an effective framework for collaboration with neighboring Gulf states. The UAE has since become a constructive force within the region and beyond, exemplifying the principles of national unity, regional solidarity, international cooperation, and religious tolerance.

This book adopts a scholarly approach in analyzing the UAE's unique federal experience, its phenomenal achievements and His Highness Shaikh Zayid's far-sighted policies. It is an in-depth study of the birth of a progressive nation and the pivotal role of its leader, based largely on unpublished historical records and documents. The factual foundation of the book and its meticulous documentation make it a valuable record covering an important era in the contemporary history of the Arab Gulf region.

Dialectical Integration in the Gulf Co-operation Council
Fred H. Lawson EOP10 (1997)

Lawson explores the dynamics that have characterized regional integration among the smaller Arab Gulf countries. He begins by assessing two conventional ways to account for the comparatively high degree of integration that has emerged among the GCC states over the last two decades. These arguments (which may be labeled structural and historical institutionalist) were originally formulated to explain trends in western Europe, but provide insight into the causes and concomitants of integration in other regions of the world. Lawson then proposes a more satisfactory alternative explanation for the shape that regionalism has taken in the contemporary Gulf. This perspective, inspired by recent work that highlights the importance of gauging the unintended consequences of interactions among sovereign states, not only offers an innovative way to explain the origins and developmental trajectory of the GCC, but also sheds light on the sources of multilateralism in other parts of the globe.

The United Arab Emirates: Nationalism and Arab-Islamic Identity
Sally Findlow EOP39 (2000)

Concepts of identity vary widely within the Islamic world and among Arab countries in general. Although this diversity is widely recognized, much of the recent discussion on modern Muslim identity has been focused on narrow images. However, the manner in which the national identity of the UAE federation has emerged illustrates the drawbacks of such restricted definitions. Emirati concepts of self and national identity defy the vague but monolithic pictures of modern Muslim identity often described in Islamic studies literature, or in the global media. Since its federation in 1971, the UAE has evolved into a progressive Arab-Islamic nation with unique characteristics that challenge prevalent theories pertaining to modern Muslim identity and nation-building. While contributing substantially to the quest for pan-Islamic and pan-Arab unity, the country has succeeded in building up a national image and consciousness that is distinct from these commitments. The UAE has also evolved its own solutions to the challenges of globalization and indigenization. This modern, Muslim, Gulf Arab nation-state retains strong elements of traditional conservatism while embracing technological sophistication. It is receptive to outside knowledge while endeavoring simultaneously to preserve its indigenous cultural authenticity. With a social infrastructure largely dependent upon natural wealth, the country also invests vigorously in industrial development, as well as individual and corporate enterprise.

This study examines the extent to which general observations on modern religious and national identities correspond to the UAE's collective identity. Surveys were conducted to find out empirically the impact of various identity components (shared religion, shared language, regionalism, pan-Arabism etc.). It concludes that the collective identity of the modern UAE is a positive, cohesive force, which generally does not rely on the antithetical model that appears to characterize many modern cultural and nationalist movements.

The Arab Gulf States: Old Approaches and New Realities
Abdulkhaleq Abdulla EOP40 (2000)

The six Arab Gulf States (AGS), comprising Bahrain, Kuwait, Oman, Qatar, Saudi Arabia and the UAE are universally recognized as a distinct group with particular socio-economic features, regional concerns and political priorities that are relatively independent of the rest of the Arab world. More importantly, these states have acquired over the last 30 years a unique international prominence. However, despite their global significance, the AGS are little, or even grossly misunderstood by the outside world.

The central purpose of this analysis is to provide answers to some key questions such as: Why is it important to study the AGS? How do we best approach and analyze them? What are their unique characteristics? How did they acquire such an imposing strategic value? The author discusses, among other aspects, three compelling reasons and three different approaches to assess the AGS. The study examines the changing national, regional and international developments affecting these states and the rationale behind their strategic and economic importance, concluding that the conventional oil-dominated approaches to the AGS do not adequately reflect their individual complexities and current realities.

Health Development in the United Arab Emirates from a Global Perspective
Hans Rosling ELS23 (1999)

The UAE has seen phenomenal improvement in health development over the last four decades. The country has registered a quantum leap from the dismal situation in the 1960s when it was counted among the ten countries with the highest child mortality rates. Today, the health of its population, as measured by the child mortality rate, ranks among the most healthy billion of the world population and is comparable to levels in Western Europe and the US. This dramatic progress, which is the fastest ever recorded in the history of mankind, is attributable not only to the country's rapid economic development, but also to the judicious allocation of national resources, the universal provision of basic amenities such as housing, water and food supplies, the high educational levels of women and the good quality of health services, which include preventive and curative primary health care as well as advanced referral services.

The health transition in the UAE has been unique and is reflected in the changes in disease patterns. The low incidence of alcohol and drug abuse and the low occurrence of AIDS are noteworthy factors. While many diseases have decreased to almost zero level, others which were formerly rare have increased in incidence. This health transition is also associated with a fall in fertility rates and one of the lowest proportion of elderly citizens in the world. In combination, these factors have resulted in a dramatic change in the age composition of the population. Taking into account the steady growth in the proportion of the elderly and the possibility of higher occurrence of chronic diseases in the middle-aged population, the per capita cost of health care is likely to increase. The main challenge confronting the country's health sector will be to maintain the present high quality of health services despite these negative trends.

The United Arab Emirates: Dynamics of State Formation
John Duke Anthony ELS35 (2002)

The tale of the UAE's birth is an inspiring account of how the constituent polities were able to achieve unity despite a historical backdrop of failed Arab confederal experiments. Two distinctive attributes marked the birth and evolution of the United Arab Emirates: the non-violent process of its establishment and the nature of the agreements wrought by the member-states on how the union would function and responsibilities be apportioned, as well as what degree of autonomy would be retained by the constituent emirates. Undoubtedly, certain external factors facilitated the UAE's nation building, among which were a window of relative regional peace, the support of Great Britain for the process, and the desire of most of the emirates' neighbors for a successful outcome.

Equally as important as these and other factors were the personality and skills of one man who is credited with being the real unifying force behind the federation: the late founding father of the UAE, Sheikh Zayed bin Sultan Al Nahyan (may Allah have mercy on him).

Women, Education and Development in the Arab Gulf Countries
Ghada Hashem Talhami EOP53 (2004)

Women's education only became an element of modernization when the Gulf countries experienced the oil revolution. However, Gulf rulers launched a revolution of their own by developing modern social infrastructure, mostly before independence. Rulers in the region accepted the notion of women's education as a pre-requisite for development, and male elites wanted compatible educated partners.

However, women's integration in the labor market was another matter. The state had to contend with a common traditional culture, which was opposed to the mixing of the sexes or the diversion of women's energies away from domestic and maternal duties. Higher education, which was normally offered on a co-educational basis and sometimes meant study abroad, provoked opposition.

With the exception of Saudi Arabia, there are no legal barriers to integrating women in the economy on a large scale. However, there are cultural issues that work against women's employment, like the lack of incentive to work in a welfare system. The drive to end the dependence on foreign labor is often countered by the pro-birth policies of countries. Perhaps the greatest obstacle to advancing women's participation in the labor market has been their absence from advisory councils and parliaments. Thus, the world of political decision-making still seems closed to women, who must rely on the commitment and reformist zeal of some enlightened rulers.

Foreign Direct Investment in the UAE: Determinants and Recommendations
Sophia Qasrawi EOP57 (2004)

Foreign Direct Investment (FDI) in a country can mean the difference between wealth or poverty, growth or stagnation. A survey of 101 Transnational Corporations operating in the United Arab Emirates (UAE) aimed to provide insight on the incentives for foreign investors to operate and invest in the UAE business environment.

The findings suggest that the main reasons for their decisions to invest are, in a decreasing order of importance, political stability in the UAE and telecommunications (92 percent), the availability of banking services (87 percent), no tax (83 percent), regional potentially profitable operations (77 percent), the fact that English is spoken widely, and 100 percent repatriation of profits (75 percent).

The main disincentives or barriers to FDI are perceived to be, in decreasing order of importance, the limitation of 49 percent ownership on foreign investors (69 percent), regulations on the foreign ownership of real estate (57 percent), the UAE's agency law (34 percent), government red tape (33 percent), and government charges and fees (21 percent). Views on these disincentives are less strongly held, ranging from 69 to 21 percent of all respondents. However, a growing interest by global companies to expand their investment beyond national frontiers is being constrained by the above-mentioned factors. Other barriers mentioned by the respondents were the ambiguity of labor law, which incurs potential costs for foreign investors, and the limitation of three-year work permits granted to professionals, which deprives the UAE economy of some well-qualified people. Most respondents thought that a combination of two or more factors, not any single factor, was important as a barrier or disincentive to FDI in the UAE.

The following proposed FDI policy for the UAE was developed: Certain industries are recommended for the UAE: fashion, water sport, filming, marine products, pharmaceutical subsidiaries, maintenance, transport, cargo, temporary storage, manufacturing of cosmetics, tourism and leisure, financial support services (e.g. rating agencies), health care, hospitals, universities, electronics, construction consultancies, process engineering and telecommunications. A part of the oil sector should be made more competitive by opening it to participation by UAE nationals and not only to the UAE's government.

The government should preferably also waive the 51 percent limitation on ownership for related foreign investment projects, subject to the number of UAE employees, training provided and type of project; impose a flat rate of five to eight percent corporate tax at a national level and abolish the UAE offshore and onshore system; encourage transparency in labor law; provide longer or permanent visa permits for qualified professionals and foreign investors in the sectors recommended above, based on capital flow, project type or qualifications; focus on developing the specialization in specific skills among UAE nationals in order to offset the lack of endowment in human capital; issue longer-term work permits for skilled labor and other required categories; impose restrictions on work permits for unskilled labor; create a short-term marketing strategy aimed at promoting the UAE as an investment destination; prioritize the involvement of local elements in the activity of firms to promote backward linkages; and promulgate an investment law to regulate the relationship between foreign investors and the government.

US FOREIGN POLICY

Beyond Dual Containment
Kenneth Katzman EOP6 (1996)

Kenneth Katzman analyzes the "dual containment" policy of the US in terms of classic balance-of-power theory and looks at how this approach represents an integral part of American strategic thinking in the Gulf region. His thesis is that while dual containment might offer some improvement on previous US policy in the Gulf, it has severe limitations which cast doubt on its overall applicability. The policy is unlikely to significantly transform the security structure in the Gulf to the point that the region is intrinsically stable and no longer on the edge of perpetual crisis. An option that needs to be considered is a US-led multilateral peace initiative, involving the GCC states as well as Iran and Iraq. There are significant obstacles to such an initiative, but the author believes its pros and cons need to be openly and seriously considered, if the Gulf region is to attain a permanent security balance.

US Sanctions on Iran
Patrick Clawson EOP8 (1997)

Patrick Clawson examines US policy on sanctions against Iran. In particular, he analyzes the background and international reaction towards sanctions on the Islamic Republic, their economic and political impact, and the existence of alternative policies such as the European Union's "critical dialogue." The sharp divisions in opinion over sanctions both within the US and among its allies are closely considered. Clawson states that although sanctions have produced some modest results, they have come about at the price of strained inter-allied relations. Indeed, the disagreement between the US and the EU over the efficacy of engaging Iran in a "critical dialogue" is an example of this. Given the present domestic politics in both Iran and the US, Clawson does not foresee a significant breakthrough in relations between the two nations. He believes the US will maintain sanctions on Iran for the indefinite future, and that the current level of hostility between the two powers will endure. Even with the impact that US sanctions have had on the Iranian economy, the author remains unconvinced that Tehran has any intention of altering its policies.

The United States and the Gulf: Half a Century and Beyond
Joseph Wright Twinam EOP11 (1997)

Joseph Twinam's study offers a rare insight into US–Gulf relations. The paper covers America's involvement in the region from the arrival of American medical missionaries from the Dutch Reformed Church in the early part of the twentieth century, through Washington's early connections with Saudi Arabia in the 1950s, its association with the Shah in the 1960s and 1970s, the Iranian Revolution in 1978–79, to the Iran-Iraq war of the 1980s, and continues up to Desert Storm and the liberation of Kuwait in 1991.

In Twinam's opinion, American involvement with the Gulf should be viewed with mixed emotions. The development of US interests in and relations with GCC states has been truly remarkable. He illustrates this by highlighting America's long and successful economic and political ties with Saudi Arabia. But among the Arab Gulf littoral countries, only about a quarter of the people live in GCC states, while the overwhelming majority are in two countries with which Washington has wretched relations. As Twinam does not see any immediate change taking place regarding Washington's approach to either Baghdad or Tehran, a continued US presence in the region seems inevitable. The author concludes by stating that America's connection with the Gulf promises to be a challenging adventure which will endure well into the twenty-first century.

US Policy in the Gulf Region
Lincoln Bloomfield ELS4 (1997)

This lecture sheds light on American foreign policy in the Gulf region by surveying American–Gulf relations since World War II and, in particular, the fact that those relations have moved from cooperation to coalition since the Gulf War. Bloomfield stresses that President Clinton will continue to concentrate primarily on domestic issues in his second term. However, foreign policy, particularly Gulf security, is of utmost importance to the American administration, especially with the current threats posed by Iran and Iraq. He also stresses that regardless of who governs the US, Gulf security will remain an American priority. Bloomfield argues that the US should look forward, articulate a vision for Gulf security and help mobilize support for common objectives.

The 1998 United States Elections
Peter Gubser ELS20 (1999)

This lecture reviews the general political environment in the US and the major issues debated by candidates in the 1998 Congressional election, in addition to those running for State and local government offices. It presents an analysis of the mid-term election together with its outcomes and implications for US policies. The effects of the state of the economy, trade and investment, the end of the Cold War, the isolationist trend in foreign policy and the Lewinsky case are explored as factors relevant to the campaigns.

The United States and Iran: Analyzing the Structural Impediments to a Rapprochement
Robert S. Snyder ELS32 (2001)

The US and Iran have had hostile relations for over two decades, yet there are some signs of a thaw. What are the prospects for a reconciliation between the two states? Although Washington and Tehran are likely to improve relations, certain structural impediments will probably keep the two from embracing each other as friends any time soon. An analysis of the breakdown in relations between the US and a set of Third World revolutionary states (including Iran) found that these revolutionary states initiated conflicts with the US largely for domestic reasons, and the US deepened the antagonism because their foreign policies challenged Washington's Cold War interests. With respect to a current rapprochement between Tehran and Washington, domestic politics still prevent Iran from seeking friendly ties with the US, and Washington has likewise been hindered from changing its stance due to its rigid containment policies in the Gulf. This paper explores these structural impediments, focusing on Iran as a revolutionary state and the US as the lone superpower. For Iran, a reconciliation would challenge the regime's theocratic institutions. For the US, a rapprochement would require that Washington accept greater limits to its power in the Middle East.

Sailing Without an Anchor? Contemporary Determinants of US Policy in the Gulf
Clive Jones ELS33 (2001)

The end of the Cold War has brought US foreign policy under close scrutiny. The old tension between isolationism and internationalism that has always framed debates over foreign policy in Washington has found new expression in debates over unilateralism and multilateralism. Proponents of these two schools of thought seek to influence a hierarchy of values over what constitutes the "national interest." The debate offers interesting insights into determinants of US policy towards the Gulf. It is easy to define US interests in the Gulf; it is more difficult to identify the means or policies that may best serve to secure these interests. A marked reluctance to incur casualties among its military forces has implications for US influence in the Gulf region. When coupled with shifts in regional alliance patterns since the defeat of Iraq in 1991, the ability of Washington to present a credible security profile throughout the region has inevitably been impaired. The extent to which US policy towards Iran and Iraq has been influenced by domestic lobby groups, not least the pro-Israel lobby groups, has also undermined any rational analysis of Washington's interests and policy objectives in the region. Jones concludes that US policy towards the Gulf lacks a unity of purpose and clarity of thought that has left its strategy of dual containment struggling to adjust to changing alliance patterns throughout the region. With the demise of dual containment, and changing patterns of bilateral relations throughout the Gulf, Washington's policy in the region is in danger of 'sailing without an anchor.'

US Policy towards Iraq in the Aftermath of September 11
Gregory Gause ELS39 (2002)

Since the attacks of September 11, 2001, the Bush administration has reoriented American foreign policy toward the fight against terrorism. The Bush administration is also very determined to address the situation in Iraq.

US Policy Towards Political Islam
Graham E. Fuller ELS45 (2003)

Political Islam is growing and diversifying in the Middle East and Central Asia. Many Islamist parties now believe that Islam and democracy are compatible. Muslims may too readily blame the West for their own problems, but their frustrations and current grievances are real. Washington should not limit itself to a merely punitive agenda, but should engage in dialogue with Islamic clerics and representatives of moderate political forces in order to support regional democratization.

US Intelligence after September 11: Closing the Gaps
Ellen Laipson ELS48 (2004)

The terrorist attacks on the United States, the pervasive feeling of national crisis and failed warnings, followed by the Bush Administration's decisions to go to war against Al Qaida and the Taliban in 2001 and against Iraq in 2003, create a compelling new context in which to review US intelligence, its strengths and weaknesses, and the many ideas of how to reform or change the complex set of agencies and offices that comprise it.

The US War on Terrorism: Impact on US–Arab Relations
Mr. James Noyes ELS49 (2004)

The "war on terrorism" has had a dramatic impact on US – Arab relations. Some of the results are positive; many are negative, at least in the short term. The US has broken down doors to enter where it has not been invited. Washington seeks and in some cases demands levels of security cooperation that transcend traditional state-to-state relationships. Are these engagements bold and courageous or foolhardy and imperial as defined by critics both in America and abroad?

The initial phase of the war on terrorism has passed. Battle lines are clearer. America has had some early success, but progress in the battle for minds is less certain. Many Arab countries, locked in this same battle, also have cause for introspection. The war on terrorism has certainly compelled the Arab world to look inwards more critically and to examine some difficult issues. All parties involved in the war on terrorism should look inward and weigh the extent to which their actions are helping or hurting each other.

The Religious Right and US Middle East Policy
Josef Braml EOP59 (2005)

The Christian Right in the USA has developed considerable financial and organizational clout over the years. With George W. Bush's victory in 2000, for the first time, a Republican presidential victory rested on a religious, conservative, southern-centered coalition led by a bloc of white Protestant fundamentalists and Evangelical Christians. The election results in November 2004 confirmed this trend. Assuming that the fight against terror will continue for a long time, it is probable that the Christian Right will continue efforts to keep "existential" issues of national security, as well as moral and religious concerns, high on the political agenda. Both the Christian Right and neo-conservatives want to create a world in which the US and Israel can feel secure against forces portrayed as "evil." They can also count on support from pro-Israeli PACs, especially the influential American Israel Public Affairs Committee (AIPAC).

The Gulf and US National Security Strategy
Lawrence Korb ELS58 (2005)

No region of the world currently has a larger influence on US security strategy than the Arabian Gulf. The importance of Gulf oil and the struggle against terrorism and religious extremism guarantee the region a prominent place in American strategic planning. With the occupation of Iraq, the Gulf now hosts the largest concentration of American troops in the world, and the region will be central to American security strategy in the near future. The two most uncertain and far-reaching variables in the Gulf are the circumstances of its two strongest powers: Iran and Iraq. As long as energy and terrorism are at the top of the American security agenda and the United States remains the world s preeminent military power, the interests of the United States and the Gulf will be deeply intertwined, and this region will remain the focus of any national security strategy.

INTERNATIONAL PEACEKEEPING

NATO's Growing Role in the Greater Middle East
Philip Gordon

In August 1995, NATO intervened militarily for the first time in Bosnia. At the time, few could have envisaged that a decade later NATO would be deploying over 10,000 troops to Afghanistan, training Iraqi military forces in Baghdad and increasing its political and military cooperation with the Gulf Cooperation Council (GCC). As a region, the Greater Middle East is viewed by the West as an area of concern in terms of issues such as WMD proliferation; terrorism; interstate conflict; failed states; immigration; and civil war. Therefore, European and North American leaders and popula-

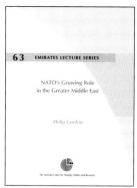

tions have a strong strategic self-interest in promoting security in the Greater Middle East. NATO has launched the Istanbul Cooperation Initiative (ICI), to expand dialogue and provide a forum for practical cooperation between NATO and the countries of the Gulf region. NATO began by offering ICI membership to the countries of the GCC. The offer was initially accepted by Bahrain, Qatar and Kuwait, while the UAE followed in June 2005. The story of NATO's involvement in the Greater Middle East over the past decade is one of increasing activity, which points to a potentially significant future role in the region. It would be naïve, however, to conclude that NATO's growing involvement in the region is a linear or irreversible trend. Many of the missions undertaken so far are quite limited in scope and have all led to serious controversy among NATO members. There is still no consensus within the Alliance on the precise role it should play in the Greater Middle East and on major challenges that must be met if NATO's role is to continue to grow.

Newsletters

In addition to the aforementioned work of the Publications Department, the Media Department at ECSSR publishes a number of bulletins and newsletters and plans to publish the Gulf Strategic Report. The newsletters, the daily *Akhbar Al-Sa'ah* and the bimonthly *Al-Nashra*, analyze important political, military and economic developments at domestic, regional and international levels and are usually addressed to senior UAE officials and diplomatic missions. The objective is to highlight current events that are of concern to the UAE and the region, and to interpret these events conceptually.

The Media Department is also in charge of the electronic archiving system for major Arab and international newspapers and magazines. The system comprises CD-ROMs, microfilms and monthly reels.

Akhbar Al-Sa'ah

Akhbar Al-Sa'ah (News of the Hour) is a daily, analytical bulletin covering important news events. It aims to provide an overview of the most pertinent political, economic and military events. Editorial priority is given to the main interests of the UAE, the Gulf and the Middle East.

The bulletin is divided into two parts: a detailed analysis of major political, economic and military events closely related to the UAE and a series of short news items on salient domestic, regional and international events. Occasional "country profiles" provide a statistical summary of basic information, economic indicators, social and religious conditions, and political and military capabilities for a particular country. An "Issue Profile" focuses on political groups, concepts and issues of specific interest to the Center, while relevant book reviews are a regular feature.

Akhbar Al-Sa'ah relies on various sources of information including international news agencies, regional and international newspapers, international TV networks, the Internet, data banks and other electronic networks. This newsletter, which is issued six times a week, is an unbiased, comprehensive source of current events worldwide.

Al-Nashra

Al-Nashra (The Bulletin) is a bimonthly newsletter which provides analysis of one specific issue, or, in certain cases, a limited number of issues. The emphasis is on providing background information and future prospects. An objective, issue-oriented commentary is also included. Articles in *Al-Nashra* are written according to the same scholarly standards as those observed in other ECSSR publications. *Al-Nashra* is addressed to senior UAE officials and UAE diplomatic missions. It includes a translation of selected international studies papers and research reports, published in accredited world periodicals, which are believed to be of interest to our readers.

Afaq Al-Mustaqbal (Future Horizons)

This bimonthly magazine is issued by the Media Department at ECSSR. It serves two main purposes:

- to cover the activities of the different departments and sections at ECSSR
- to convey ECSSR opinion on major political, economic and social issues.

The magazine is distributed to senior officials, ministries and other institutions in the UAE.

GULF STRATEGIC REPORT

The Strategic Studies Department, in coordination with other units, is planning to issue an annual *Gulf Strategic Report* which analyzes and assesses important strategic developments relevant to the UAE and the Gulf. Its purpose is to provide a Gulf perspective in contrast to the writings of foreign scholars and researchers dealing with the region. The *Gulf Strategic Report* will feature three sections:

National

This section will cover the UAE with emphasis placed on significant local events that shape developments within the country.

Arabian Gulf

This section will focus on important strategic developments within the Gulf, specifically addressing developments within the GCC at general, political, military and economic levels, as well as important domestic events in each individual state.

Regional

This section will analyze critical external issues which influence and affect the UAE and the GCC states. Areas of interest will include Iran, South West Asia and the broader Middle East.

Pamphlets and Brochures

The Center issues a variety of booklets and brochures providing detailed information on ECSSR conferences, symposiums, round table discussions, publications, and visits of such prominent personalities as Mikhail Gorbachev, Margaret Thatcher, John Major, Caspar Weinberger and Richard Cheney. Brochures covering its books and monograph series include details on the relevant publication procedures.

Awards

AWARDS RECEIVED BY ECSSR

Although a relatively new institution, ECSSR's achievements and activities have received local, regional and international acclaim. In addition to its publications, conferences, workshops, symposiums and other outreach activities, the Center has organized several courses in scientific research methodology, computing and the English language in which ECSSR employees, and members and employees of the Armed Forces and different ministries have participated.

ECSSR has been awarded several prizes:

- Al-Owais Foundation's Cultural Institution of the Year award (1995).

- Best Book Prize at the 16th Annual Sharjah Book Fair (1997) for *Iran and the Gulf: A Search for Stability*, edited by ECSSR Director General Dr. Jamal S. Al-Suwaidi.

- Bin Turki Award for Research and Future Planning awarded by the Intellectual Research, Poetry and Heritage Organization in Cairo on 20 September 1998 for *Gulf Security in the 21st Century*, edited by Dr. David E. Long and Dr. Christian Koch.

- ECSSR's webpage won a prize as one of the five best websites on the Internet. The award was given by Jayson Bamear, Director of the Suite 101 organization.

- "The Economic Conditions in the Coastal Emirates 1862-1965" which was published by the Center in Arabic, won the Best National Author Award at the 20th Annual Book Fair in Sharjah in 2001.

- The Center was awarded the Sharjah Award for Arab Publishers during Sharjah's annual World Book Fair 2004, The award honors publishers whose contributions are distinguished and whose efforts in the field of publishing and translation are outstanding.

The Center plans to participate in competitions organized by prominent Arab and international research institutions. For further enquiries please contact:

The Emirates Center for Strategic Studies and Research
Distribution and Exhibitions Section
P.O. Box: 4567 – Abu Dhabi, UAE
Tel: +9712 4044445
Fax: +9712 4044443
E-mail: books@ecssr.ae
Website: www.ecssr.ae

AWARDS GRANTED BY THE ECSSR

With a view to achieving its goals and translating them into reality, ECSSR promotes scientific research, especially research related to national issues. In this regard, ECSSR has offered valuable awards and prizes to encourage such research. Among these are the 1996 awards for the Best Research on the 25th Anniversary of the Federation, and the 30th Anniversary of the Accession of His Highness Sheikh Zayed bin Sultan Al Nahyan, the late President of the UAE. ECSSR specified the two themes of the competition as follows:

- The Leadership Role of His Highness Sheikh Zayed bin Sultan Al Nahyan, President of the UAE.
- The Federation Experience in the UAE.

Since the inception of the ECSSR in March 1994, the Center has attracted attention as a committed, forward-looking and growth-oriented academic institution. The Center is an important venue for political leaders, thinkers, administrative officials, scholars, professors and researchers visiting the UAE, many of whom have indicated their admiration for its ambitious objectives and sound achievements. Numerous guests have had the opportunity to deliver speeches, lectures or engage in discussions with the administration of the Center and its researchers.

The Center has been honored to receive visitors to the UAE from many Arab and foreign countries. Several of these visits have culminated in the establishment of close academic ties, particularly with visiting officials from research centers and academic institutions. The following pages contain photographs of some of the dignitaries and delegations that have visited the Center over the years.

Visits

(1994–2006)

H.H. Gen. Sheikh Mohammed bin Zayed Al Nahyan, Crown Prince of Abu Dhabi, Deputy Supreme Commander of the UAE Armed Forces and President of the ECSSR, receives former British Prime Minister Baroness Margaret Thatcher at the ECSSR (June 20, 1994)

H.H. Gen. Sheikh Mohammed bin Zayed Al Nahyan, Crown Prince of Abu Dhabi, Deputy Supreme Commander of the UAE Armed Forces and President of the ECSSR, H.E. Mr. Richard Cheney, the Vice-President of the USA and ECSSR Director-General H.E. Dr. Jamal S. Al-Suwaidi hold discussions (March 19, 1996)

A VIP visit by Their Highnesses the Sheikhs and Their Excellencies the Ministers,
headed by the Personal Representative of H.H. the President of the UAE
(July 6, 1997)

H.H. Gen. Sheikh Mohammed bin Zayed Al Nahyan, Crown Prince of Abu Dhabi
Deputy Supreme Commander of the UAE Armed Forces and President of the ECSSR,
accompanies H.E. Atef Oubeid, the Egyptian Prime Minister
(November 2, 1997)

ECSSR Director General H.E. Dr. Jamal S. Al-Suwaidi talks to the former US Secretary of Defense, The Honorable Caspar Weinberger (April 16, 1994)

The President of the former Soviet Union, Mikhail Gorbachev, is welcomed at the Center (December 4, 1994)

The Honorable Lord David Owen (November 21, 1995)

Prof. Lawrence Klein, winner of the Nobel Prize in Economics (foreground right)
(May 4, 1997)

Former Chief of the South African National Defence Force, Lt. Gen. George Meiring
(October 1, 1997)

A delegation from the Bahrain Center for Studies and Research
(October 13, 1997)

H.H. Sheikh Abdul Rahman bin Saud Al-Thani (third from left) from Qatar
(November 3, 1997)

Dr. Kurt Waldheim, former UN Secretary-General and former President of Austria
(December 1, 1997)

H.R.H. Prince Turki bin Sultan bin Abdul Aziz Al-Saud, Under Secretary for Foreign Information, Kingdom of Saudi Arabia (March 2, 1998)

*A delegation from the UAE Federal National Council
(March 23, 1998)*

A delegation from the French Ministry of Defense holds discussions
(April 4, 1998)

ECSSR Director General H.E. Dr. Jamal S. Al-Suwaidi talks to the Director
of the Euro-Asian Studies Center in Norway, Professor Kjell Eliassen (June 16, 1998)

*H.R.H. Staff Major General Khalid bin Bandar bin Abdul Aziz Al-Saud
(October 4, 1998)*

*ECSSR Director General H.E. Dr. Jamal S. Al-Suwaidi accompanies the French Joint Chief-of-
Staff, General Jean Pierre Kelch
(December 13, 1998)*

Visit of H.E. Ural Latypov, Deputy Prime Minister and Minister of Foreign Affairs in the Republic of Belarus (January 17, 1999)

H.M. Queen Rania Al-Abdullah (second from left), of the Hashemite Kingdom of Jordan, accompanied by H.R.H. Princess Aisha bint Al-Hussain (far right) (April 11, 1999)

H.E. Engineer Saif Al-Islam Muammar Al-Qaddafi
(May 10, 1999)

Syrian President H.E. Dr. Bashar Al-Assad pays a visit to the ECSSR
(November 13, 1999)

H.H. Sheikh Saud bin Saqr Al-Qassimi, Crown Prince and Deputy Ruler of Ras al-Khaimah, UAE (April 11, 2001)

H.E. Anatoliy Zlenko (Center), Minister of Foreign Affairs, Ukraine, heading a high-ranking Ukrainian delegation (January 15, 2002)

H.R.H. Princess Aisha bint Al-Hussain of the Hashemite Kingdom of Jordan
(November 21, 1999)

H.E. Counsellor Abdul Aziz M. Al-Rawwas, Advisor for Cultural Affairs
of H.M. The Sultan of Oman (January 23, 2002)

A delegation from the Ministry of Foreign Affairs of Bosnia-Herzegovinia
(May 18, 2002)

A delegation of media specialists from the BBC
(July 17, 2002)

Staff Colonel Nasser bin Jumaa Al-Zadjali, Director of the Center for Defense Studies,
Sultan's Armed Forces of the Sultanate of Oman (June 23, 2003)

Dr. Azmi Bishara, Leader of the National Democratic Rally
(April 28, 2003)

Mr. Hamed Ansari from New Delhi
(September 10, 2003)

A delegation from Purdue University, USA
(July 16, 2003)

A military delegation from Taiwan
(September 29, 2003)

A delegation from the National Defense College, USA
(October 25, 2003)

H.E. Mr. Hassan Awreed, Official Spokesman of the Moroccan Royal Palace and Director of the Tarik bin Ziad Center for Studies (December 22, 2003)

Omani women's delegation led by H.E. Sheikha Aisha bint Khalfan bin Jumail Al-Siyabi, Chairperson of the General Commission of Artisan Industries (January 7, 2004)

Ambassador Dr. Gunter Mulack, Commissioner for the Dialogue with Islam/Dialogue among Civilizations at the German Foreign Ministry (January 19, 2004)

H.R.H. Prince Abdul Aziz bin Bandar bin Abdul Aziz, Director General of the National Research Center, Kingdom of Saudi Arabia (February 18, 2004)

H.E. Mohammed Al-Ashaari, Minister of Culture - Morocco
(February 23, 2004)

H.E. the Chinese Ambassador to the UAE
(April 25, 2004)

Turkish media delegation
(April 26, 2004)

A delegation from the Institute of Foreign Affairs and National Security, Republic of Korea
(May 2, 2004)

H.E. Eldar Salimov, Azerbaijan ambassador to the UAE
(June 26, 2004)

Admiral Giampaolo di Paola, the Italian Defense Chief of Staff
(October 10, 2004)

Visit of HRH Prince Faisal bin Abdullah bin Mohammed Al-Saud
(December 6, 2004)

A delegation from the Ministry of National Security of Azerbaijan
headed by the Minister H.E. Alder Mohammedov (February 16, 2005)

H.H. Prince Rado Du Hu Hayns Willern, Member of the Royal Family of Romania
(February 20, 2005)

Dr. Ahmed Al-Teebi and Mr. Mohammed Barakah, Arab Deputies in the Israeli Knesset
(February 22, 2005)

A delegation from the UAE Diplomatic Institute, headed by the Instititute's Scientific Coordinator, Dr. Nassreddin Al-Ayadi (February 23, 2005)

Dr. Mohammed Salem Weld Sidi Ahmed, the Arab African Center for Media & Development - Moritania (March 5, 2005)

Dr. Theodor Karassac, RAND Institute in the United States of America
(March 6, 2005)

A deligation from the Ministry of Foreign Affairs of Finland, headed by H.E. Aaeopo Polho,
Director General of Africa and Middle East Affairs in the Ministry (March 14, 2005)

HRH Prince Ali bin Naif, Special Secretary to the Jordanian Monarch and the Chairman of the Board of Trustees, the Royal Hashimite Jordnian Center for Documentation (March 23, 2005)

Prof. Vitaly V. Naumkin, President of the International Center for Strategic and Political Studies, Moscow, Russian Federation (March 29, 2005)

H.E. Amb. Jawad K. Al-Hindawi, Dean of the Iraqi Institute for Foreign Services
(April 18, 2005)

Gen. Holmi Ouzok, Chief of Staff of the Turkish Armed Forces
(May 3, 2005)

Dr. Richard N. Haass, President, Council on Foreign Relations, USA
(May 4, 2005)

H.E. Ankussazana Dlamina Zuma, Foreign Minister, Republic of South Africa
(May 10, 2005)

A delegation from the University of National Defense in the USA,
headed by Lt. Gen. Michael Dunn, President of the University (May 15, 2005)

A delegation from the American University of Sharjah, head by Dr. Bassel Salloukh
(June 15, 2005)

A delegation from the UAE Ministry of Economy and Planning, headed by H.E. Abdullah Bin Ahmed Al Saleh, Assistant Undersecretary for International Economic Affairs (June 28, 2005)

A delegation from the UAE Foreign Ministry, headed by the Undersecretary H.E. Amb. Abdullah Rashid Al-Nuaimy (July 13, 2005)

H.E. Sheikh Talal Al-Khalid Al-Ahmed Al-Sabah, Official Delegate for Petroleum Services at the Kuwaiti Petroleum Association (September 25, 2005)

A delegation from the Strategic Observations Center at the Afghani Foreign Ministry, headed by Mr. Munir Ghayathi, the Center's Deputy Director (October 3, 2005)

A delegation from the Embassy of Egypt to the UAE, headed by
H.E. Amb. Mohammed Saad Obeid (November 19, 2005)

A delegation from the Argentinian Ministry of Foreign Affairs, International Trade & Religions,
headed by the Deputy Minister H.E. Georgi Tayana (November 22, 2005)

A delegation of the Lecturers of the symposium entitled: Turkey & the Arabian Gulf (December 19, 2005)

Dr. Philip H. Gordon, Director, Center on the United States and Europe, The Brookings Institution, USA (December 20, 2005)

*Mr. Hussein M. Mohammed, Consultant for Administrative & Consular Affairs,
the Embassy of Somalia to the UAE (December 25, 2005)*

*A delegation of the participants of the symposium entitled:
Iraq's Constitution: Implications for Iraq and beyond (December 27, 2005)*

H.E. Abdullah Bin Mohammed Al-Othman, Ambassador of Qatar to the UAE
(January 2, 2006)

Mr. Omigh Bhatia, Director, Political Islam Studies Unit, Foreign Ministry of Singapore
(January 22, 2006)

Dr. Charles Kupchan, Senior Fellow & Director of European Studies, Council on Foreign Relations, Prof. of International Affairs, Georgetown University, USA (January 29, 2006)

A delegation from the Iraqi Ministry of Culture, headed by the Minister H.E. Nuri F. Al-Rawi (February 6, 2006)

Prof. Jassim Al-Khloufi, Director, Department of Studies & Research, Court of the UAE Deputy Prime Minister & Minister of State for Foreign Affairs (February 7, 2006)

A student delegation from the Harry Truman Foundation, USA (February 8, 2006)

*A delegation from the China Research Institute on Contemporary International Relations
(February 11, 2006)*

*A delegation of the participants of the workshop entitled:
Earthquake Disaster Mitigation: Why is it Necessary? (February 12, 2006)*

A delegation from the Embassy of Sweden to the UAE, headed by
H.E. Amb. Bruno Pager (February 13, 2006)

A delegation from the Algerian People's National Army,
headed by the Chief of Staff Maj. Gen. Ahmed Q. Saleh (February 19, 2006)

*A delegation from the Yemeni Central Service for Control & Auditing,
headed by the Service's Chief, Dr. Abdullah Al-Sanafi (February 19, 2006)*

*Ms. Patricia Henderson, Director of Middle East Relations,
Mandarin Oriental, Hyde Park, UK (February 21, 2006)*

H.E. Mirza Basik, Charge D'Affaires, Embassy of Bosnia-Herzegovna to the UAE (February 21, 2006)

A delegation of the participants of the symposium entitled: Iran's Nuclear Program: Realities & Repercussions (February 26, 2006)

*Mr. Mohammed Abdul Rahman Mohammed, Director of Cooperation & Foreign Relations,
Shanqit Center for Studies & Media, Moritania (March 8, 2006)*

*A delegation of the participants of the ECSSR 11ᵗʰ Annual Conference
(March 12, 2006)*

Dr. Philip Andrew, Director, Center for Energy, Petroleum & Mineral Policy Law,
Dundee University, UK (March 26, 2006)

A delegation from the Afghani Senate,
headed by Mr. Hamed Kilani, First Deputy Speaker (April 2, 2006)

H.E. Abdul Qader Zawi, Ambassador of Morroco to the UAE
(April 3, 2006)

A delegation from the Strategic Research Center of the Turkish Armed Forces,
headed by the President of the Center, Brig. Gen. Suha Taniri (April 5, 2006)

Mr. Idriss A. M. Adam, Director, Center for Middle East & African Studies, Sudan
(April 11, 2006)

A delegation from the Russian Academy for National Economy,
headed by Prof. Vladimire Mao Sibl (April 16, 2006)

A delegation from the Institute for Strategic Studies at the US War College,
headed by Dr. W. Andrew Teriel (April 23, 2006)

Mr. Nahedd Abdul Wahed, Director, Department of Media Planning
Palestinian Ministry of Interior (April 29, 2006)

Dr. Saturu Nakamura, Political Science Specialist on Saudi Affairs, COB University, Japan
(May 9, 2006)

Senator Daniel Gulette, Member, Committee of Foreign Affairs & National Defense,
President, Committee of French - GCC Relations, French Senate (May 15, 2006)

A delegation from the Indian National Defense College,
headed by Brig. Gen. Ashuk Senha (May 15, 2006)

Index

SUBJECTS AND PLACES

PEOPLE

Al-Qaddafi, H.E. Engineer Saif Al-Islam Muammar 230
Al-Qasemi, Dr. Hanif Hasan 94
Al-Qasim, Dr. Ahmed 86
Al-Qassimi, H.H. Sheikh Saud bin Saqr 231
Al-Qudsi, Dr. Sulayman 83
Al-Rashid, Mr. Abdel Rahman 89
Al-Rawdan, H.E. Staff Lt. General (Ret.) Eid Kamil 109
Al-Rawwas, H.E. Counsellor Abdul Aziz M. 232
Al-Rumaihi, Dr. Mohammed 74, 89, 123
Al-Rumaithi, Dr. Mohammed Ibrahim 85, 87, 88
Al-Sabab, Staff Colonel Ahmed 125
Al-Sabah, H.H. Sheikh Salim Sabah Al-Salim 124
Al-Sabah, Ms. Rasha Al-Humoud 126
Al-Saud, H.R.H. General Prince Khaled bin Sultan bin Abdul Aziz 123
Al-Saud, H.R.H. Prince Turki bin Sultan bin Abdul Aziz 226
Al-Saud, H.R.H. Staff Major General Khalid bin Bandar bin Abdul Aziz 228
Al-Sayed, Dr. Adnan 122
Al-Sayegh, Mr. Ahmed Ali 102
Al-Shamsi, Dr. Fatima 86
Al-Sharafi, Mr. Abdullah 106
Al-Share, Dr. Monther 92
Al-Shiryan, Daoud 95
Al-Shuaibi, Dr. Ali Qasim 88, 95
Al-Siyabi, H.E. Sheikha Aisha bint Khalfan bin Jumail 237
Al-Sulayti, H.E. Dr. Hamad Ali 92
Al-Sulh, Dr. Ragheed 144
Al-Suwaidi, Dr. Abdullah N. 106
Al-Suwaidi, H.E. Dr. Jamal S. 10, 102, 103, 116, 119, 122, 126, 127, 129, 137, 188, 189, 201, 216, 220, 222, 227, 228
Al-Tadmuri, Dr. Ahmed Jalal 118
Al-Thani, H.E. Sheikh Hamad Bin Jassim Bin Jabr 129
Al-Thani, H.H. Sheikh Abdul Rahman bin Saud 124, 225

Al-Zaid, Mr. Saleh 100
Alami, Tarik H. 162
Alawi, Dr. Mustafa 94
Aleklett, Prof. Kjell 104
Allam, Major General Fouad Mohammed 126
Aloofy, Dr. Abdellatif 89
Amirahmadi, Dr. Hooshang 120
Anani, H.E. Dr. Jawad Al 72
Anderson, Jon W. 167
Andrews-Speed, Mr. Philip 102
Anis, Dr. Mamdouh 128
Ansari, Mr. Hamed 235
Anthony, Ian 202
Anthony, John Duke 206
Arif, Mr. Muhammed 90
Arnett, Dr. Eric 74
Arnett, Peter 89, 167
Atrissi, Dr. Talal 105
Awreed, H.E. Mr. Hassan 237
Ayesh, Dr. Mohammed 89, 94
Aziz, H.R.H. Prince Abdul Aziz bin Bandar bin Abdul 238
Babu, Dr. Suresh 100
Badrakhan, Abdel Wahab 95
Badran, Dr. Adnan 91
Baghish, Dr. Ali Ihsan 115
Baktiari, Dr. Bahman 120
Balakrishnan, Mr. K. S. 73
Barber, Mr. Benjamin R. 129
Barber, Ms. Elizabeth 127
Barrari, Hassan 152
Barton, Mr. Andrew 97
Barylski, Dr. Robert 121
Beaver, Dr. Paul 125
Becker, Dr. William 92
Beech, Mr. Mark 116
Belhassa, H.E. Ahmed Saif 85
Bell, Mr. Ken 99
Benjamin, Dr. Roger 92
Bennis, Dr. Warren 114
Bergsten, Dr. Fred 79
Beyoghlow, Dr. Kamal A. 135
Bill, Dr. James A. 120
Birol, Fatih 104

The Emirates Center for Strategic Studies and Research

P.O. Box 4567 - Abu Dhabi, United Arab Emirates
Tel +9712 4044444 Fax +9712 4044404
E-mail info@ecssr.ae Website www.ecssr.ae